THE MUSIC OF THE JEWS

THE
MUSIC OF THE JEWS

An Historical Appreciation

ARON MARKO ROTHMÜLLER

A. S. Barnes and Company, Inc.

New York

A Perpetua Book ∞

First American edition
Published in 1954
by the Beechhurst Press, Inc.

PERPETUA EDITION 1960

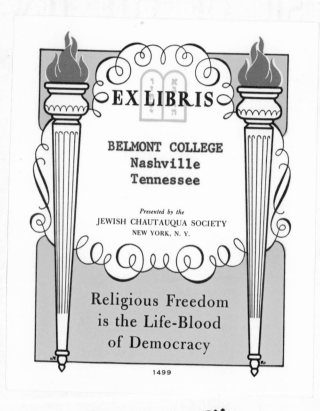
Printed in the United States of America

CONTENTS

PART ONE

FROM THE EARLIEST TIMES TO THE DESTRUCTION OF THE SECOND TEMPLE

PART TWO

THE SYNAGOGAL SERVICE AND JEWISH MUSIC FROM THE FIRST TO THE TWENTIETH CENTURY C.E.

PART THREE

THE NEW JEWISH MUSIC: NINETEENTH AND TWENTIETH CENTURIES

ACKNOWLEDGMENTS

Acknowledgments are due to C. C. Birchard and Co., Boston, U.S.A., for permission to reproduce the illustration on page 175; to Elkin & Co. Ltd., London, for the musical example No. 7, page 232, and to Edition Naidat, Tel Aviv, for the musical example No. 7, page 232; also to Mr. Y. Admon-Gorochov, Mr. Menachem Avidom, Mr. P. Ben-Haim, Mr. D. Sambursky, Mr. L. Saminsky, Mr. J. Stutschewsky, and Mr. J. Weinberg for permission to use quotations from their compositions in Chapter XVII.

Acknowledgments are also due to Mr. Curt Sachs for certain of the early plates; to Pan Verlag, Zürich, for the illustrations on Plate VI (2); and to the management of the Israel Philharmonic Orchestra for Plates IX and X.

FOREWORD

WHEN, early in 1941, I made preparations to write a book on the Music of the Jews, I set out with the firm intention of confining myself to an historical survey of the subject, avoiding all polemic regarding the nature or, for that matter, the existence of 'Jewish music.' For I consider that Jewish music must provide its own testimony to its existence, and must justify its right to be regarded as a genuine and intrinsic art form. Like all other works of art, it must achieve its own effect; it is to be brought to the music public's notice, but not to be defended to that public. Whether and how it has developed and will develop depend entirely on those who create, practise, and promote it.

Yet it did seem to me that there was room for an historical sketch which, besides providing a survey of Jewish music, could also serve as an introduction to the subject. To perform its task adequately such a sketch must aim at historical continuity; but this was far from easy to achieve, for I lacked the material, in the form of musical history or even of musicological works generally, to cover the subject exhaustively. This book treats some four thousand years of the cultural history of the Jews, but for many periods contemporary details of their music and music-making are completely lacking. Moreover, for long periods the Jews have been scattered into different communities, existing in various environments and geographically isolated from one another; even to-day there is not adequate contact among the various Jewish cultural centres in which music, like the other arts, is cultivated. Because of this there are many phenomena which I am unable to discuss in this book, interesting though they are from the aspect of cultural history, simply because they are outside my ken; they relate to Jewish cultural centres which the difficulties of geographical dispersal have made it impossible for me to study.

From the beginning my purpose has been to write an outline that would be simple and straightforward enough for anyone, even with little or no knowledge of musical technique, to understand; my aim was to avoid undue specialisation in any respect, and to deal even with the question of 'Biblical accents' for instance, in such a way that it should be intelligible to all. So no expert knowledge of music is required, and no terms are used that cannot be found in one of the popular dictionaries of music. And although it has been necessary to discuss Hebrew words and phrases to some extent, especially in the early chapters, I have always had regard for the reader who does not know the language or the characters.

None the less, I considered it necessary to make the first part of my book, relating to Biblical times, as thorough and detailed as possible within the general scope of my plan, since it is obvious that this period fundamentally shaped and directed all the musical development of the Jewish people. Similarly, the third part, in which the new, modern Jewish music is discussed, also called for detailed treatment, because it is a living and developing phenomenon of practical interest to all the present-day music world. A visit to Israel in 1951 enabled me to increase considerably the range of this section of the book.

One further remark, concerning the scope of this work, is very necessary. Throughout, I have been concerned only with music made by Jews, by which I mean those individuals who have been or are part of the Jewish community, and have had or have some organic relation with the Jewish cultural group. This applies not only to the earlier chapters, but also to those that treat of Jewish music in modern times, and it will explain the absence of certain names prominent in the making of European music. Generally I have not attempted to evalue any living composer from the point of view of the history of music ; this will be done in due course by historians. Thus, the amount of space devoted to each composer is not to be taken as an indication of their relative importance, for the extent of treatment has been governed not only by the contribution of the composer to Jewish music, but also by the amount of information I could gather about him.

The reader will quickly discern from the manner of presentation of the material that I myself am neither a theorist nor an historian of music. Rather, as an active musician and artist I have tried to provide the clearest possible account of the subject, based on the findings of historical research. In case my limitations should be regarded as a disadvantage, let me mention yet another. As I had to draw upon all kinds of works, including non-scientific ones, for guidance and information, it is quite possible that there are errors in certain of my details, especially as frequently the sources I referred to failed to agree with one another. But, with the aid of others, I have done my best to reduce such defects to a minimum.

During my work on this book I have received help from many people. Although I mention only two by name, I am deeply grateful for all the assistance and encouragement I have received, and take this opportuntiy of expressing my sincere thanks for so much inestimable support. To Dr. C. Rabin, Cowley Lecturer in Post Biblical Hebrew at the University of Oxford, I am indebted for many corrections to the text and for several valuable suggestions; he also kindly gave his advice concerning the transliteration of Hebrew names, etc. But it is chiefly Mr. H. C. Stevens to whom I must express my gratitude, both for the great pains he has taken over his translation, and for suggesting numerous improvements to the original German edition. Finally, a word of appreciation is due to the staff of the English publishers, Messrs. Vallentine, Mitchell, for their untiring and tactful assistance during the many months when this work was undergoing revision and extension.

ARON MARKO ROTHMÜLLER.

October, 1953.

PART ONE

FROM THE EARLIEST TIMES TO THE DESTRUCTION OF THE SECOND TEMPLE
(70 C.E.)

INTRODUCTORY

JEWISH MUSIC IN BIBLICAL TIMES

THE first phase of the story of Jewish music extends from the beginnings of Jewish history down to the restoration of the Jewish State in the days of Ezra and Nehemiah, and approximately to the end of Persian suzerainty *circa* 332 B.C. All the material for this part of the story is derived from Holy Scripture.

The chronology of the events narrated in the historical portions of the Bible is sufficiently well established to justify us in venturing upon a description of the musical culture of the ancient Israelites and their successors, the Judaeans. Modifications of the accepted chronology might cause difficulties in other spheres, but they could not seriously affect the sphere of music. The difficulties one has to face are rather of a different nature: there are many scriptural passages relating to music which to-day are obscure, and even words and phrases which are quite unintelligible, so, often, we have to grope in the dark. And, as Ambros pertinently remarks in his 'Geschichte der Musik,' 'where there is darkness it is easy to see phantoms.' For this reason, in the following pages I have tried to avoid unjustifiable speculation ; one has no right to build up hypotheses and opinions into an arguable reconstruction which may or may not be correct, when there is no clear contemporary reference to the point. So I have drawn only upon ascertained facts. For this reason also, wherever the Bible is quoted I have gone back to the original Hebrew or Aramaic text, and, while in this English translation the Authorised Version has been used for the main text, I have not hesitated to substitute the known correct English term where an erroneous word has been used in that version. I have very rarely ventured upon conjectures of my own, and that only

1

where they help to clarify the issue. On the other hand, it has to be presumed that the authors of the Holy Scriptures were not themselves musicians, and so were not primarily interested in making precise statements about music and musical instruments. We have to accept the lack of precision that arises in consequence, and this is bound to restrict our hypotheses and reconstructions. Even so, we can build up a picture of the music and music-making of the Jews in Biblical times which, though not clear in every detail, will certainly be accurate in its general outline.

CHAPTER I

THE BEGINNINGS

(*Down to Thirteenth Century* B.C.)

AS in the case of the other peoples of antiquity, it is not possible to establish the first beginnings of music and music-making among the ancient 'Children of Israel.' Musical notation did not come into existence until long after the Bible was written, and so we can get little or no idea of the kind of music they produced, apart from the literary references we find in the Scriptures. All we can do is to consider the various cultural influences that must have affected their music-making, drawing on the available historical sources and the results of archæological research, and deducing what we can from the descriptions and pictorial representations of instruments and so on that have survived. And so, for the long period in which the Jewish nation was in process of formation and development, from its earliest forefathers down to the destruction of the Second Temple, a large part of our task will consist in sketching Jewish cultural history with special reference to its music.

We also accept that it was only at a comparatively late stage in the history of the Jewish people that the Israelite religion acquired its dominating rôle as their spiritual centre, and its overwhelming influence in their cultural activity. This would appear to have come about as the result of their need for a Cult peculiar to themselves, and after they had become a homogeneous people. It is a striking fact that there is nothing to show that any of the Israelites' musical activities in pre-Canaan times were borrowed from religious practice, or introduced into secular from religious spheres. On the contrary, as we shall see later, there seem to be indications that various secular usages and customs were introduced into religious practice; for instance, the use of silver trumpets, and sounding the trumpets as a summons to warfare, to the assembly of the congregation, to break up the camp, and so on, all undoubtedly had their origin in secular life.

According to the Biblical account the Hebrews entered

Canaan from Mesopotamia. Recent discoveries have thrown much light on the civilisation of that area during the second millennium B.C., but it is as yet impossible to estimate what culture the Hebrews brought with them or what they took over from the very advanced material culture of Canaan and carried with them when they 'went down to Egypt.'

According to the Bible narrative the final formulation of the Israelites' Cult, the establishment of their religious faith and practice, and the codification of their laws into a system occurred shortly after the Exodus from Egypt. It may be, as higher criticism maintains, that the five books of Moses which form the Jewish Law or *Torah* came into being in their written versions long after the Exodus. None the less, the few passages in these books which refer to music or musical instruments throw some light on this subject. To begin with, they provide a few details of musical instruments and musical practices relating to the days before the Israelites' conquest of Canaan. We know, too, that during the period between the Exodus and the invasion of Canaan the Children of Israel developed into an Israelite nation, with all the constitutional, religious, and legal institutions appertaining to nationhood. Their arrival at the bounds of the land of Canaan, which they were now to go up and possess, connoted their arrival at the threshold of their own national and cultural history.

Our only source of information for the music of the ancient Hebrews or Israelites is the Bible. Their history down to and including the conquest of Canaan is covered by the Five Books of Moses (the Pentateuch). Although some scholars do not consider that these books were written by contemporaries, for our purpose this does not matter. We can accept that they do provide details of the kind of music made and the musical instruments used by the Israelites in those days. Nor does it matter that opinions vary as to the comparative chronology of the Biblical books, and especially of the Pentateuch. We shall follow the generally accepted chronology, for any modifications that might become necessary in the light of future research could not fundamentally affect the story of the development of Jewish musical culture.

On examining the books of the Pentateuch for references to

music, we find the first mention in Genesis 4, 20-22, which tells us that *Yaval* (Jabal) was the first shepherd, *Yuval* (Jubal) 'the father of all such as handle the harp and the pipe' (*kinnor* and *ugav*), and *Tuval* (Tubal) *Cain*, the first ' forger of every cutting instrument of brass and iron.' But it is very unlikely that Jubal was a musician who actually lived ; it is much more probable that the word *yuval* is intended to convey the generalised conception of a musician.[1]

We have no description of either of the two instruments mentioned in connection with *Jubal*: the *kinnor,* and the *ugav.* Usually *kinnor* is translated as ' harp,' ' cythara,' or ' lyre ' ; and *ugav* as flute or pipe. So the *kinnor* was a plucked-string instrument and the *ugav* a wind, probably a wood-wind instrument, such as are depicted in Egyptian representational art and, later, on Jewish coins in the second century C.E. So far as we can judge from excavations, etc., the flute and harp were also the earliest instruments of the Egyptians.

Later in Genesis occurs the passage in which Laban sets out after Jacob, who had departed without taking leave of his father-in-law. Laban upbraided Jacob with the secrecy of his departure, saying: '. . . I might have sent thee away with mirth, and with songs, with tabret [or timbrel] (*tof*), and with harp (*kinnor*)' (Genesis 31, 27). This suggests that singing and music were the normal accompaniment to an escort of honour, and were part of the bridal procession when the newly wedded couple departed with the blessing of their parents. The *tof*, here mentioned for the first time, was probably a hand percussion instrument, similar to the present-day Oriental tambourine, (in Arabic, *duff*).

Exodus 15 gives the text of a ' Song to the Eternal,' sung by Moses and the Children of Israel ; it is a hymn of praise and thanksgiving for their salvation from the might of the Egyptians. In verse 20 we are told that Miriam, Aaron's sister, ' took a timbrel (*tof*) in her hand, and all the women went out after her with timbrels (*tuppim*) and with dances (*mecholot*). *Tuppim* is

---

[1] There is an etymological similarity between *Yuval* and *Yovel*, 'horn,' used to signify the blowing of the horns to announce the *Yovel*, or jubilee year ; and so it may well be that *Yuval* was a personification of music-making, or of a festival which had music as its chief characteristic. For *Hayovel*, see page 16.

the plural of *tof* and *mecholot* the plural of *machol* or *mecholah*. The authorities disagree as to the meaning of *mecholah*. Some translators of the Bible render it as ' flute ' or ' shawm ' (e.g., Torczyner) ; others as ' round,' or ' round dance ' (*e.g.*, Luther, Kautzsch, and Buber). If it originated from Egypt we must take both senses into account, for there are contemporary Egyptian representations of girls playing the tambourine and also a kind of flute, and others dancing to a tambourine. On the other hand, among the Canaanites the ritual dance of maidens was a very important feature of religious ceremonial. It follows that if the passages which mention the *mecholot* relate to Egyptian culture, then possibly both a musical instrument and a kind of dance are implied. But if they relate to Canaanite culture they indicate rather a dance. The word may be related to *machalat*, as used in Psalms 53 and 88, but this probably indicates some kind of musical instrument.

One instrument still in use to-day in the Jewish synagogal service is of very ancient origin. This is the *shofar,* the wind instrument always made of ram's horn, which is first mentioned in Exodus 19, verses 16 and 19 ; it was sounded when Moses went up Mount Sinai to receive the Tablets of the Law from God.

We must also note the use of small bells, obviously giving a musical effect, mentioned in Exodus 28, 33-34, and 39, 25. The bells, *Pa'amon* (plural *Pa'amonim*), of gold, were to be on the hem of the robe of the ephod ; ' and Aaron shall wear it when he ministers, and his sound shall be heard when he goeth in unto the holy place before the Lord, and when he cometh out, that he die not.' It seems that certain customs of a partly super-stitious nature were responsible for this ordinance. But we may safely assume that bells made of other materials were also known to the Israelites, besides the *pa'amone zahav* (golden bells) on Aaron's vestments.

From Exodus 32 we can deduce that music-making was an accompaniment of Israelite feasting, for as Moses and Joshua were returning from Mount Sinai and drew near to the camp they heard voices ; and as they entered the camp they saw the golden calf, and *mecholot*. Even here, however, some authorities translate the word as ' dances,' others as ' shawms.'

The Book of Leviticus contains various prescriptions for the sounding of the *shofar* to announce various days of feast. Leviticus 23, 24, prescribes: 'In the seventh month, in the first day of the month, shall ye have a solemn rest, a memorial proclaimed with the blast of horns.' This feast corresponds with the present-day *Rosh Hashanah*, or Jewish New Year.

The Book of Numbers adds further to our knowledge of Israelite instruments, and their manner of use. Chapter 10, verses 1 to 10, relate that God gave Moses the following instructions:

'Make thee two trumpets (*chatzotzerot*) of silver, of a whole piece (other authorities: 'of chased work') shalt thou make them; that thou mayest use them for the calling of the assembly, and for the journeying of the camps. And when they shall blow (*taqe'u*) with them, all the assembly shall assemble themselves to thee at the door of the tabernacle of the congregation. And if they blow but with one trumpet, then the princes, which are heads of the thousands of Israel, shall gather themselves unto thee. When ye blow an alarm (*teqa'tem teru'ah*) then the camps that lie on the east parts shall go forward. When ye blow an alarm the second time, then the camps that lie on the south side shall take their journey; they shall blow an alarm for their journeys. But when the congregation is to be gathered together, ye shall blow, but ye shall not sound an alarm. And the sons of Aaron, the priests, shall blow with the trumpets. . . . And if ye go to war . . . ye shall blow an alarm with the trumpets. . . . Also in the day of your gladness, and in your solemn days, and in the beginnings of your months (*i.e.*, new moon days) ye shall blow with the trumpets over your burnt offerings, and over the sacrifices of your peace offerings.'

Although the instrument mentioned in this passage is probably not to be regarded strictly as a musical instrument, but rather as a means of giving signals, we must consider it in more detail, establishing certain features of its construction and performance. Clearly the *chatzotzerah* is a very different instrument from the *shofar*, for it is to be fashioned of silver, and so 'trumpet' is certainly the most accurate translation. The *shofar* was and still is fashioned of a ram's horn. We note also that the *chatzotzerah* could be blown strongly, as is indicated by *teru'ah*, and also gently, as is indicated by *teqoa*; the difference is not so much that of *forte* and *piano*, as of blaring and blowing.

Further, it is expressly demanded that Aaron's sons, the priests, shall be responsible for sounding the instrument; this must have been an innovation at the time, for otherwise it would not have been specified as an absolute command.

As we know from Egyptian representations, trumpets were extensively used in that country, and we should not interpret this passage as indicating that trumpets were invented at this time, but only that the Israelites instituted their use for special purposes.[1]

Two other passages in the Pentateuch are of interest from the musical aspect. The first, at Numbers 29, 1, is really a repetition of Leviticus 23, 24, for it also deals with the institution of the feast later known as *Rosh Hashanah*. But here it is called *Yom Teru'ah*, 'the day of the (violent) blowing of trumpets' (horns). The other reference, at Numbers 31, 6, describes how Moses sent out an army to war against the Midianites: 'a thousand of every tribe, them and Phinehas, the son of Eleazar the priest, to the war, with the holy instruments, and the trumpets to blow in his hand.'

In the Pentateuch there is remarkably little, strictly speaking, no reference at all, to musical practice, though there is detailed description of the sanctuary, the service of sacrifice, and other religious ritual and usages. The occasional references to the manner of blowing instruments, 'vigorously' or 'gently,' are chiefly in connection with the giving of signals, and seldom have any symbolical significance (perhaps Numbers 29, 1: 'a day of the blowing of the horn'). Exodus, chapters 25 to 31, give details of the sanctuary, the altar, the priestly vestments, the service of sacrifice, and even the tributes to be paid to the priests, etc., all in the form of divine prescriptions; Leviticus, chapters 1 to 3, describe the sacrifices and the manner of their offering;

---

[1] In his 'Antiquities of the Jews,' 3rd book, 13th chapter, section 6, Josephus gives a description of these 'signal trumpets': 'They were a full ell long, and their tube was narrow, rather thicker than a flute. The mouthpiece was so large that it could take the player's breath comfortably, and it ended in a bell, like a trumpet.' Josephus does not tell us where he obtained this description; it is possible that he was speaking of instruments in use in his day. A trumpet resembling Josephus' description is depicted among other cult objects on the Arch of Titus. See Plates V and VI.

chapters 4 to 7 detail the various forms of sacrifice for the expiation of various sins; chapter 8 the consecration of Aaron and his sons; and chapter 16 the exact procedure in regard to the sin offering. In fact Leviticus contains all the religious, juridical, hygienic and other enactments of the Israelites, and is remarkably detailed and precise on all these matters. Yet it contains not one passage permitting of the deduction that music was an accompaniment of the religious service of that time, or played any rôle in that service. The blasts on the *shofar* and *chatzotzerah* and the small golden bells on Aaron's vestments were of no musical significance. Nor is there any passage entitling us to presume the existence of any kind of dance in Israelite religious practice, before the conquest of Canaan; if there were we might also assume that it had musical accompaniment. This applies to the mention of '*mecholot*' also; even if it does imply a dance as well as a musical instrument, it is nowhere mentioned in connection with the Cult.

It follows that as the ordinances in the passages we have cited governed all communal and public life, but not private and secular activities, there was nothing of a musical nature in the Israelite religious practice, apart from the blasts on the *shofar* and *chatzotzerah*.

On the other hand, it would appear that ordinary merry-making included singing, playing, and possibly dancing (*i.e.*, *mecholot* ?). For instance, Exodus 32, 6, reads: 'The people sat down to eat and drink, and rose up to make merry.' Again, as Moses and Joshua were returning from Mount Sinai they heard 'the noise of them that sing'—*qol 'annot* (ibid., v. 18); and saw 'the calf and *mecholot*' (v. 19). This clearly refers to some kind of profane music or dancing. The passage we have already quoted from Genesis 31, 27, in which Laban tells Jacob he would have sent him away 'with songs, with *tof*, and *kinnor*,' obviously refers to profane music. The blast of the 'trumpets' in Numbers, chapter 10, is clearly of profane origin; it was obviously introduced into religious practice from secular life. Thus, the chapter specifies that the trumpet was to be sounded for summoning the assembly and for breaking up camp (v. 2); for gathering together the congregation (v. 7); for summons to war against enemies (v. 9); and for heralding days of festivity,

the feasts, and the days of the new moon (v. 10). These are all
secular activities, secular institutions of the Children of Israel. On
the other hand, the ordinance that 'the sons of Aaron, the priests,
shall blow with the trumpets' (v. 8) indicates, as we have said, that
this was an innovation, instituted by this special ordinance. From
all of which it would seem that according to the Pentateuch, our
one available source, all the musical instruments then used by the
Israelites were of secular origin, and borrowed by the Cult.

We can thus safely say that as the Israelites' religious
usages and ritual took shape they incorporated in them certain
customs of their secular life. This musical practice (in the
present-day meaning of the words) was without any special,
religious significance.

Because of the paucity of the sources at our disposal we cannot
get any complete picture of Jewish musical culture prior to the
conquest of Canaan, in the 13th century B.C. On the other hand,
we do have definite information on certain instruments:

(a) *Musical Instruments.*

Kinnor (כנור)	A harp or lyre (cythara).	A plucked string instrument.
Ugav (עונב)	A flute or shawm.	Wood-wind instrument.
		It is mentioned only four times in all the Bible (Genesis 4, 21; Psalm 150, 4; and Job 21, 12, and 30, 31). No definite information concerning it is available.
Tof (תף)	Small hand-percussion instrument, apparently similar to the present-day tambourine, usually played by women.	Percussion instrument.
Machalat (מחלת)[1] *Machol, Mecholah* (מחול, מח. לה)		The nature of this instrument cannot be established, but it was probably a wood-wind, as it was played by women. Some authorities also take the word to mean a round dance.

---

[1] *Machalat*—מחלת is also a girl's name (II Chron., 11, 18).

(b) *Non-musical Instruments.*

Shofar (שופר)	*i.e.*, Ram's horn.
Pa'amon (פעמן)	Bell.
Pl. *Pa'amonim* (פעמנים)	Bells.
Chatzotzerah (חצוצרה)	An instrument used primarily for signalling, and corresponding to the present-day valveless trumpet. In Moses' time it was made of chased silver.

We may add in conclusion that at times of secular festivity both singing and dancing (perhaps indicated by *mecholot*) appeared to be customary.

CHAPTER II

IN THE LAND OF CANAAN
(The Days of the Judges)

ALTHOUGH we have only scanty details of the musical activities of the Israelites before their arrival in the 'Promised Land,' the Books of the Pentateuch do reveal that there was considerable development in building up the fundamentals of culture generally. But the Children of Israel were not yet a really settled people, and the forms of their cultural life were determined by their nomadic existence.

The land of Canaan, in which they were now to dwell, approximately corresponded in situation and area to the Palestine of Mandate times. The peoples already living there were not culturally homogeneous. Canaan had been entered and inhabited by various peoples at various times, and thus had come under differing cultural influences. In the days immediately before the arrival of the Children of Israel the country was inhabited by various tribes, chiefly Semitic. Each of these tribes probably had its own culture, worshipping various gods, and practising various cults.

These cultural peculiarities by no means came to an end with the arrival of the Israelites, nor even when they had conquered the land. The days of Joshua, in the thirteenth century B.C., were filled with wars, and the historians of the time devoted their narratives almost exclusively to reporting the various campaigns. However, from Joshua 24 and Judges 2 we learn that, although Joshua had instituted an Israelite form of worship at *Shiloh,* basing it on usages dating from the wanderings in the wilderness, the Children of Israel were far from unaffected by the religious customs of the surrounding tribes, and were serving Baal and Ashtaroth. The same thing was reported as happening in the times of Samuel (I Samuel 7, 3-4). Again, the book of Judges (21, 19-23) refers to a 'Feast of *Yahve*' in the temple which was founded at *Shiloh* about 1175 B.C.; this feast included a ritual 'dance of Maidens,' a custom hitherto unknown among the Jews.

It was natural enough that the cults already existing in Canaan should have influenced the Israelites ; when these nomads took to a settled existence they gradually assimilated the higher forms of life of their environment. It is true that spiritually they were no poorer than the Canaanites, but the relative pomp and splendour of the latter's settled conditions must have had a strong attraction for them, inspiring a feeling of admiration. But their own Cult, and their more developed ethical conceptions had such deep root that the new accretions had necessarily to be harmonised with their fundamental beliefs and characteristic ways of life, and not vice versa. And in order to preserve their religion and its practices in their integrity it was obviously necessary to impose certain restrictions on themselves, to isolate their Cult from those of the strangers around them. The other peoples cultivated the representation of various divinities, and pictorial representations were a strong element in their cults ; but the Israelites went to the other extreme, they condemned and forbade any kind of graven or pictorial image. The ornamentation on their utensils and buildings, and, at a much later date, the representations on their coins which archæology has revealed, have to be attributed to outside influence ; in any case they are of no religious significance. On this question Auerbach remarks:
' This absence of pictorial representation in Israel is not to be explained as due purely to artistic incapacity, as sometimes happens ; no people on earth has ever shrunk from worshipping quite primitive pictorial representations of their gods. As the Decalogue shows, even in the time of Moses it was far more a conscious revolt against Egypt, the land of wholesale and highly developed image-worship. This rebellion of a poor Bedouin people against the Egyptians' rich culture, which had spread all over Canaan, was in fact a vital expression of its religious originality and genius.'[1] If we could assume that the Israelites had not accepted laws forbidding the pictorial representation of God, but, on the contrary, had fostered such activities, there is good reason for thinking that they would certainly have accomplished a great deal in this direction ; but how far they would have gone would have depended on general cultural and social

---

[1] 'Wüste und gelobtes Land,' vol. 1, p. 148, Berlin, 1932.

trends. However, on the evidence before us we can accept that the ancient 'Children of Israel' were more attracted to historical writing, to prophecy, and to poetry, especially the poetry of psalms; in other words, they were drawn more to ethics than to æsthetics.

In a folk community such tendencies are often modified, frequently through outside influences. This is especially the case when the spiritual and intellectual forces have been expended in a certain direction and have arrived at a dead end; then the opportunity arises for these forces to concentrate on another form of culture, and so a different branch of culture is cultivated and flourishes. We can confirm that the second commandment, which forbade the making of any image of God, was not an absolute, or the sole, hindrance to the development of representational art,[1] and that the reason rather seems to be that there was no demand for it, by asking the closely related question: how was it that the Israelites produced no equivalent of a representation of God? If there had been any impressive demand for pictorial representation generally they could have found many opportunities, apart from the representation of divinity. It is possible that historical writing, which perhaps had all the attraction of novelty, meant so much to them that their intellectual powers were entirely absorbed in it and in the task of maintaining their religion against their environment, and so they would not dissipate their creative powers on the cultivation of representational art.

The foregoing remarks, which relate to the period between the sojourn at the oasis of *Kadesh* (where their religion and the Cult took final shape) and the time of the conquest of 'the promised Land,' are not based on information concerning the Israelites' music-making, which is extremely scarce. In this sphere we must argue by analogy, so far as is permissible, and apply what we have said about the absence of representational art to their music. During this transitional period (thirteenth century B.C.) their spiritual and intellectual powers

---

[1] It is true that later, under the Greeks and Romans, the Jews would not tolerate any pictorial representation, even on the Roman military standards. But this does not vitiate the argument, for by that time they regarded this as a national idiosyncrasy.

were fully absorbed in the practice of their religion, and in historical writing. Possibly their taste for music was first aroused by outside influences, in particular by the religious usages of the peoples among whom they dwelt, as we shall see later, in the times of the Kings.

In all the Book of Joshua there is only one reference to the use of a musical instrument, and then, it would seem, for the purpose of intimidating an enemy. At the siege of Jericho the Lord said unto Joshua: '. . . Seven priests shall bear before the ark seven rams' horns (*shoferot ha-yovelim*) and on the seventh day ye shall compass the city seven times, and the priests shall blow with the horns. And it shall come to pass, that when they make a long blast with the ram's horn (*qeren ha-yovel*), and when ye hear the sound of the horns, all the people shall shout with a great shout; and the wall of the city shall fall down flat, and the people shall ascend up every man straight before him' (Joshua 6, 4-5). Here the exact phrase used for 'rams' horns' in the original text is *shoferot ha-yovelim*.[1]

In those troublous times the *shofar* was used extensively. In the Book of Judges it is almost the only instrument mentioned. As it was used in wartime, it was sounded frequently. For instance, when Ehud returned home after killing the king of Moab, 'he blew a horn in the mountain of Ephraim, and the Children of Israel went down with him from the mount, and he before them' (Judges 3, 27). The *shofar* is mentioned in several other passages in Judges, and always it is in connection with warfare (6, 34; 7, vs. 8, 18, 20, 22). The passage in chapter 7 relating Gideon's defeat of the Midianites is worth noting, especially verse 20: 'And the three companies blew the *shoferot*, and brake the pitchers, and held the torches in their left hands, and

---

[1] Martin Buber translates this phrase 'Heimholerposaunen'; Luther 'Sound-year trumpet,' because the *shofar* was used for announcing the Jubilee Year. Kautzsch gives 'ram's horn trumpet,' or simply 'trumpet.' *Shofar* and *qeren* (in verse 5) are clearly identical, or else the historian is inexact in his choice of words. In any case, *shofar* refers not to a trumpet, which is always an instrument made of metal, but to the ram's horn. Assuming that the *shoferot* used to announce the *Yovel* (Jubilee) year, which came after seven times seven years, i.e., every fifty years (the number seven played an important rôle at the siege of Jericho, be it noted), were larger than those used in divine service, we can see why these horns were particularly used for sounding the alarm in wartime.

the *shoferot* in their right hands to blow withal. . . .' So each of the three hundred warriors carried a *shofar,* giving the impression that the attacking force was much stronger than it was.

The oldest surviving example of the Israelite heroic poem, the ' Song of Deborah,' also has some interesting references to music. We read in the fifth chapter of Judges: 'Then sang Deborah and Barak, the son of Abinoam on that day (after Sisera had been vanquished and murdered), saying: ' I, even I, will sing unto the Lord ; I will sing praise to the Lord God of Israel.'

Only two passages in Judges refer to musical usages already mentioned. The first is in chapter 11, 34, after Jephthah had smitten the children of Ammon: ' And Jephthah came to Mizpah unto his house, and behold, his daughter came out to meet him with *tuppim* and *mecholot.' Tuppim* are, of course, ' timbrels,' or ' tambourines ' ; while, as in previous instances, *mecholot* is variously translated, by Buber as ' round dances,' by the Authorised Version as ' dances,' and by Torczyner as ' shawms.' *Mecholot* occur again in the second passage, Judges 21, 21. Here the word clearly seems to indicate a dance. ' And see, and behold, if the daughters of *Shiloh* come out to dance in dances,' says the Authorised Version. The original reads: *la-chul ba-mecholot.* As *chul* means ' to spin round,' ' to spin in the dance,' here *mecholot* may indicate either a definite dance or the musical accompaniment to a dance. We may note that examples of a dance taking its name from a musical instrument can be adduced from the vocabularies of other peoples, e.g., ' Musette,' in French, and ' Hornpipe,' in English.

Apart from the reference to *qeren ha-yovel* already mentioned, (in which connection we must remember that *ha-yovel* is sometimes also attached to *shofar*) the musical instruments we have specified above are the only ones to be found in the books relating to this period. *Qeren ha-yovel* could have been a bull's horn prepared for blowing, while the *shofar ha-yovel* may have been an extra large ram's horn. But this is only conjecture. However, both expressions indicate a wind instrument with a very powerful sound.[1]

---

[1] *Ha-yovel* is also the Hebrew equivalent of ' bell-wether,' i.e., the ram that leads the flock.

CHAPTER III

THE TIMES OF THE EARLY KINGS

S O far, we have dealt with Israelite music during the times when they lived a nomadic or semi-settled life in the inhabited areas of the 'fertile crescent,' or in the wilderness between Mesopotamia and Egypt, and then while they were conquering Canaan and gradually taking to a settled existence in their own country. Now we come to the days when the Kingdom of Israel was established, to the reign of its first three kings, who represented the culmination of Israelite national and political power, and the culmination of Israel's cultural and spiritual life. It is true that the time of highest development of musical culture did not coincide with the period of greatest political power ; politically, Solomon was the greatest king of Israel ; whereas David's reign was of more importance in musical respects. But on the whole the times of the first three kings were times of construction ; though there were interruptions for wars, civil wars and unrest, they were marked by material prosperity.

The Biblical books dealing with these years provide a clear picture of the way in which the Israelites absorbed the Canaanite culture, and were influenced and stimulated by other cultures through international commerce ; the picture also reveals the great difficulties they had in fusing the new with the old and the traditional, and bringing them into harmony. Undoubtedly, so far as ostentation and splendour of ceremonial were concerned they had much to learn, for their wilderness tradition was homely, nor could it have been otherwise in such conditions. Now, in their own powerful kingdom, they developed a more brilliant form of worship and more sumptuous festivals. The Canaanites and other neighbouring peoples provided them with examples in plenty.

The reign of the first king of Israel, Saul, was unusually turbulent, filled with continual wars. Such times are not conducive to the cultivation of music, or any other art. None the less, at the very beginning of his reign we are told of musical training in connection with the education of the young men. This was so especially in the south, in the part known as Judah. The case of the young harpist, David, could not have been an exception.

In this connection we come upon a factor which is quite new in our study: music is recognised as having an effect on the human spirit. The peculiar power of music, its manifold effects on man, are especially realised even to-day in the Orient and in central Europe, wherever the oriental influence has reached. In addition to its purely æsthetic qualities, it has an emotional power to stimulate the imagination,[1] to exalt the spirit, to pacify or provoke the soul, etc. All these evocations of a specific reaction required the accompaniment of a certain degree of ecstasy. In this respect the methods used by the *nevi'im* (singular *navi,* ' inspired,' ' possessed by the spirit') are of particular interest. The *nevi'im,* the forerunners of the greater prophets of later days, are said to have been groups of ecstatics who wandered about the country under a leader, and drew the impressionable onlookers after them by their furious dancing.[2] This state of ecstasy was deliberately evoked by the *nevi'im* in order to exalt themselves into a mood in which their religious feelings could find expression, and to bring the strongest possible influence to bear on the crowd around them. As Samuel anointed Saul as king and sent him on his homeward journey he said to him: '. . . Thou shalt meet a company of inspired (*nevi'im*) coming down from the high place with a *nevel* (a harp), a *tof* (tambourine), a *chalil* (pipe), and a *kinnor* (cythara) and they shall behave inspiredly. And the spirit of the Lord will come upon thee, and thou shalt be inspired (*vehitnabbita*), and shalt be turned into another man.' (I Samuel 10, 5-6.) These *nevi'im* are often mentioned in the Scriptures and, in those days, they played an important part in the religious life. As we see from the passage quoted, they went with music, and music was one of their most effective means of achieving ecstasy. Unfortunately, the Bible provides no details as to the nature of their music; it simply mentions the names of their instruments, and the circumstance that they danced or whirled in furious dances.

---

[1] Cf. II Kings 3, 15. ' But now bring me a minstrel (*menaggen*). And it came to pass, when the minstrel played, that the hand of the Lord came upon him ' (i.e., Elisha).

[2] Auerbach, op. cit., vol. I, p. 287.

For the source of this development of religious ecstasy among the Israelites we must turn to the cults of Asia Minor, whence this form of exaltation penetrated into Syria and Phœnicia, where we find it in the Adonis cult. The Israelites acquired it from the peoples of Canaan, and Auerbach says that 'among the Israelites it was always regarded as something foreign, regarded with shrinking and a slight contempt rather than with respect, and finally was driven out from among them by the classic prophets.'[1]

The Israelites repeatedly took steps to suppress the Canaanite custom of achieving religious ecstasy through music, but at the same time they recognised its beneficent effect on the human spirit. Evidently they used the sounds of the harp as curative treatment for moods of melancholy, sentimentality, and spiritual depression, for we find that king Saul's servants appealed to him: 'Behold now, an evil spirit from God troubleth thee. Let our lord now command thy servants, to seek out for thee a man who is a cunning player on the *kinnor* (cythara). And it shall come to pass, when the evil spirit from God is upon thee, that he shall play with his hand, and thou shalt be well.' (I Samuel 16, 15-16.) The Bible goes on to relate how David was brought for this purpose. He was 'a mighty valiant man, and prudent in matters,' but above all else he was a youngster with musical training, and talented. According to tradition David found favour in Saul's eyes because with his skill on the harp he was able to mitigate the king's spiritual depression and melancholy. 'And it came to pass, when the evil spirit from God was upon Saul, that David took the cythara (*kinnor*) and played with his hand; so Saul was refreshed, and was well, and the evil spirit departed from him.' (Ibid. v. 23 also ch. 18, 10; ch. 19, 9.)

The custom already referred to, of going out to meet the victor of a battle with song and music, was still practised at this time. For as David returned from his duel with Goliath (I Samuel 18, 6) 'the women came out from all the cities of Israel, singing (*la-shir*) and dancing (*mecholot*),[2] to meet king

---

[1] Loc. cit.

[2] Translated variously. Buber, 'sounds of joy'; Torczyner, 'playing of flutes'; Kautzsch, 'dancing.' But note the natural association of 'singing and dancing,' and the fact that only percussion instruments are mentioned.

Saul, with timbrels (*tuppim*), with joy (*simchah*), and triangles (*shalishim*).

In the religious sphere also music began to play an important part in the days of David. He gave especial attention to the ordering of divine worship. It was king David who had the Ark of the Covenant brought to Jerusalem and set it up there in that part called ' the City of David,' to conform with the wilderness tradition. He had the Ark of the Covenant brought into the city amid scenes of great festivity. (II Samuel 6, 15.) ' So David and all the house of Israel brought up the ark of the Lord with shouting, and with the sound of the horn,' and (verse 5) they ' played before the Lord on all manner of instruments made of cypress wood, on cytharas (*kinnorot*), harps (*nevalim*), tambourines (*tuppim*), bells (*mena'ane'im*), and cymbals (*tzeltzelim*). Understandably enough, David's wife, who was Saul's daughter Michal, was astonished at this foreign manner of glorifying God, which had not been customary among the Israelites. But David was greatly influenced by the contemporary *nevi'im* (just as his predecessor, the passionate and unstable Saul, had succumbed to them), and he paid homage to the God of Israel with ecstasy, with dancing, and music. We can, perhaps, ascribe this innovation to the influence of Canaanite culture in the musical sphere. The king himself came under that influence, and associated it with Israelite traditions and customs some of which dated back to the years in the wilderness. Thus, although David had the Ark of the Covenant set up in the ' City of David,' it was still kept in a tabernacle, in the tent of the wilderness era.

The king's next step was to order the temple service with great precision ; and although, so far as the musical aspect is concerned, the details given are inadequate, we can partly reconstruct it. David appointed Abiathar to the office of high priest, and later added Zadok to him, but he retained supreme authority in his own hands, even in the sphere of ordinance of divine worship. He gave Asaph instruction and set him ' as head (of the singers and instrumentalists) and as his deputy Zechariah ' (I Chronicles 16, 5). The leaders of the instrumentalists were king David himself, Asaph, Jeduthun, and Heman (ibid., 25, 1-6). Asaph played the cymbals (*metziltayim*) ; Asaph's sons, Zaccur, Joseph, Nethaniah, and Asarelah, were under their father (ibid.,

25, 2).[1] Jeduthun played the *kinnor* (cythara) 'to give thanks and to praise the Lord,' and under him were his sons Gedaliah Zeri, Jeshaiah, Hashabiah, and Mattithiah (ibid., 25, 3). Yet another group was formed by the sons of king David's seer, Heman: Bukkiah, Mattaniah, Uzziel, Shebuel, Jerimoth, Hananiah, Hanani, Eliathah, Giddalti, Romamti-ezer, Joshbekashah, Mallothi, Hothir, and Mahazioth. All these 'were under the hands of their fathers for playing in the house of the Lord, with cymbals (*metziltayim*), harps (*nevalim*), and cytharas (*kinnorot*) for the service of the house of God' (ibid., 25, 6). Verse eight adds: 'And they cast lots on their duties, both the youngest and the oldest, the teachers and the scholars.' In the following twenty-three verses we are given the order in which the lots came out. Altogether two hundred, fourscore and eight persons were devoted to the service of music in the temple (ibid., 25, 7).

From the description of the Levites' functions given in I Chronicles 15, vs. 17 and 19, we learn that Heman, son of Joel, Asaph, son of Berechiah, and Ethan, son of Kushaiah, all 'brothers of the first degree,' were appointed to sound with 'cymbals of brass' (*metziltayim*). A number of 'brothers of the second degree' were appointed gatekeepers (v. 18), and among these Zechariah, and Aziel, Shemiramoth, Jehiel, Unni, Eliab, Maaseiah, and Benaiah, were to play 'on harps on *alamot*,' *bi-nevalim al-alamot*.[2] Mattithiah, Elipheleh, Mikneiah, Obed-edom, Jeiel, and Azaziah were to accompany on the *kinnor*, the eight-stringed cythara. To these must be added Shemiramoth, Jehiel, Eliab, and Benaiah, who played on harps and cytharas, *nevalim uvekinnorot* (16, 5). Chenaniah, chief of the Levites, was to supervise the performance, as he was skilful in the art (15, 22). The priests Shebaniah, Jehoshaphat, Nethaneel, Amasai, Zechariah, Benaiah, and Eliezer 'did blow with the trumpets (*chatzotzerot*) before the ark of God' (15, 24), while the priests Benaiah and Jahaziel were posted with trumpets before the Ark of the Covenant (16, 6). When the ark of God had been set up

---

[1] Herodotus (Bk. 6, 60) tells that among the Egyptians it was customary for the son to follow his father's occupation, so that family trades were practised. Among the Israelites this custom applied also in the musical profession.

[2] For discussion of *alamot*, see p. 25.

in the tent that David had pitched for it, and the Levites had been established in their functions, 'then on that day David delivered first this psalm, to thank the Lord through Asaph and his brethren' (ibid., 16, 7-9):

> 'Give thanks unto the Lord, call upon His name,
> Make known His deeds among the peoples.
> Sing unto Him, play unto Him,
> Talk ye of all His wondrous works. . . .

The fact that certain names occur more than once, in connection with various functions, suggests either that there were several Levites of the same name, or that the same Levites were assigned to different functions at different times, or—least acceptable hypothesis of all—that the chronicler was inexact. However, the point is of no importance. That all these various functions were specified shows the pomp with which king David surrounded the worship of God in the temple established in the city of David at Jerusalem. As Ambros says: 'This temple music differs from its contemporary Egyptian counterpart by the essential circumstance that in Egypt music was already entirely the women's function, whereas in Jerusalem only men were appointed to its performance.'[1]

As already said, the first mention of religious dancing among the Israelites relates to this period. As king David brought the ark of God out of the house of Obed-edom to the city of David he danced (*mekharker*)[2] 'with all his might before the Lord' (II Samuel 6, 14).

The Bible contains many references to David's encouragement of the art of singing. We cannot definitely assert that singing was common among the Israelites apart from the temple service, but the story of David playing before king Saul indicates its probability. Of course, it is quite likely that the songs David sang to Saul to dispel his depression were of a religious nature, some kind of psalm. But there is also evidence that under king David song was common in the royal court. When he summoned the eighty-year-old Barzillai to go with him to be maintained at the

---

[1] Op. cit., 1, p. 199.
[2] *Mekharkes* (II Samuel 6, 14): to hop, to spring; *meragged* (I Chronicles 15, 29): to spring, to dance.

king's expense in Jerusalem, Barzillai declined in the words: '. . . can I hear any more the voice of singing men and singing women ?' (II Samuel 19, 35). The tenor of the answer indicates singing of a secular nature.

One of the royal acts of king Solomon was to command the erection of a magnificent temple and, when this was completed, a royal palace, both of which were built mainly by foreign workmen. Unlike his predecessors, Solomon reigned in a manner similar in many respects to the rule of contemporary wealthy oriental kings and princes.[1] However, this outward pomp and splendour was not accompanied by any corresponding cultivation of music. There is no mention of any innovations in the sphere of music during his reign ; on the contrary, we are told expressly of his adherence to the established order, to the temple service as arranged by his father, David, who had had a much simpler court (II Chronicles 7, 6, and 8, 14). Solomon himself showed more interest in architecture than in music ; however, it is said of him that 'his songs were a thousand and five' (I Kings 4, 32). It is also recorded that he was the first to import a particularly costly wood, *almug* wood (traditionally said to be red sandalwood, but more probably juniper wood) for the making of cytharas (*kinnorot*) and harps (*nevalim*) for the singers (I Kings 10, 12 ; II Chronicles 9, 11).

When the temple was finished, the ark of God was brought out of the city of David into the temple, and the service continued in the place where king David had instituted it (II Chronicles 5, 12). 'Also the Lévites, the singers, all of them, of Asaph, of Heman, of Jeduthun, with their sons and brethren, being arrayed in byssus, with cymbals (*metziltayim*), harps (*nevalim*), and cytharas (*kinnorot*) stood at the east end of the altar, and with them a hundred and twenty priests sounding with trumpets (*chatzotzerot*).'

By this time the transformation in Jewish music which Ambros describes in his ' History of Music ' can be regarded as fully

---

[1] Ecclesiastes (*Kohelet*—the Preacher) declares: 'I gathered me also silver and gold, and the peculiar treasure of kings and countries ; I got me men singers and women singers, and the delights of the sons of men, such as musical instruments, and that of all sorts' (2, 8) Even if this was not written by Solomon, it characterises his reign.

accomplished: 'It is very strange and remarkable how, in the case of the Hebrews (Israelites) the miraculous effects of music as described in most of the sagas and myths of the peoples of antiquity acquired a theosophical character. . . . Among the Phœnicians, or the Phrygians, music was used simply as a pathological means of stimulation and exaltation, it was regarded simply as a physiological effect of sounds and their dynamic strength, and music revealed power over the mind only in so far as it itself is a constant component of the great life of nature, in whose violent currents every people is irresistibly carried away and submerged. But for the Hebrews music was a *musica sacra*, a bridge linking humanity to the spiritual world that is above nature; it was the bearer of prayer, and, as a gracious return gift, it brought from the God of Abraham, Isaac, and Israel (Jacob) prophetic illumination, a benediction on the land and its fruits, miraculous victory over the enemy. Because of this exceptional tendency of Hebrew music it does not matter whether or not they regarded it as an art, a representation of beauty through sound, as the Greeks did later. It was not art, but service to God; and not æsthetics but religion determined its value.'[1]

Turning to a consideration of the various musical instruments in use during the reigns of the kings Saul, David, and Solomon, we find that for this period we have more details than before. Even so, many of the instruments mentioned are not described at all, and there are certain terms, e.g., *alamot*, which are obscure; we cannot say whether they refer to musical instruments, are musical expressions, or some kind of notation, and, if an instrument is indicated, whether it is string, wind, or percussion, and so on. Some of the instruments have, of course, been mentioned in previous chapters.

1. *Musical Instruments*

Kinnor (כנור), pl. *Kinnorot* (כנרות). A harp or cythara; a plucked string instrument having, it is conjectured, eight strings,[2] played with the hand.[3]

---

[1] Op. cit., vol. 1, p. 195.
[2] Cf. I Chronicles 15, 21: *be-kinnorot al ha-sheminit,* i.e., on the cytharas, on the eight-string.
Cf. I Samuel 16, vs. 16 and 23 ; 18, 10 ; 19, 9.

Nevel (נבל), pl. *Nevalim* (נבלים). Apparently a simple, primitive harp or cythara with few strings. It is first mentioned in II Samuel 6, 5. This may signify that the Israelites had not known the instrument in Babylonian days or during the period in Egypt, but first met with it and adopted it in Canaan. On the other hand, from earliest times the Egyptians were acquainted with a guitar, mandoline, or lute form of instrument with the Coptic name of *nabla*.[1] The Greeks regarded the *nabla* as an invention of the Phœnicians and more precisely of the Sidonians.[2] We have no reliable details concerning the nature or quality of the instrument.

It must have been simpler and perhaps more primitive than the *kinnor*. This is indicated by, for instance, the reference in Amos 6, 5, *ha-poretim al-pi ha-navel*, of which the meaning is more or less ' to bring out (strum) single notes according to the *nevel.*' The fact that the word *nevel* also means a pitcher or leather bottle may indicate that the instrument was so named because of its shape as a whole, or of its resonator-body. It is possible, but unlikely, that it was a higher-pitched percussion instrument for providing accompaniments. On the other hand, there are biblical passages favouring the presumption that it was similar to the *kinnor*, e.g., I Chronicles 15, 28, *mashmi'im bi-nevalim ve-kinnorot*, ' making a noise with harp and cythara instruments.' As the *kinnor* and *nevel* are thus mentioned in close association it is possible that they were akin and similar.

We must also mention that the *nevel* is found in association with the word *alamot*. In I Chronicles 15, 20, we find *bi-nevalim al-alamot*. Torczyner translates this ' on harps on *alamot,*' suggesting that *alamot* is a musical instrument. On this two observations are worth making. Firstly, in the very next verse we read *be-kinnorot al ha-sheminit*, which means ' on cytharas, on the eight-string.'

Further, the analogous manner of writing in these two consecutive verses suggests that just as *al ha-sheminit* is a more precise indication of the kind of *kinnor*, so *al-alamot* is a more precise indication of the *nevel*. And, secondly, *almah*, pl. *alamot*, means ' a maid,' ' maidens.' From which we could

---

1 Uhlemann, ' Handbuch der ägyptischen Altertumskunde,' Part Two, p. 302.
2 Gressmann, H.: ' Musik und Musikinstrumente im Alten Testament,' p. 23, Giessen, 1903.

deduce that *alamot* in association with *nevalim* would have the sense of 'slight,' 'tender,' or 'high' (young women's voices, sopranos, trebles). In that case *bi-nevalim al-alamot* would indicate high-pitched *nevalim*. In his 'Antiquities of the Jews' Josephus describes the *kinnor, nevel,* and *metziltayim* in the following words : ' The *kinyra* had ten strings and was struck with a small stick (i.e., it was a kind of cythara) ; the *nabla* had twelve notes and was played with the fingers (a kind of harp) ; finally, the cymbals were of brass and were large and broad.'[1] Later he says that the *nabla* and *kinyra* ' were fashioned from electrum.'[2] According to Pliny, electrum was a metal of an amber colour, consisting of four parts of gold and one of silver.

Chalil (חליל) . A flute ; a wood-wind instrument.

Chatzotzerah (חצצרה), pl. *Chatzotzerot* (חצצרות). A trumpet ; a metal wind instrument.

Tof (תֹף), pl. *Tuppim* (תפים). A tambourine ; a percussion instrument.

Metziltayim (מצלתים)[3]. Cymbals ; a percussion instrument made of brass or copper.[4]

Tzeltzelim (צלצלים). Small bells, or small cymbals ; an instrument for producing a rustling or tinkling noise.

Mena'aneim (מנענעים)[5]. Bells ; a shaken instrument.

Shalish (שליש)[6]. A triangle ; a percussion instrument.

It must be added that possibly the phrase in II Samuel 6, 5, *be-khol atze beroshim,* ' all manner of instruments of cypress wood,' may refer to some kind of percussion instrument (a xylophone ?) made of cypress wood. Buber translates the phrase ' cypress-wood wind instruments.'

2. *Non-musical Instruments*

In this category we class those instruments which were employed either for signalling, particularly in warfare, or were otherwise used outside the sphere of music-making, and justify

---

[1] Op. cit., Book, 7, chap. 12, section 3.
[2] Op. cit., Book 8, chap. 3, section 8.
[3] Always in dual form.
[4] Cf. I Chronicles 15, 19.
[5] From *nua* to shake.
[6] From *shalosh* three.

classification here because of the details given in biblical passages relating to the first period of the Israelite kings. Consequently this class varies a little from that at the end of chapter one.

Shofar, ram's horn.

The *qeren* is also mentioned, e.g., in I Chronicles 25, 5 ; I Kings 1, 50, and 2, 28 (cf. Genesis 22, 13). But it would appear that by this period a difference was drawn between the *shofar* and the *qeren* (=horn), a *shofar* being made of a ram's horn, and a *qeren* of a bull's horn. During the epoch of the three kings, Saul, David, and Solomon, the *qeren* is never referred to as a musical instrument ; but in later writings (Joshua 6, 5, and Daniel 3, vs. 5, 7, 10, and 15) it is.

There is also mention of *machalat* (I Samuel 18, 6) and *mecholot.* As we have said, the authorities are uncertain whether this word means an instrument or a dance.

CHAPTER IV

THE TWO KINGDOMS

THE religious ceremonial which David introduced and Solomon continued was in musical respects so rich and varied that, as we have already indicated, it must be regarded as the central feature of Israelite musical life. In addition, we have to take note of the poems and 'Lamentations' of various prophets, but these can only be thought of as supplementary to the main stream. It was the Cult that decisively influenced not only state, political, and cultural life, but life generally, to a perhaps unprecedented extent; every political, and indeed every intellectual and religious movement immediately found outward expression in the observances of the Cult. Broadly speaking, two fundamental trends now developed in Israelite life: that of the southern (Judaean), and that of the northern (Ephraimite or Israelite), branch. Although neither of these groups exhibited a single, uniform tendency, the two trends were fundamentally and clearly distinct: the southern kingdom, with its centre at Jerusalem, held fast to the Cult as established by the two great kings David and Solomon, while the northern kingdom, with its centre at Samaria, reverted to the Cult of the times of the Judges, and was influenced to some extent by the cults of the contemporary non-Jewish peoples, such as the Aramaeans of Damascus, the Phœnicians, Egyptians, and, later, the Syrians.

When Solomon died the State of Israel was split into two, to form the northern kingdom of Israel and the southern kingdom of Judah, the former being much the larger. Jeroboam, the first king of Israel, revolted against the Cult of the southern kingdom, broke away from the worship of a 'single,' 'eternal' God, and set up two golden calves as divinities. The Cult which he established at Bethel and Dan was closely akin to the usages of the patriarchal days of the Judges, which were largely of

Canaanite origin. (See chapter II.) On the pretence of meeting the northern Israelites' objections to religious dependence on Jerusalem and its priests, Jeroboam achieved his aim of securing not only religious, but intellectual and political independence of Judah. Rehoboam, the first king of this southern kingdom, began his reign with the intention of observing the forms of religion established by his predecessors, David and Solomon. In consequence, all the Levites in the northern kingdom fled to him in Judah (II Chronicles 11, 13-17), and there maintained the temple tradition in its integrity. However, in the long run the Judaeans were no more able to resist the alien religious influences than their northern kinsmen.

All the stresses in the national life had corresponding reactions in religious life. In both kingdoms the forms of belief which had been firmly established in the temple at Jerusalem began to be affected by pagan cults. None the less, king David's religion and its outward observances remained the ideal for all Israelites, and all else was regarded as a deviation and error. But in practice Jeroboam's defection was not an isolated incident, it was repeated again and again by his successors. In the northern kingdom the worship of Baal and other idols had the consequence that princes of Israel married women of alien nations ; for instance, king Ahab married the Phœnician princess, Jezebel. These foreign women often brought their own priests with them into the country, and always held to their own beliefs. And even though in those days the practice of an alien form of religion by no means excluded honour to Yahve as the supreme God, yet the worship of idols was bound to displace Jewish religious culture and song in all essentials.

All these developments affected the music-making of the time. We cannot do more than mention the influence of the strange cults, through the introduction of ' chambers ' devoted to the cults, the introduction of Baal, Astarte, and other idols ; of two golden calves, or bulls, as divinities ; the worship of sacred trees ; divination by clouds ; spells, magic, battle magic, and exorcisms, for we cannot estimate exactly what influence these had on musical developments. None the less, we can see that music still played a large part in the national life. Following the tradition of their fathers, the Judaeans still used music in the temple service at Jerusalem ; and for all the Israelites music formed part of the coronation ceremony, of religious ceremonial before and after battle, and of popular festivities and customs. Then there were the songs of lamentation and the songs of the prophets, with which we shall be dealing later. The worship of Baal and other idols also must have had some effect on Israelite musical life.

As we have said, during this period of religious, or, to be more exact, of cult error (for, so far as the practice of the cult was concerned, the common people were primarily affected), one ideal was held high: David's form of religious service, and his songs. Of course, as time passed much was added, to correspond with new conditions ; we know, for instance, that many psalms were written after David's death, since they refer to later experiences. Yet the tradition that originated from the Temple of David in Jerusalem was always decisive as the model to be followed.

In II Kings 12, 12-14, we find it expressly mentioned that in the time of king Jehoash no trumpets (*chatzotzerot*) were made of the gold ' that was brought into the house of the Lord,' the gold which was kept in a chest standing on the right-hand side of the altar. So it is evident that at this period trumpets also were in use in the temple. We find them mentioned, too, in the descriptions of coronation ceremonies. When, during the reign of Asa, the Israelites renewed the covenant with the Lord, in other words, ' put away the abominable idols out of all the land of Judah and Benjamin, and out of the cities' (II Chronicles 15, 8) and ' entered into a covenant to seek the Lord God of their fathers' (ibid, v. 12) ' they sware unto the Lord with a loud voice, and with blasts (*bi-teruah*) on trumpets (*chatzotzerot*) and horns (*shoferot*)' (v. 14).

Again and again we are told that the ordinances instituted by king David were regarded as sacrosanct in the temple service. For instance, II Chronicles 23, 18, says that the priest ' Jehoiada appointed the offices of the house of the Lord by the hand of the priests the Levites, whom David had distributed in the house of the Lord, to offer the burnt offerings of the Lord, as written in the law of Moses, with rejoicing and with singing as it was ordained by David.' Similarly, king Hezekiah (720-690 B.C.) ' set the Levites in the house of the Lord with *metziltayim* (cymbals), *nevalim* (harps), and *kinnorot* (cytharas) according to the commandment of David, and of Gad, the king's seer, and Nathan the prophet; for so was the commandment of the Lord by his prophets. And the Levites stood with the instruments of David (*bi-khele David*) and the priests with the *chatzotzerot* (trumpets). Then Hezekiah commanded to offer the burnt offering upon the altar. And when the burnt offering began, the song of the Lord (*shir Adonaï*) began also, with the *chatzotzerot* (trumpets) and with the instruments ordained by David, king of Israel. And all the congregation worshipped, and the singers sang, and the *chatzotzerot* (trumpets) sounded. . . . Moreover, Hezekiah the king and the princes commanded the Levites to sing praise unto the Lord with the words of David and of Asaph the seer. And they praised him with gladness.' (II Chronicles 29, 25-28 and 30.) The same Hezekiah arranged a feast of the Passover, for which the Israelite tribes who had turned away from the faith were invited to Jerusalem, and 'the Levites and the priests praised the Lord day by day, with loud instruments unto the Lord.' (II Chronicles 30, 21.)

In a passage narrating events that occurred in king Hezekiah's reign, Isaiah 36, 3, says: 'Then came forth unto him Eliakim, Hilkiah's son, who was over the house, and Shebna the scribe, and Joab, Asaph's son, the precentor (A.V.—recorder).' Joab the precentor, the son of Asaph, is also mentioned in verse 22 of this same chapter as well as in the parallel passage in II Kings 18, 18. There are many references in scripture to the 'sons of Asaph,' both in the historical books and in superscriptions to various psalms, and in view of the association with 'precentor' in these passages we may hazard the conjecture that the 'sons of Asaph' were assigned to the office of precentor.

King Hezekiah followed his great predecessor, David, in other respects too, for Isaiah 38, 20 attributes to him a song of thanksgiving for recovery from sickness, in which occur the lines:

> 'The Lord, the Lord was ready to save me,
>   Therefore we will sing my songs to the
>   stringed instruments. . . . (*u-neginotai nenaggen.*)'

However, Dubnow considers that this psalm was 'really written by the chronicler himself, as is common in rhetorical history, or else was borrowed from the Temple, from the psalm appointed to be read on restoration to health.'[1]

But after Hezekiah, king Menasseh, the son of this energetic follower of the tradition of David and Solomon, turned away from the path. After a disastrous war against the king of Assyria he was taken in chains to Babylon, but then was set free. He repented of his backsliding and returned to the faith of his father (and his fathers), abolished idol-worship, and reintroduced the temple worship of the Eternal. And in the reign of his grandson Josiah, the Levites Jahath and Obadiah, Zechariah and Meshullam were expressly named not only as overseers of the workmen in the house of God, but as versed in instruments of music. (II Chronicles 34, 12.)

During the reign of Josiah, Hilkiah the priest was emptying the chest containing the temple money, when he found in it the ' Book of the Law' given by Moses. This incident had important consequences. The book was read out to the king, who realised how far they had departed from the law of Moses and took steps to bring its ordinances once more into effect. Among his other acts he arranged for a celebration of the feast of the Passover according to the ancient customs. During the ceremonies in the house of the Lord, ' the singers, the sons of Asaph, were in their place, according to the commandment of David, and Asaph, and Heman, and Jeduthun, the king's seer. . . ." (II Chronicles 35, 15.) This mention of Asaph, Heman, and Jeduthun in association, as on previous occasions, is a clear harking back to the days of king David and his ordinances, when the temple service was originally instituted, and these three priests were appointed, with their sons under them, to various offices. But it is also possible that, as we have suggested in regard to the ' sons of Asaph,' each of these three names represented a separate musical office, instrumental or vocal, in the temple service, in accordance with the original ordinances of David. (cf. I Chronicles 25, etc.). These offices may, at least at first, have been held hereditarily.

One of the outstanding features of this period was that the vocal aspect of religious worship greatly increased in importance. Instruments were more and more relegated to superficial

---

[1] Weltgeschichte des jüdischen Volkes, Berlin, 1930, vol. 1, p. 277.

functions, acquiring a symbolic significance, providing a musical background, accompanying the vocalists, or introducing the announcement of important occurrences, all these functions being in harmony with tradition. Singing becomes more important in religious worship. God's praises were still sung and religious feeling and devotions were still expressed in the manner of king David, but many new songs and hymns were composed in honour of the Lord. Thus developed a clear allocation of functions to instrumental and vocal music: instruments being used to enhance the outward splendour of the temple service, while the words sung in the service gave direct expression to the people's moods of devotion and worship, and their attachment to the religion of their fathers.

The prophetic books frequently refer to music in connection with the temple service, and from these references we obtain a clearer picture of the manner in which the people of those days expressed their singing to the Lord. In Isaiah 12, 4-6, we read:

' And in that day shall ye say, praise (*hodu*) the Lord.
Call upon his name, declare his doings among the people,
Make mention that his name is exalted.

Sing (*zammeru*) unto the Lord, for he hath done
    excellent things ;
This is known in all the earth.

Cry out and shout (*tzahali va-ronni*) thou inhabitant of
    Zion ;
For great is the Holy One of Israel in the midst of thee.'

It would seem that the distinctions drawn between *hodu*, *zammeru*, *tzahali*, and *ronni* refer to variations in the manner of expression, and do not imply completely different conceptions. In his vision of the liberation from the Assyrian yoke the same prophet says (Isaiah 30, 29-32):

' Ye shall have a song, as in the night when a holy
    solemnity is kept,
And gladness of heart, as when one goeth with a pipe
    (*chalil*) to come into the mountain of the Lord,
To the mighty One of Israel.
And the Lord shall cause his glorious voice to be heard. . . .

For through the voice of the Lord shall the Assyrian be
beaten down,
Which smote with a rod.
And in every place where the grounded staff shall pass,
Which the Lord shall lay upon him,
It shall be with tambourines (*tuppim*) and cytharas
(*kinnorot*).'

In those days there was a fresh outburst of religious poetry
and song, as Isaiah says in chapter 42, verse 10:[1] 'Sing unto the
Lord a new song . . . (*shiru ladonai shir chadash*).' And, rejecting
the sacrificial feasts of the erring Israelites, the prophet Amos
declared the words of the Lord (Amos 5, 23):

'Take thou away from me the noise of thy songs,
And your harps (*nevalecha*) I will not hear their playing.'

The 'Vision of Ezekiel' reveals that singers still had official
functions to perform in the newly built temple: 'And without
the inner gate were the chambers of the singers in the inner
court.' (Ch. 40, 44.) His description of the Temple and the sacrifices
recalls the former times, but it also reflects the changed conditions
of national tutelage and poverty. So far as we can gather
from the sparse and incidental references to the question in this
description of the new temple, it would seem that song now
played a more restricted part in the temple service than in the
days of kings David and Solomon. These modest conditions might
well have applied in the days of the first restoration also.

In those days the coronation was neither a purely religious
nor a purely political ceremony. Yet either the actual coronation
or the proclamation of the king was always carried out in the
temple, and on these occasions musical instruments were
employed. When Jehu was proclaimed king (II Kings 9, 13) 'they
blew on the *shofar*.' At the coronation of Joash, Athaliah, who had
been queen, looked, 'and behold, the king stood by a pillar, as
the manner was, and the princes and trumpeters (*chatzotzerot*) by
the king, and all the people of the land rejoiced, and blew with

---

[1] This passage falls within chapters 40-66, which it is generally accepted
were written by an Isaiah (Deutero-Isaiah) of the next era, that of the
Babylonian exile and the Persian domination. In addition, chapters 56-66
have been attributed to a 'Trito-Isaiah.'

trumpets' (II Kings 11, 14). We get further details of this ceremony in II Chronicles 23. This was during the time when the
priest Jehoiada was reorganising the service of Levites on the
model of David's original ordinances. Joash, the seven-year-old
son of king Ahaziah, and grandson of Athaliah, was brought out,
and they 'put upon him the crown, and gave him the regalia'
(v. 11). And Athaliah looked, 'and behold, the king stood at his
pillar at the entering in, and the princes and the trumpets
(*chatzotzerot*) by the king; and all the people of the land rejoiced,
and sounded with trumpets, also the singers with instruments of
music (*bi-khele ha-shir*) and such as taught to sing praise' (v. 13).

War also, then a frequent occurrence, was begun and ended
to the sound of musical instruments; e.g., in the struggle between
Jeroboam, leading the Ephraimite-Israelites, and Abijah, the
Judaean, when the Judaeans 'looked back, behold, the battle
was before and behind; and they cried unto the Lord, and the
priests sounded with the trumpets' (*machtzerim ba-chatzotzerot*)
(II Chronicles 13, 14). When Jehoshaphat was attacked by the
superior might of the Moabites and Ammonites, he found himself
in great danger. 'And the Levites, of the children of the
Kohathites, and of the children of the Korhites stood up to
praise the Lord God of Israel with a loud voice on
high. . . . And when he had consulted with the people, he
(Jehoshaphat) appointed singers unto the Lord, and that should
praise the beauty of holiness, as they went out before the
army, and to say, "praise the Lord; for His mercy endureth for
ever." And now, as they began to cry and sing His praises, the
Lord set ambushes.' This passage suggests some kind of religious
ceremony before the battle. After the battle had been won 'they
came to Jerusalem with harps (*nevalim*) and cytharas (*kinnorot*)
and trumpets (*chatzotzerot*) unto the house of the Lord
(II Chronicles 20, 19-22 and 28). Needless to say, the *shofar* was
the instrument chiefly used before a battle, and it is also mentioned in straightforward descriptions of warfare. The *shofar*,
with its fear-instilling roar, was an essential part of the prophetic
concept of the 'Day of the Lord,' and was also used for announce-
ments and proclamations, especially of risings to achieve freedom
against the foreign yoke, even when this was to be achieved by
God's intervention. This is referred to again and again in the

prophets.[1] But the *shofar* is never used as a musical instrument, and the references to it in the prophets are equally clear on this point. When Isaiah writes, in chapter 58, verse 1:

> 'Cry aloud,
> Spare not,
> Lift up thy voice like a *shofar* . . .'

he is thinking of the powerful, penetrating note of the instrument.

There is one very expressive form of song which is frequently described, and exemplified, in the prophets. We shall be discussing this, the 'lament,' or 'lamentation,' later in this chapter, but meanwhile we may quote II Chronicles 35, 25, which speaks of the prophet Jeremiah's lament for the death of king Josiah, who had been killed in the struggle against the Egyptian king Necho: 'And Jeremiah lamented for Josiah, and all the singing men and singing women spake of Josiah in their lamentations.'

So far as the kingdom of Judah was concerned, the end of this historical era came in the days of the prophet Jeremiah, when Judah, which had retained its independence one hundred and fifty years longer than the northern kingdom, was conquered by Nebuchadnezzar. The great majority of its population were carried off to Babylon, while a small remnant, including Jeremiah, went to Egypt (586 B.C.). The factor of decisive importance in the cultural and religious spheres during this era (eighth to sixth century B.C.) was that it saw the advent of classical prophets, men of a very different quality from the original 'inspired,' the *nevi'im.*

During the stormy days of the two kingdoms and the invasions of the Assyrians and Babylonians there was a great change in the nature and functions of the *nevi'im.* From now on they could rightly be called 'prophets,' though at times they were simply 'preachers.' It was they who took on the task of defending and

---

[1] See Isaiah 18, 3 ; 27, 13 (even *shofar gadol*—large *shofar*), Jeremiah 4, vs. 5, 19, 21 ; 6, vs. 1, 7 ; 42, 14 ; 51, 27 ; Ezekiel 7, 14 (here the phrase is *taqeu va-taqoa*—which commonly means 'wind instrument' [from *taqa*—to blow an instrument]) ; 33, 3 ; Amos 2, 2 ; 3, 6 ; Zephaniah 1, 16 ; Zechariah 9, 14 ; Hosea 5, 8 (here both *shofar* and *chatzotzerah* are mentioned) ; 8, 1 ; Joel 2, 1 and 15.

preserving the Israelite religion of their fathers, it was they who became the spiritual leaders of the people, expressing their views strongly in speech and writing, in prose and poetry. Very often they exerted a profound influence on politics. Exercising all these functions, they were in close affinity with the *shofetim* or judges, of the days before the kings. Thus in a sense they tended to complete the circle of the development of the ' Congregation of Israel,' which at one time had longed for a king, but then had had to suffer many disadvantages from this excursion into power-politics.

The prophets relied on three main forms for conveying their revelations: speeches and sermons, poems (frequently of an allegorical nature) and lamentations (*qinot*). In addition, they were active in originating the type of religious poetry called psalms, and the ' Songs of the House of Yahve ' for which king David's compositions served as a prototype. Their speeches and sermons, partly put into writing by the prophets themselves, partly by their followers, contain many allusions to the conditions of their times, and from them we draw certain brief passages relating to music. These prophetic compositions in poetic form may well have been sung, or ' cantillated,'[1] even in those days. The prophetic books have many references which permit us to conclude that in many cases the utterances of the prophet were sung, while in other cases they were declaimed, or ' said.' For instance, Isaiah 26 opens: ' In that day shall this song be sung in the land of Judah.' But in other passages (e.g., Isaiah 13, 1 ; 14, 28 ; 15, 1 ; 17, 1 ; 19, 1 ; 21, 1) we find the word used is *massa*, which is best translated ' declaration,' ' dictum ' (though Buber translates it ' burdenword,' like the A.V.). Chapter 3, verse 19, of Habakkuk ends: ' to the accompanist on my stringed instruments ' (*la-menatzeach bi-neginotai*),[2] which Luther translates ' to sing to my string-playing.' This chapter is generally recognised as a psalm.

In this respect not only these poetic prophecies, but the songs

---

1 ' Cantillation ' is a term generally used to denote the kind of chanting peculiar to the Jewish religious service, especially to the cantor's and reader's musical renderings.
2 On *la-menatzeach* see Appendix.

of lamentation (*qinot,* singular *qinah*) also, have affinities with the psalms. The lamentations of the prophets developed out of the laments for the dead which were a customary feature of the mourning rites of the time. Undoubtedly the laments were originally confined to funeral obsequies, being sung, groaned, and wailed over the corpse, special bands of wailing women being appointed for the purpose. But the prophets exalted the form into a lament over the unhappy lot of the people, particularly at the time of the deportations to Babylon. The prophets greatly favoured them as a form of expression; many of the *qinot* melodies have been handed down from generation to generation even to the present day. The Lamentations of Jeremiah are well known, but laments are to be found in the writings of other prophets, though they are not always designated as such in the text. They vary greatly in their content, but in the majority of cases they express a tenderly lyrical mood. Instrumental music is frequently drawn upon to provide similes. For instance, Isaiah 16, 11: 'wherefore my bowels shall sound like a harp (*ka-kinnor*) for Moab'; or Jeremiah 48, 36: 'Therefore mine heart shall sound for Moab like pipes (*ka-chalilim*) and mine heart shall sound like pipes (*ka-chalilim*) for the men of Kir-heres.' Here, too, we may cite the later passage from Job 30, 31:

'My cythara (*kinnor*) is turned to a song of lamentation,
And the shawm (*ugav*) to notes of mourning.'

Again, in Lamentations 5, 14-15, we read:

'The elders have vanished from the gate,
The young men from their stringed playing (*mi-neginatam*)
The joy of our heart is ceased,
Our shawm (*mecholenu*) is turned to mourning.'

We learn of music-making in the secular life of the people mainly from indirect references, as, for instance, later, from the passage in Job 21, 12: 'They take up the tambourine (*tof*) and cythara (*kinnor*); they rejoice to the sound of the shawm' (*ugav*). There is frequent reference to instrumental playing and singing in the royal palace, (e.g., Amos 8, 3: 'And the songs of the palace shall be wailings in that day,') and also among the people. Amos laments: 'They that pluck the harp (*ha-poretim al-pi ha-navel*), like David have they invented themselves instruments of music (6, 5). Note that here *ha-poretim*, from *parat*, means to produce single notes, to pluck, used in a rather contemptuous sense. It is noteworthy that the instrument mentioned is the *nevel*, the more primitive type of harp, as also previously in Amos 5, 23. Jeremiah remarks (31, 4):

> 'Thou (Israel) shalt again be adorned with thy tabrets (*tuppayich*)
> And shalt be drawn forth with the merry shawms (*bi-mechol mesachaqim*).

In describing the forthcoming return from Babylonian exile he says (31, 13): 'Then shall the virgin rejoice in the playing of the flute' (*be-machol*). As we have said before, there is no unanimity among the authorities as to the meaning of *machol* and *machalat*.

Isaiah (14, 11) laments the decay and disappearance of the sound 'of thy (Israel's) harps' (*nevalecha*). In Isaiah 23, vs. 15, 16, we are even told of a 'Song of the Harlot': 'after the end of seventy years shall Tyre go forth as with the Song of the Harlot':

> 'Take the cythara (*kinnor*)
> Go about the city;
> Thou forgotten harlot!
> Make sweeter melody,
> Sing more,
> That man may remember thee.'

This short song or snatch of song must have been popular at this time, if Isaiah did not deliberately compose it to use in this context, where the wantonness of the king of Tyre is compared with the wantonness of a harlot.

In any case, we can be quite sure that song was a feature of popular festivities and an accompaniment of wine-drinking. Isaiah says in chapter 5, 1:

> 'Now will I sing to my beloved,
> My friend, a song concerning his vineyard.'

And then (chapter 5, 11-12):

> 'Woe unto them that rise up early in the morning,
> That they may follow after strong drink ;
> That sit on till late at night ;
> The wine heats them.
> And the cythara (*kinnor*), the harp (*nevel*), the tambourine
> (*tof*), the flute (*chalil*) and wine
> Are in their revels.'

Again :

> 'In that day sing ye unto her,
> A vineyard of red wine' (27, 2).

> 'The mirth of tabrets (*tuppim*) ceases,
> The noise of them that rejoice endeth, ,
> The joy of the cythara (*kinnor*) ceaseth ;
> They shall not drink wine with a song,
> Their strong drink shall be bitter' (24, 8-9).

Continually stimulated by the example of king David, religious compositions also flourished. In the service of worship and during religious (*Yahve*) festivals psalms played a very important part. We devote all chapter six to discussion of the psalms, so will not enlarge on the matter here.

None of the writings relating to this period of Israelite existence mentions any instrument we have not met with before. But one change has to be noted. A number of passages in which *qeren* is used indicate that it did not now refer to a wind instrument as in earlier passages,[1] but was simply an expression symbolising power ; it also referred to temple ceremonies.

---

[1] Except in Joshua 6, 5 ; and Daniel 3, vs. 5, 7, 10, and 15.

CHAPTER V

THE BABYLONIAN EXILE
and
THE RESTORATION OF THE TEMPLE
(586-332 B.C.)

AS the deportations to Babylon affected chiefly the upper
strata of the Judaeans, it was natural that even in that
distant land they were not assimilated in cultural, and
still less in religious, respects. Truly, their forefathers had
originally dwelt in the basin of the Euphrates ; but centuries
had passed since then, they had adopted and absorbed some
elements of the Egyptian and rather more of the Canaanite
cultures ; but above all else, they had carried through a national,
cultural and religious development specific to themselves.
Consequently, during their sojourn in Babylon they felt spiritually
' in a strange land,' and they struggled to preserve their own
culture and to prepare for its revival and further development.
Apart from the verbal expression of the religious service,
the foreign influence affected their speech much more than the
content of their lives, and this must also have applied in the
sphere of music. But the references in Daniel 3, especially verses
5, 7, 10, and 15, reveal the pressure of the Babylonian influence:
' That at what time ye hear the sound of the horn (qarna), flute
(mashroqita), cythara (qatros), harp (sabbekha), psaltery
(psanterin), bagpipe (sumponya) and all kinds of music (ve-khol
zene zemara) ye fall down and worship the golden image. . . .'
It is striking that nearly every one of these names is to be found
only in this chapter, and nowhere else in the Scriptures.

The brief period of the Babylonian exile, down to the first
restoration of the Temple at Jerusalem, about 536 B.C., gave the
Judaeans time in which to recall their national heritage of spiritual
and cultural achievement, and, forgetting all their former backsliding and disunity, to recognise that heritage as a national

treasure which it was a sacred obligation to preserve. They unhesitatingly accepted all the ancient prescriptions as obligatory upon them, and all their knowledge of the past ordinances, legends, and stories was preserved in the faith that some day they would be handed down to coming generations in their ancestral homeland. They looked forward full of hope to the future in their own national land.

The country of Judah itself was devastated; inhabited only by a sparse and poverty-stricken population, it was in spiritual and economic chaos. The Israelite culture was moribund. In the north of Judah the Samaritans, only half Hebrew, predominated.

About 539 B.C. Babylon was conquered by King Cyrus of Persia, and, acting in accordance with his conceptions of tolerance for the subdued peoples, and for political considerations, he set the Jews free to return to Judaea and to rebuild their temple. ' Also Cyrus the king brought forth the vessels of the house of the Lord, which Nebuchadnezzar had brought forth out of Jerusalem, and had put them in the house of his gods ' (Ezra 1, 7). Led by Zerubbabel, grandson of king Jehoiakim, who had died in Babylon, and by the priest Jeshua ben Jozadak, grandson of the Jerusalem priest Seriah, who had been executed by Nebuchadnezzar, some 50,000 Jews wandered back to their homeland. And among them were ' two hundred singing men and singing women' (*meshorerim u-meshorerot*) (Ezra 2, 65; see also Nehemiah 7, 67).

Thus they returned home with music, with song and with the playing of instruments. For we read:

' Now in the second year of their coming unto the house of God at Jerusalem, in the second month, began Zerubbabel the son of Shealtiel, and Jeshua the son of Jozadak, and the remnant of their brethren the priests and Levites, and all they that were come out of the captivity unto Jerusalem, and appointed the Levites, from twenty years old and upward, to set forward the work of the house of the Lord. Then stood Jeshua with his sons and his brethren, Kadmiel and his sons, the sons of Judah, together, to set forward the workmen in the house of God: the sons of Henadad, with their sons and their brethren the Levites. And when the builders laid the foundation of the temple of the Lord, they set the priests in their apparel with trumpets (*chatzotzerot*) and the Levites the sons of Asaph with cymbals (*metziltayim*) to praise the Lord, after the ordinance of David king of Israel. And they sang together by course in praising and giving thanks unto the Lord, because he is good, for his mercy endureth for ever toward Israel. And all the people shouted with a great shout, when they praised the Lord, because the foundation of the house of the Lord was laid. But many of the priests and Levites and chief of the fathers, who were ancient men, that had seen the first house, when the foundation of this house was laid before their eyes, wept with a loud voice ; and many shouted aloud for joy, so that the people could not discern the noise of the shout of joy from the noise of the weeping of the people ; for the people shouted with a loud shout, and the noise was heard afar off ' (Ezra 3, 8-13).

This yearning for a 'house of the Lord' and the urge to restore it so soon after their return to Judah were very natural, for in religious respects the Jews had felt constrained 'in the strange land' of Babylon. When the temple was destroyed and the people were deported they were no longer able to observe the temple ordinances, nor could they offer up sacrifices, whether in exile or in Judah. In Babylon the one substitute for the temple worship was the religious assembly which each apparently auto-nomous local community organised. Now they had returned to their native land, and once more they could have their true temple, in full accordance with tradition. From all the narratives of the time we learn that Moses' prescriptions and David's temple ordinances, as they had been handed down by oral and written tradition, were accepted as decisive and binding. However, owing to the intrigues of the Samaritans and of the alien tribes dwelling in the land—in which connection the political unrest and the Persian wars must also have had considerable influence—the work of building the temple was not completed at this time. The task was not taken up again until sixteen years later, in the reign of king Darius, and was completed in 516 B.C. And then 'the Children of Israel, the priests, and the Levites, and the rest of the children of the captivity, kept the dedication of this house of

God with joy. . . . And they set the priests in their divisions and the Levites in their courses, for the service of God, which is at Jerusalem ; as it is written in the book of Moses' (Ezra 6, 16 and 18). This 'second temple' was not on such a magnificent scale as that of Solomon's. None the less, as we learn from the contemporary prophets Haggai and Zechariah, it stimulated the Judaeans to fresh spiritual and intellectual development.

So Jerusalem again became a vital centre of religious life, and—seventy years after the destruction of the 'first temple'—seemed to have regained its former place as the home of the Israelite Cult. But, despite this religious restoration, the Jews were unable to accomplish either a religious renaissance, or even moderate political independence for their country. The local indigenous life had been overborne by too many foreign elements. Thus their hopes of revival were disappointed, until Ezra son of Seraiah, 'a priest and learned in the writings' (ha-kohen ha-sofer), organised a second return and restoration. He obtained plenipotentiary powers from king Artaxerxes I, Longimanus, and entered Jerusalem in the year 457 B.C., bringing with him 'of the Children of Israel, and of the priests, and the Levites, and the singers, and the porters, and the servants' (Ezra 7, 7), altogether some 1,500 men with their families. He rallied the national aspirations and endeavours around himself, and set to work at once to reform and renew the religious life of the people, which, as is always the case at such times, was hardly separable from their public and private life.

To assist him, king Artaxerxes himself appointed his own cupbearer, Nehemiah son of Hachaliah, as governor, with full powers, in 444 B.C. The twelve years Nehemiah spent in Jerusalem as governor were very fruitful for Jewish spiritual, political and social revival. His first step was to set about the rebuilding of the city wall, in order to separate and secure the people and their cult from the outer world. He tells us that during the rebuilding of the wall, 'for the builders, every one had his sword girded by his side, and so builded. And he that sounded the shofar was by me' (Nehemiah 4, 12). When the wall and the city gate were completed, he appointed 'porters and singers and the Levites' (7, 1) ; and together with Ezra he set about complete restoration. They dedicated the wall with great pomp, once more, it appears,

44

in the desire to follow the example of king David and king Solomon. 'And at the dedication of the wall of Jerusalem they sought the Levites out of all their places, to bring them to Jerusalem, to keep the dedication with gladness, both with thanksgiving, and with singing, with cymbals (*metziltayim*), harps (*nevalim*) and cytharas (*kinnorot*) (ibid., 12, 27). And Nehemiah 'brought up the princes of Judah upon the wall, and appointed two great choruses of thanksgiving and festivity, one on the right hand upon the wall towards the dung-gate. And after them went Hoshaiah, and half of the princes of Judah. And of the priests' sons with trumpets (*chatzotzerot*) Zechariah . . . And his brethren . . . with the musical instruments of David (*bi-khele shir David*) the man of God, and Ezra the scribe before them . . . But the second chorus of thanksgiving went to the other side, and I (Nehemiah) after them, and the half of the people upon the wall, over the tower of the furnace as far as the broad wall. . . . So the two choruses of thanksgiving stood still in the House of God, and I, and half of the rulers with me ; and the priests . . . with the trumpets (*chatzotzerot*) . . . And the singers sang, with Jezrahiah, their overseer . . . and both the singers and the doorkeepers kept the ward of their God . . . according to the commandment of David, and of Solomon his son ' (Nehemiah 12, vs. 31-2, 35-6, 38, 40-42, 45). The worship of God was reinstituted in the Temple, and music and song were again cultivated. As Nehemiah says :

'And Mattaniah the son of Micha, the son of Zabdi, the son of Asaph, was the principal to begin the thanksgiving in prayer ; and Bakbukiah the second thereafter of his brethren, and Abda the son of Shammua, the son of Galal, the son of Jeduthun.' We are not in a position to determine whether these genealogies, tracing the line back to the two singers, Asaph and Jeduthun, of David's time, are imaginary or real, though it must be pointed out that only three generations are mentioned in each instance, to cover some five hundred years. But in any case they indicate an hereditary interest in a musical profession. This passage also justifies the deduction that at this period the service of prayers provided for a soloist (precentor), i.e., Mattaniah, and a choir. Altogether there were two hundred and eighty-four Levites in the holy city, and we are told that their overseer ' was Uzzi, the son of Bani, the son of Hashabiah, the son of Mattaniah, the son of Micha, of the sons of Asaph, the singers in the service of the house of God. For it was the king's commandment concerning them, and the singers were obliged by covenant: the day's honorarium for his day' (ibid., 11, 17-18, 22-23). 'Mattaniah, he and his brethren, were for the giving of devotions . . . And the chiefs of the Levites . . . with their brethren over against them, to praise and give thanks according to the commandment of David . . . ' (ibid., 12, 8, 24).

Social reforms and reforms in religious practices were carried through at the same time. The *Torah*, or Teaching (i.e., the Pentateuch), was recognised as binding more perhaps than ever before in Israelite history. In the temple service great trouble was taken to follow David's and Solomon's ordinances as faith-fully as possible. The prophets yielded place to the scribes (*soferim*). The scribes, of whom Ezra was the first to be called by that name as well as priest (*ha-kohen*) conducted the religious assemblies, called by the Greek word 'synagogues,' at which the *Torah* was taught and expounded. The reading and singing of psalms also formed an essential part of the devotions in these assemblies. Undoubtedly the Jews brought this institution from Babylon, where the 'synagogues' had been a substitute for divine service in the temple, and it was Ezra who developed it on a larger scale. We know that at a later period in Jewish history these synagogues took over the observance of the temple sacred service and its service of sacrifice.

Apart from this revived national, spiritual, and religious centre in Jerusalem, a temple also existed for those whom Judah rejected and regarded as unclean. The Samaritan leader Sanballat erected a temple on Mount Gerizim, in which the priests, Levites, and scribes expelled from the Jewish community at Jerusalem con-ducted the service. Their cult consisted of a mingling of ancient Israelite and later Judaic elements.

However, by this time there were Jewish colonies outside Palestine: in Babylon, Syria, Iran, Asia Minor, and Egypt, in each of which Jews were developing their own communities. For all these communities the restored Jerusalem was the model and symbol ; it was the object of all their aspirations, it was the light in their darkness. But these colonies, especially those in Babylon and later that at Alexandria, had a reciprocal influence on the Judaean homeland, for a number of them were at times very strong not only economically but culturally. After the exile to Babylon a part of Jewry was always broken into geographically sundered groups, with their spiritual centre in Judah, but living scattered among alien peoples, in the Diaspora. Outside influence on the Israelites' musical culture had probably been quite strong in the past; but, as is always the case, such influence was exerted even more strongly on the Diaspora. Yet, as time passed, the communities scattered in the Diaspora saw more and more clearly that it was their task to maintain the tradition, and so they increasingly became the conservators of the ancient music of their ancestral homeland.

CHAPTER VI

THE PSALMS

A S we have remarked in previous chapters, there was a great development of religious poetry in ancient Israel. Of course, many of the songs we have discussed were not included in the collection known as the ' Psalms,'[1] but they come within the same category, of songs of praise and devotion to God. Many passages in the Book of Psalms are to be found elsewhere in the Scriptures, in Chronicles, for instance. This is because the recording, or perhaps the collection of the psalms into a single book, occurred at a comparatively late period, when the texts were already well known orally, and so it was easy to insert passages from them in other writings.[2] We can do no more than make some attempt to determine the original source of such a passage by studying its character or its allusions, such as point to definite historical events. For instance, the ' Psalms of the King,' i.e., those which praise God as king, could hardly have been composed before the times of the Israelite kings, for previously the entire conception of kingship had been alien to Israelite thought. Thus, the phrase ' He (*Yahve*) is become king' would signify that the people of Israel had once more placed themselves under Yahve, and had recognised him as their ' highest' king, as their God (the most High Lord).

The oldest of the psalm poems date back to the earliest days of the Children of Israel, and had their beginnings at the time of the first religious lyrics. We know that the Israelites must have been influenced by the hymn and psalm poetry of the Babylonians and Egyptians when they dwelt among these peoples. Also, in

---

[1] The ' Psalms'—songs of praise—are called *Tehillim* in Hebrew ; the word is derived from *hallel*, to praise, exult, rejoice.

[2] In the eighth volume of ' Dissertazioni preliminari alla traduzione de' Salmi,' published by Saverio Mattei at Padua, 1780, Father Metastasio expressed the opinion that the Psalms were copied out from the temple choirbooks together with all the musical terms. This view was undoubtedly based on the corresponding Christian practice.

recent years a great deal of information on the religious poetry of the Canaanites has come to light, and there is little doubt that it exerted a profound influence on Israelite poetry and music. The psalms waxed and waned in popularity among the Children of Israel in accordance with their attitude to their religion at any moment; when alien, non-Israelite religious practices had less hold upon them, then their own Israelite psalms were more in favour as an essential part of the temple service and of religious worship generally. This is shown, for example, by the fact that the composition and dissemination of psalms were most marked in the days of the prophets.

In any case, no matter how strongly the Israelites were influenced by the poetry of non-Israelite peoples, in their psalms they achieved such a high development of poetic language and imagination that a new kind of poem was bound to result. They themselves realised that their psalms contained much that was new, otherwise they would not so often have described them as new. For instance, Psalm 40, 4, says:

> 'He hath put a new song in my mouth,
> A song of praise unto our God.'

Similarly Psalm 96, 1 (also 98, 1):

> 'O sing unto the Lord a new song,
> Sing unto the Lord, all the earth.'

It is impossible to determine exactly when each psalm or group of psalms was created, or who was its author, but we can be sure that the form dates back to the earliest days of Israelite lyrical poetry. And we do know that the first kings of Israel did much to foster the art, irrespective of whether they themselves wrote and sang psalms, or whether they encouraged others to write them. For instance, even if we accepted the opinion that the Book of Psalms as we know it to-day includes none by king David himself, we can still take it for granted that he had a considerable influence on the psalmists of his time. As the Israelite Cult took stronger hold of the nation and as the prophets grew in influence there was increasing resort to the writing and singing of psalms, and the art came to its finest flower contemporaneously with the great age of prophecy, from the eighth to the fifth centuries B.C. It can hardly be said that there was any development or change in the character of the psalms after the states of Judah and Israel were overthrown and the people were carried off into exile ; but this may be due to a spiritual attitude which we find expressed in Psalm 137, verse 4: 'How shall we sing the Lord's song in a strange land ? ' In their exile, all the past achievements of Jewish national and religious life came to be regarded as a cultural heritage which was their one spiritual surety, their one rallying-point in defence of national solidarity. In exile the Jewish community, holding itself apart from the alien environment, lived in the strength of the past days of glory, defending the ancient traditions. On the return from exile they rallied still more strongly around their traditions, and probably only a few psalms and hymns were written in the ensuing period. Psalms were generally appreciated and sung or recited in public after 500 B.C., but their poetic quality was already declining. The writing of psalms probably came to an end in the days of the Maccabees, in the middle of the second century B.C.

The Book of Psalms contains 150 songs.[1] The Septuagint[2] includes a 151st psalm, which has the duel between David and Goliath as its subject ; but it is regarded as apocryphal. The book as we know it to-day consists of various groups of psalms brought together to make the one collection. Thus, there are the psalms of Korah, the psalms of Asaph, and the psalms of David, differentiated from one another chiefly by their superscriptions. In addition there are isolated psalms ascribed to Solomon, and others which have no ascription at all. The psalms of Korah and Asaph, and certain of those of David were probably appointed for the temple service and sung or otherwise rendered during the service. On the other hand, the psalms of David include a number of poems that could not have been written for religious use. Most of these have a superscription which includes a brief biographical note indicating

---

[1] The designation of the whole collection as a ' psalter ' is derived from the Greek *psalterion*, a large harp with twenty strings.

[2] I.e., the translation of the Hebrew Scriptures into Greek, made in the third century B.C., and so called because it was said to have been made by seventy-two elders in seventy-two days (Josephus, Antiquities, 12, 2).

when and where David composed them. (Psalms 51, 52, 54, 56, 57, 59, 63.) Apparently the circumstances in which they were composed and first publicly presented were not connected with religious practice. Professor N. H. Tur-Sinai (formerly Torczyner) of Jerusalem, has recently put forward the theory that the psalms are songs which the writer of the story of David interspersed with his narrative of historic events, in order to illustrate them, just as later the Latin historians of Roman times inserted speeches into their histories.[1] We have no certain knowledge of the original purpose of the psalms bearing the superscription: *shir ha-maalot* or *shir la-maalot*, as the meaning of the word *maalot* is unknown. The Talmudic commentaries assume that it means 'pilgrimages,' signifying that the psalms bearing this superscription are among those that may have been sung on the occasion of the three festivals of Passover, Pentecost, and Tabernacles during the pilgrim's journey to Jerusalem, or on similar occasions.

Authorities divide the entire collection of psalms into five books. Gunkel, in his 'Einleitung in die Psalmen,' distinguishes the following types: hymns, songs of Yahve's ascent of the throne, people's songs of lamentation, psalms of the king, individual songs of lamentation, individual songs of thanks, and various smaller classes (expressions of victory, of malediction, the pilgrimage songs, the songs of victory, the songs of thanks of Israel, legends, and the *Torah*). Like most classifications, the foregoing is only approximately correct, as it is rare for any one poem to fall exclusively into one class.

On studying the psalms for ideas and terms that may have connection with music, we must turn first and foremost to the psalms of David. The majority of these (53-62, 68, 69) have superscriptions containing terms which, it is generally accepted, indicate the manner in which they are to be rendered. Unfortunately, we do not know exactly what these terms signify, especially those which are assumed to point to the musical interpretation. (We give a list of these terms in the Appendix.) Even the Septuagint fails to provide any satisfactory information on the subject. Consequently, authorities have hazarded various opinions as to their application to the musical aspect or interpretation of

---

[1] Tur-Sinai, Halashon Vehasefer II, Jerusalem, Mosad Bialik, 1951.

the psalms in which they are used. Some would confine certain of them, e.g., *al ha-gittit* (A. V. 'upon Gittith,' Psalms 8, 81, 84); *al mut* (A. V. Psalm 9, 'upon Muth'); *al alamot* (Psalm 46, 'upon Alamoth'); *al yonat elem rechoqim* ('like doves the distant trees,' Psalm 56); *al tash-chet* ('ruin not,' A. V. Al-Taschith, Psalms 57, 58, 59, 75); *al shushan edut* (Psalm 60); *al shoshannim* (Psalm 69); *el shoshannim edut* (Psalm 80) to the place where the melodies came into being, others to the melody to which the given psalm was to be sung; while there are yet other explanations. Many of the obscurities are perhaps to be ascribed to errors in transcription, which now cannot be cleared up. So no light can be thrown on this group of problems.

In the work already mentioned[1] Tur-Sinai has recently propounded new explanations of a number of these terms. Thus he suggests that the word *shoshan* is the *cyperus papyrus* on which the scribes indited the poems (cf. Accadian *shishnu, shishanu,* and Syrian *shishna*). The expressions *anot, shir, hazkir, lammed,* etc., are to be understood only by reference to the history in which the particular psalm was inserted: i.e., the song which David ordered to be sung, remembered, taught, etc. Musical directions such as *el hanchilot, al hashminit, al hagittit, al alamot,* etc., are simply abbreviations for: 'David ordered the songs to be sung on Nehilot'; or: 'David ordered the maidens (*alamot*) to sing this and that.' (One may recall David's words in his lamentation over Saul: [II Samuel 1, 24] 'Daughters of Israel, weep over Saul.') *Shire Hama'alot* are songs to accompany the lifting of the Ark of the Covenant, sung by David and Solomon when the Ark was kept in Jerusalem. Other poets later wrote further poems on the same subject (see Psalm 132), including poets of the generation which returned from the exile to Babylon, especially when they began to rebuild the Temple. Tur-Sinai comments that the Psalms can only be understood by having regard to the situation to which their authors or modifiers fitted them.

Certain internal allusions can reveal what was the purpose for which the particular psalm was written (they have very differing functions) and where it belongs. Thus, verse four of

---

[1] Tur-Sinai, op. cit.

Psalm 49 indicates that it was said when questioning an oracle:

> 'I incline mine ear to the verdict,
> Unveil my questions upon the harp (*kinnor*).'

But the most usual subject is the expression of homage, and gratitude to and yearning for the 'Eternal,' to God:

> 'My soul longeth, yea, even fainteth for the courts of the Lord;
> My heart and my flesh crieth out for the living God.'
>
> (Psalm 84, 2.)

> 'Blessed are they that dwell in thy house;
> They will be always praising thee.'
>
> (Psalm 84, 4.)

> 'Praise waiteth for thee, O God, in Zion.'
>
> (Psalm 65, 1.)

> 'O come, let us sing unto the Lord;
> Let us make a joyful noise to the rock of our salvation;
> Let us come before his presence with thanksgiving,
> And make a joyful noise unto him with psalms.'
>
> (Psalm 95, 1-2.)

> 'I will sing unto the Lord as long as I live;
> I will sing praise (*azammera*) to my God, while I have my being.'
>
> (Psalm 104, 33.)

> 'Sing unto him (*shiru lo*)
> Make music unto him (*zammeru lo*).'
>
> (Psalm 105, 2.)

> 'While I live I will praise the Lord;
> I will make music unto my God while I have any being.'
>
> (Psalm 146, 2.)

We can turn now to discussion of the manner in which the psalms were rendered, at least, in so far as we find indications in various passages of the psalms themselves. So far as we can tell from such passages, they were sometimes spoken, 'said'; sometimes they were cantillated, in a rising and falling tone; and sometimes they were sung. There could not have been a very great difference between these various techniques, and the difference depended not so much on the text itself as on the occasion (holy days, days of mourning, days of festivity, and so on); and on the place in which they were rendered and the person rendering them. The rendering of a Levite must have been very different from that of a layman. Despite the great length of time which has elapsed since the heyday of Jewish psalm-writing, their melodic settings have to some extent survived to our times; many of them were even taken over by the early Christian church together with the words, and were perpetuated in Roman Catholic ritual. We shall deal with this question in chapter nine, when discussing the *neginot,* or synagogal tropes, and the *teamim,* the accent marks found in the Jewish scriptures. Much of what we have said in previous chapters about Jewish music is applicable to the problem of performance of the psalms, and in fact much is applicable exclusively to them. Moreover, the Biblical texts can themselves help to fill out our knowledge of the circumstances and background in which psalms were rendered.

' I have seen the procession for thee, O God,
  The procession into the sanctuary for my God, my King.
  The singers went before,
  The string-players (*nogenim*) followed after,
  Among them the maidens beating the timbrels (*be-tokh
    alamot tofefot*).'

(Psalm 68, 24-25.)

Here ' maidens ' seems rather a strained translation of *alamot,*[1] since neither maidens nor women generally were allowed to take any part in the ' sanctuary.'

' Then come I unto the altar of God,
  Unto God my exceeding joy,
  And do homage to thee with the cythara (*kinnor*)
  O God my God.'

(Psalm 43, 4.)

On *Alamot,* see Appendix.

' I will also praise thee with the harp (*nevel*)
Because thou preservest, my God,
To play on the cythara (*kinnor*).'

(Psalm 71, 22.)

The psalms, whether sung, said, or chanted, could be rendered by various combinations of voices. All the text might be delivered by a soloist, or distributed between a soloist and a choir (consisting of Levites, or priests), or the congregation, in the manner of versicles and responses ; or the soloist might deliver the body of the text, while the congregation would end with an *Amen* ('The truth—so it is!'). Psalm-singing was the frequent accompaniment of processions on special occasions, as we see for instance in Psalm 68 already quoted, and in Nehemiah 12, 27-28 and 31 :

'And at the dedication of the wall of Jerusalem they sought the Levites out of all their places, to bring them to Jerusalem, to keep the dedication with gladness, both with thanksgiving, and with song, cymbals (*metziltayim*), harps (*nevalim*) and cytharas (*kinnorot*). And the singers gathered together . . . and (I) appointed two great companies of them that give thanks, whereof one went on the right hand upon the wall toward the dung gate. . . .'

According to II Chronicles 20, 19, it was usually ' The Levites of the sons of Kohath, and of the sons of Korah,' who ' praised the God of Israel with a loud voice on high.' Thus we can deduce that it was the descendants of Kohath and Korah who were responsible for the religious performance of the psalms. This also elucidates the frequency of the words *bene Qorach* (Sons of Korah) in superscriptions to various psalms. It is possible that the psalms with this superscription were originally performed by the Korahites, and that when the Book of Psalms was collected later this fact was indicated. On the other hand, in Chronicles and elsewhere there is frequent mention of the singers Asaph, Heman, and Ethan-Jeduthun, the descendants of the three Levitical families of Gershom, Kahat, and Merari. In ' The Old Testament, its Origin and Tradition,' Sir William Smith concludes that after ' The singers, the children of Asaph, a hundred twenty and eight ' (or alternatively an hundred forty and eight) (Ezra

2, 41, and Nehemiah 7, 44) had returned from exile they were the only singers in the Temple, while in Chronicles the sons of Korah are referred to as doorkeepers, so that in the days of Nehemiah they were not yet, and in the time of the Chronicles, no longer singers in the Temple. Gunkel challenges this view, being rather of the opinion that, conformably with I Chronicles 6, 18; 9, 19 and 31; and II Chronicles 20, 19, the Korahites have to be reckoned among the Levites.

Instrumental music was prominent in the temple service generally, but especially in the rendering of the psalms. This is evident from the following passages (although the exact meaning of certain phrases cannot now be established, we give the translations of these):

'Praise the Lord with cythara (*kinnor*)
Make him music on the ten-stringed harp (*benevel asor*).
Sing unto him a new song (*shir chadash*);
Play finely with jubilant sound (*hetivu nagen bi-teru'ah*).'

(Psalm 33, 2-3.)

'. . . I sing, play up (*ashira va-azammerah*).
Awake, my praise,
On harp (*nevel*) and cythara (*kinnor*).'

(Psalm 57, 7-8.)

'Sing aloud unto God our strength,
Make a jubilant noise to the God of Jacob.
Sound out the music, strike the timbrel (*tof*),
The cythara (*kinnor*), play loud on the harp (*nevel*)
Blow the *shofar* at the new moon,
For the full moon, on the day of our festival.'

(Psalm 81, 1-3.)

'It is a good thing to give thanks to the Lord,
To sing to thy Name, Lord most high.
To announce thy loving kindness in the morning,
And thy faithfulness every night,
On the ten-stringed instrument (*ale asor*) and on the harp (*nevel*)
To sound the cythara (*al higgayon be-kinnor*).'

(Psalm 92, 1-3.)

Make a joyful noise unto the Lord, all the earth;
Make a loud noise, and jubilate, and make music;
Play to the Lord on the cythara (*kinnor*)
With the cythara, and the voice of a song.
With trumpets (*chatzotzerot*) and the *shofar* sound,
Rejoice to the Lord, the King.'

(Psalm 98, 4-6.)

'I sing a new song unto thee, O God,
On the ten-stringed harp (*benevel asor*)
I play to thee.'

(Psalm 144, 9.)

'Praise ye Yah!
For it is good to sing praises unto our God . . .
Sing unto the Lord with devotion,
Make music to our God on the cythara (*kinnor*).'

(Psalm 147, 1 and 7.)

'Praise ye Yah!
Sing unto the Lord a new song,
His song of praise in the congregation of the devout!
They shall praise his name with shawms (*machol*[1])
Make music to him with timbrel (*tof*) and with cythara
(*kinnor*).'

(Psalm 149, 1 and 3.)

'Praise him with the sound of the horns (*be-teqa shofar*)
Praise him with timbrel (*tof*) and shawm (*machol*)
Praise him with the music of stringed instruments (*minim*)
    and flute (*ugav*)
Praise him with clashing cymbals (*be-tziltzele teru'ah*).'

(Psalm 150, 3-5.)

---

[1] Several translations of Psalms 149 and 150 translate *machol* as 'dance,'
e.g., the A.V., Buber, Luther, and Gunkel (in his 'Einleitung in die
Psalmen'). Kautzsch goes so far as to give it the meaning of a (liturgical)
round dance. Yet it is possible that an instrument is meant, as only
musical instruments are listed (see also pp. 6, 10, 16). It is, however,
striking that in Psalm 150 *machol* follows the *tof* (tambourine). Moreover,
as Egyptian pictorial representations show, tambourines were especially
used with dances, and here *machol* might signify a religious dance.

As we have already said, the psalm belonged to Zion, to the Temple at Jerusalem, for which it was appointed. We get a striking affirmation of this in Psalm 137, 1-4:

> ' By the rivers of Babylon, we sojourned,
> Ah, we wept,
> When we thought of Zion.
> There on the willow trees
> We hung our cytharas (*kinnorotenu*)
> For there our captors demanded of us a song,
> And our tormentors mirth:
> " Sing us one of the songs of Zion."
> How shall we sing the Lord's song
> In a strange land ? '

Even to-day there are many, chiefly orthodox and conservative Jewish communities which, influenced by this psalm, will not allow any musical instrument to be played in synagogues outside Palestine, except perhaps at weddings, although all the psalms are included in the present-day synagogue service and many of them contain references to instrumental playing.

In conclusion, we may repeat that all we have said about Jewish music in scriptural times essentially applies to the Psalms also ; even the instruments mentioned are the same. But as it is accepted by all authorities to-day that the Book of Psalms contains poems from various periods of Israelite history, that is quite natural.

CHAPTER VII

THE GREEK AND ROMAN CULTURAL EPOCHS
(332 B.C. to 73 C.E.)

THE detailed consideration we have given to the music of the Children of Israel has enabled us to make a very wide survey of the origin and development of their cultural life in the sphere of music, in so far as it is at all possible to reconstruct that life. In the course of our survey we have seen that during the first thousand years of Israelite history in their own country the Cult peculiar to them became the chief centre of musical activity. Accepting the assumption that the Jewish scriptures came into being and were recorded either before or during the Babylonian exile, we can make two alternative deductions in regard to the music of pre-exile times. Either the tradition as thus recorded faithfully communicated the nature of the music in those bygone days, in which case we still have the actual details of that music ; or, on the other hand, the details have, truly, been passed down to us, but modified by the forms of expression current at the time of recording. In the latter case we would have to accept that the scriptural records of Israelite music for any period before the Babylonian exile were not entirely true to the past, but were affected by contemporary musical custom. On the other hand, if the books of the Pentateuch did in fact come into being before the rest of the scriptures, as the great majority of biblical authorities consider, they contain the oldest records of Israelite music.

In any case, so far as the majority of the other books now included in the biblical canon—covering chiefly the histories and the books of the prophets—are concerned, we appear to be justified in accepting as a fact that they were committed to writing not later than in Ezra's day ; and that this was one of the tasks assigned to the *soferim*, or scribes, by the *Keneset ha-Gedolah*, or Great Assembly, which is said to have been founded by Ezra after the return from Babylon. They were taken down wholly or partly from oral tradition, which perhaps was modified by reference to various accepted written versions. This justifies the assumption that details of music given in these writings cover the period down to the times of Ezra. So far as the Books of Ezra and Nehemiah are concerned, these are purely historical records, compiled from accounts supplied either by Ezra and Nehemiah themselves, or by circles in close touch with them. So here we find ourselves on contemporary ground, and we need no longer consider the possibility of great deviations from the actual state of affairs, so long as we accept the reliability of the historians themselves. This is one reason why we shall not consider the next cultural period (which in any case really consists of more than one period) in such great detail as those preceding it ; for we no longer need to consider various possible hypotheses, nor do we have to supply so many conjectural details. We must add that most of the available sources for details of the next period of Jewish culture are in Greek, and that references to music are extremely scanty.

Down to the last third of the fourth century B.C. the Jewish religion, and its forms, usages, and practices were being developed and extended ; it was in process of creation by the Children of Israel themselves. But with Ezra came a fundamental change in the direction of organisation of the state, and this entailed a momentous cultural change. Under Ezra and Nehemiah the people of Judah cut themselves off from the outer world in both racial and cultural regards ; and they became the chief exponents of the Israelite cultural and religious heritage. On the other hand, on the periphery, so to speak, there were now Jewish centres in the Diaspora, primarily in Babylon and Egypt, and at various times these centres came to have great importance. Some indication of their importance can be gained from the fact that the rabbis of the Babylonian community produced their own version of the Talmud, much fuller than that of the Jerusalem community, and that the Alexandrine Jews were responsible for the Septuagint translation of the Jewish scriptures. Because of this development of centres in the Diaspora we shall speak in future of the history of the Judaic, the Jewish people, who followed the Israelite religion, of which the spirit and the culture is called Judaism. By the time Ezra completed his reforming activities this people had reached a point in cultural development in which it regarded the written and oral tradition as unimpugnable, and this was bound to arrest that development to some extent. True, later generations of Jews produced a mass of writings, but with small exceptions these were essentially in the nature of commentaries, based on the Scriptural canon.

Development in the Israelite Cult, with its attendant musical practice, was dictated by the constitution of their religion. Constitutionally this was founded on the 'Covenant' which, according to tradition, the Children of Israel had concluded with their one God. Strictly speaking, the problem of *belief* in this God was not discussed in the Jewish scriptures ; so far as we know they contain no special word or verbal formula for this conception—for 'I believe in,' for instance. In the course of time this 'Covenant' acquired all the status of a treaty, with various treaty obligations. It was the prophets who first laid emphasis on the spiritual content of the 'Covenant,' and in doing so gave the Israelite religion a spiritual basis. On the other hand, even in the days of the prophets music, as a phenomenon attendant on all religious activities and institutions, and on the rite itself, provided no special impulse towards the representation of beauty in the Greek sense or towards the development of a spiritual content for itself, but continued simply to be part of the Cult. Consequently, only when there was a far-reaching and fundamental formulation of the Cult, such as occurred in king David's time, could music acquire new or deeper significance. In such circumstances the final formulation of the manner in which the psalms, for instance, were to be rendered must have opened up new possibilities in musical practice, in this case chiefly in vocal regards. We can be sure that the psalms played a very important part in the vocal aspect, i.e., the singing, of the Jewish Cult.

After the downfall of the great Persian Empire, in 332 B.C., the Jewish people were subjected to quite new outside influences, and had to struggle to maintain their traditions, while all their national character, their viability and powers of resistance were put to the proof. Previously the Israelites had come into effective cultural contact only with oriental peoples, chiefly the Babylonians, Assyrians, Egyptians, Canaanites, and surrounding tribes. During the evolutionary period of their history they acquired a great deal from these oriental peoples, while rejecting and prohibiting much more out of a spirit of opposition. As they, like the other oriental peoples to some extent, were in an evolutionary and formative phase, they were able to take over alien elements more easily. In this phase, too, they could easily refashion and spiritually subdue what they took over, if it was in accordance with their own characteristics. Thus they were able to assimilate a great deal especially from Babylonian and Canaanite cultures. By the fourth century B.C. the Jewish nation had acquired a distinctive taste for all branches of national, social, religious, and cultural life. But now non-oriental peoples, first the Greeks and then the Romans, each of whom had achieved their own distinctive development and represented quite a different world, acquired a dominating rôle in the life of the people of Judah.

The music of the Greeks and the Romans must have had only trifling influence on that of the Jews. There is nothing to show how far that influence extended or what modifications it effected. On the other hand, there are a number of sources depicting the Jewish struggle to maintain their national religion and its observances. Since we must accept that during both the Hellenic and the Roman cultural period music was of importance only in association with the Cult, we must conclude that neither the Greek nor the Roman Cult could have influenced it essentially, since the Jews were successful in maintaining their national characteristics, doing so with determination and even by resort to arms. Beyond doubt, during these periods there was a greater cleavage between the music of the Cult and secular music than ever before. Our basis for this assumption is that the Hellenists, as they were called, those who advocated the Hellenising of Judah, gradually took over a certain amount of Greek culture. As the Judaeans came into contact with Greek, and later with Roman, culture through ' gymnasia,' theatres, and other activities, they must have absorbed some of the alien song, and possibly instrumental music. But as they very zealously defended their Jewish religion and the temple music from foreign influences, it must have diverged even more from the tastes and perceptions of foreign contemporaries. In consequence the temple music must have sounded antiquated, obsolete ; yet the keepers of the temple tradition insisted that it could not be changed by one jot or tittle. We know that such an attitude could not be maintained in its entirety. But we note as a characteristic feature of the Greek and Roman epochs that the temple music grew still more antiquated and that there was an even greater cleavage and alienation between it and profane music.

How far Jewish secular music was influenced by Greek music, by the already classic concept of art as the representation of beauty, we have no means of telling. We must assume that it had some influence, for at one time the Judaeans shared very actively in the life and the customs of the Greeks, and later of the Romans. And, of course, these secular acquisitions must ultimately have had influence on Jewish religious music. Of one thing we can be certain, the devout Judaeans took nothing consciously from the Greeks and Romans, least of all in the sphere of religious music. On the contrary, they fought, even with weapons, against everything they regarded as alien and not inherent in the tradition, and continued to do so even after they had lost all autonomy in their own country.

When Alexander of Macedon conquered the Persian Empire in 332 B.C., Judah also fell under his rule. The oriental influence was rapidly replaced by the Greek. The international Aramaic language, which the Jews also used in everyday life, was gradually replaced by Greek. Judah was united politically with Syria to form ' Coelesyria ' (Lower Syria) and this also determined the direction of the country's cultural development. The Jewish community in Alexandria, the city founded by Alexander, grew to great importance. It was the first Jewish community to come into contact with Greek culture, and for a time it was the intermediary between Jews and Greeks. It was responsible for the translation of most of the Hebrew Scriptures into Greek (especially the Septuagint), with the object of disseminating them among non-Hebrew-speaking Jews, and also among the Greeks. In Judah itself the Hellenist Jews who attempted to introduce Greek culture into the country were vigorously opposed by the so-called ' Chasidim.'[1] The ' Chasidim,' or ' devout,' called upon Jews to be true to Judaism, and struggled desperately against the

---

[1] Not to be confused with the Chasidim movement founded in the eighteenth century. H.C.S.

Hellenistic trends; but from the days of the Hasmoneans (Maccabees) onward they had to fight simultaneously not only against the Hellenists but also against the foreign domination of the state. They achieved serious results only in the sphere where the influence of the Hellenists and the state authorities was least effective, namely, in religious worship.

Yet even in these times the service in the Temple at Jerusalem was conducted with great pomp. Jeshua ben Eliezer ben Sira (Jesus, son of Sirach) has left us an impressive description of the service as it was conducted in the Greek period. In 'Ecclesiasticus' he describes the priest Simon in the following words:

> ' He stretched out his hands to the sacrificial cup,
>> and poured of the blood of the grape;
> he poured out at the foot of the altar
>> a sweet-smelling savour unto the most high king of all.
> Then shouted the sons of Aaron, the priests,
>> and sounded the trumpets of chased work;
> they made a great noise to be heard,
>> for a remembrance before the most High.
> Then all the people together hasted
>> and fell down to the earth upon their faces,
> to worship their Lord God Almighty,
>> the Holy one of Israel.
> The singers also sang praises with their voices,
>> with great variety of sounds was there made sweet melody.'
>
> (Ecclesiasticus 50, 15-18.)

From this same period we also have lesser details which show that in liturgical respects and in the rendering of the ' songs of praise ' (the psalms) much that dated from former times had been preserved in its integrity. In any case all these details reveal that the Holy Scriptures provided the prototype, and we find no essential modifications of biblical usages. Thus, in the description of the festival of victory after Judith had killed Holofernes, we read: ' Then Judith began to sing this thanksgiving in all

Israel, and all the people sang after her this song of praise. And
Judith said:

> ' Begin unto my God with timbrels,
>
> Sing unto my Lord with cymbals.
>
> Tune unto him a new psalm ;
>
> Exalt him and call upon his name.'

(Judith 16, 1-2.)

During the rule of the Seleucids open conflict developed
between the Chasidim, who guarded the tradition, and the
Hellenists. This dissension culminated in the desecration of the
Temple by image worship, when Antiochus Epiphanes attempted
to force the Judaeans to follow the Greek cult. The Maccabees
(Hasmoneans) led a rising originally to secure the restoration of
the Jewish religious service, but it was so successful that the
Judaeans were able to throw off the foreign yoke and achieve
independence. Naturally, with independence came the restoration
of the Jewish religion and all its former practices. I Maccabees 4,
54-55, relates that the Temple at Jerusalem was newly consecrated
' with songs, and cytharas and harps, and cymbals. And all the
people fell on their faces, worshipping and praising toward
heaven him who had given them good success.' This festival is
again mentioned in II Maccabees 10, 7. During the Maccabean
wars there were frequent opportunities to purify the ritual from
the use of idols and image worship. (I Maccabees 13 ; 47, 51.) In
the descriptions of such ceremonies we are struck by the part
played by the ' songs of praise,' i.e., the psalms, as well as various
instruments, harps, and cytharas, and stringed instruments, and
cymbals. The Third Book of the Maccabees, which, however,
cannot be regarded as historical writing, but simply as a collection of untrustworthy legends, mentions a round dance of the
liberated Jews, who ' employed the time during the festival in
joyful thanksgiving and psalms.'

In the sphere of non-religious music the Greeks must certainly
have had a strong influence. Above all, the Jews would have
adopted a good deal of Greek secular song. The Greek philosophers and poets must have effected a steady and increasing
modification of the Judaeans' outlook on such questions. The
spirit of the Greeks, whether it spread from Hellenic Egypt or

from other parts of the Greek world, left its traces everywhere. The Second Book of Maccabees provides sufficient details to show how even influential Jews (or perhaps especially these) yielded to the Hellenic pressure. One can imagine what strength the assimilation trends acquired with the course of time, when one reads that even ' the priests had no courage to serve any more at the altar, but despising the Temple, and neglecting the sacrifices, hastened to be partakers of the unlawful allowance in the place of exercise, after the game of discus called them forth, not setting by the honours of their fathers, but liking the glory of the Grecians best of all." (II Maccabees 4, 14-15.)

Undoubtedly the assimilation process operated very powerfully in the sphere of secular music, especially as the Jews had not previously developed and cultivated the art of music to any great extent outside their religion. In the days of the Maccabees, after the achievement of political and cultural autonomy, the music of the temple service was cultivated still further (i.e., from the middle of the second down to perhaps the middle of the first century, B.C.). But as the Roman influence increased the Jewish national traditions tended to decline. And there was a corresponding decline in certain features of the temple cult, especially its characteristic splendour. When the Jews suffered national catastrophe and the destruction of the Temple, in 70 C.E., little of the musical tradition was left for the jealous and faithful guardians of the national traditions and the national cultural heritage to save, since during the struggle for national existence these musical traditions had suffered seriously and the heritage had been impoverished. They confined themselves to the task of saving and preserving the spiritual heritage and a few musical usages for the next and for the coming generations, for those who ever since, down to the present day, have had to forgo all the splendours of the Jerusalem temple service in the manner of king David and king Solomon. After that August of 70 C.E., or, in the Jewish calendar, Ab 10 (or Ab 9), 3830, when the service of sacrifice came to an end in the Temple at Jerusalem, all musical contributions to Jewish religious ritual also came to an end for many centuries. That date is an outstanding landmark in the history of Jewish music, which inevitably suffered the decline and decay experienced by Jewish national life as a whole.

PART TWO

THE SYNAGOGAL SERVICE AND
JEWISH MUSIC FROM THE FIRST TO THE
TWENTIETH CENTURY C.E.

CHAPTER VIII

THE JEWS IN PALESTINE AND BABYLON
(73-1099 c.e.)

WITH this latest destruction of their State and the loss of their political autonomy the Jews were denied all possibility of organising themselves on a political basis. This time the consequences were more serious than those that followed the deportation to Babylon in the sixth century b.c. Their first task was to recover from this disaster and to rebuild their own existence. But it was not long before they realised that they could still concentrate their forces in the sphere of their religion and the teaching of the Law.

Great changes occurred in their religious life. The service of sacrifice, which had always been the central feature of the temple worship, was replaced by prayers and devotions. So long as the service of sacrifice and the Cult were still observed in the Temple at Jerusalem, prayers and devotions had been only attendant phenomena, performed mainly through the intermediary of the Levites. The devotions and prayers which, as we saw in chapter five, had been observed in the earlier synagogues—where they had been subsidiary to the study of the *Torah*—were now incorporated in the sacred service which took the place of the service of sacrifice. A new order of service and prayers was drawn up, mainly under the guidance of Gamaliel II in the Academy at Jabneh. In the second century c.e., the Jewish sacred writings also were given their final form, in twenty-four books, as we have them to-day.

At first the Romans tolerated this continuation of Jewish religious life in a changed form, in its new and healthy development. But when they decided to rebuild Jerusalem as a Roman city and planned to erect a temple in honour of the Capitoline Jupiter in the place where the Jewish Temple had stood, in 132 c.e. the Jews revolted in one final struggle for freedom. The movement was led by Bar Kochba, who was influenced by Rabbi

69

Akiba. It met with success at first, but was swiftly suppressed. Henceforth, the Jews were forbidden to practise their religious ordinances and, under the Emperor Hadrian, 135-138 C.E., were punished with death if they defied the ban. About this same time the Pauline-Christians, followers of the Apostle Paul, and the Judaeo-Christians, who still observed certain of the Jewish ordinances, broke away more and more from the main body of

Hebrew-Yemenite and Gregorian Psalmody
(according to Idelsohn)

la - me nas-se-ab 'al hag-git-tit,_____ mi-ze-mor le - a - - saf._____

E-ruc-ta-vit cor me - - um ver-bum bo-num; di-co e-go
Lin-gu-a me - a_____ ca-la-mus scri-bae.

Jews. But as both these groups had sprung directly from the Jews and at first had only gradually become estranged from their origins, both groups took almost all the Jewish ritual and other usages into the service of their own religion. In this way the early Christians also took over the musical aspect of the Jewish religious service, out of which they later developed their own liturgical music, which continued to be based on the Jewish manner of vocal performance. The realisation of this connection has led of recent years to the investigation of early Christian music, such as the Gregorian plainsong, and its comparison with the surviving Jewish traditional religious melodies (above all, the so-called 'tropes') and to tracing their affinity. These researches, in which the Jewish musicologist Idelsohn was especially active, have furthered the endeavour to establish the many old, traditional Jewish melodies, and especially to determine the manner in which the scriptures were rendered in the ancient Jewish religious service. We shall be discussing this question in Chapter IX.

After Hadrian there were great fluctuations in the Romans' toleration of Jewish religious life. The Jewish law was expounded from Galilee, and during this period the oral teaching on the law, and the prescriptions, *halakhoth,* as established by generations of *Soferim* and *Tannaim* (scribes and teachers), were assembled, ordered, and committed to writing, under the supervision of Rabbi Jehuda ha-Nassi (about the end of the second century c.e.). The resulting collection, called the *Mishnah,* provides some details of the sacred service of the time ; and from that service all present-day Jewish religious services have developed.

This collection of rabbinical writings also contains some details of Jewish music. Though the various references consist more of opinions and interpretations relating to Biblical times and to the days of the first and second temples than of descriptions of contemporary musical life, a certain amount also applies to the time in which the Talmud and these various writings came into being, or when they were first committed to writing. This applies especially to that part of the *Mishnah,* etc., concerned with the early centuries of the Common Era, although there is some reference to the period immediately preceding.

The most important of these references is to the musical instrument called the *magrephah,*[1] which is usually taken to be a pipe organ, and which is not met with previously. The *Mishnah,* which was completed at the beginning of the third century c.e., describes the *magrephah* as a very complex musical instrument, and one which could be heard over a great distance (e.g., Mishnah Tamid 5, 6 ; B. Arakhin 10b). But in the Mishnah Tamid 3, 8, and the Jerusalem Talmud, Sukkah 5, 1, we find it stated that this latter quality applied not only to the *magrephah ;* for the singing, the sound of the *shofar,* the *chalil,* and the *tziltzal* were all so loud that from Jerusalem they could be heard in Jericho. The *magrephah,* which was said to be capable of producing a thousand different tones, does not appear to have been a water-organ, since in the Talmud we find it stated that the Temple had no such provision.

Besides the *magrephah,* we find mention of various musical instruments which we have already met with in earlier times. The *chalil* is referred to as an instrument indispensable in funeral rites, and even a poor man would hire at least two *chalil* players for the funeral of his wife. (Ketubot 4, 4.)

---

[1] From Hebrew *grophith* a reed.

71

After the destruction of the Temple the rabbis laid it down that to emphasise the national mourning for the loss of state independence and even more of the right freely to celebrate their own temple service, music was to be banned in the synagogue service, and even outside it. This interdiction had important consequences, especially for instrumental music. Even in earlier times secular music had frequently suffered condemnation, and now this was even more the case. As the result, during this period music, which formerly had been a highly important element in the religious service, was dropped from it altogether. Only much later was an exception made in the case of marriages.

On the other hand, when studying the Scriptures and the *Mishnah* it was customary to cantillate the passages read for this facilitated memorisation of the text.[1]

Meanwhile, the Cantor was becoming an increasingly important person in the synagogue. Gradually the position was reached in which he had to provide the main part of the musical element in the sacred service, for which in the days of the Temple a large musical staff had been available. Now his services alone had to suffice, and he took over more and more of the functions of the former priests. The Babylonian Talmud gives a description of the qualities demanded of a cantor. He had to be an educated man, modest, acceptable to the people, skilled in chanting, with a pleasant voice, versed in the Scriptures, the *Mishnah*, the Talmud, etc.[2]

The Talmud and the rabbinical writings contain many passages discussing musical practice in the temple service. The opinions expressed differ as to whether instrumental or vocal music played the predominant part, but the view that the instruments served chiefly to provide an accompaniment to the singing tends to prevail.[3] Sukkah 51a, b gives us an impressive picture: ' Men of piety and good deeds used to dance before them with lighted torches in their hands, and sing songs and praises. And Levites without number with harps, lyres, cymbals, and trumpets and other musical instruments were there upon the fifteen steps

---

[1] Babylonian Talmud. Megillah. 32a.
[2] Babylonian Talmud, Ta'anit, 16a.
[3] E.g., Sukkah 50b; 51a; Babylonian Talmud, Ta'anit 27a; B. T. Arakhin, 11a.

leading down from the Court of the Israelites to the Court of the Women, corresponding to the fifteen songs of Ascents (A.V. "degrees") in the Psalms. It was upon these steps that the Levites stood with their instruments of music and sang their songs.'[1] This description refers, of course, to the former musical practice in the Temple, which no longer existed at the time the passage was committed to writing.

Each 'synagogue,' in Hebrew called 'Bet Keneset' or House of Assembly, managed its own affairs, in which it was headed by the 'Rosh Ha-Keneset,' or 'head of the synagogue.' Beside him there was the 'Chazzan,' who had the task of ensuring order during divine service and taking the rolls of the Torah from their chest to read them to the congregation. In addition there was a 'Cantor,' the 'plenipotentiary of the Community' (sheliach tzibbur), who was the precentor of the synagogue. Later on the term 'chazzan' came to be used for the precentor, and to-day 'chazzan' and 'cantor' are used indifferently. The 'Shammash' (beadle) was the servant of the synagogue, roughly corresponding to the verger of the Christian church. While the cantor was reading or singing the prayers and the psalms he stood at the bar where the rolls of the Torah are kept, usually turning his face towards Jerusalem. After the destruction of the second temple and the final suspension of the service of sacrifice a new synagogue service had to be drawn up, based on the previous practices. For this purpose the practices of the communities in the Diaspora, and above all the rites of the Babylonian Jews, who had always had to worship without regard to the Services of the temple and the sacrifice, were drawn upon, as well as certain traditional rites, prayers, and psalms which could be taken from the forbidden services. Moreover, new religious poems were written and added to the service.

These new forms of service were centred in the synagogue, which had survived, especially since Ezra's time, chiefly as a kind of school for instruction in the Torah, as a centre for public reading of the Torah, and for devotions. One new factor in regard to the synagogue service was of importance: unlike the temple service, which could be celebrated only at Jerusalem, it could

---

[1] Babylonian Talmud. Soncino Press translation.

be practised wherever there was a Jewish community. Now the rendering of the psalms (which, as we know from the continuity of tradition, were chiefly sung) and the reading of the Torah (which also had a specific musical rendering which we shall discuss in the next chapter) became prominent features of the service. And they became the chief vehicle for preserving the traditional Jewish religious melodies for future generations.

At some time after the talmudic period, probably in the fifth century, a new artistic movement appeared. A number of *poytanim* or *paytanim*,[1] *chazzanim* by profession, composed poetical pieces which were introduced into the traditional services of special sabbaths and other outstanding days in the calendar, and particularly of the high holy days. These pieces, the *piyyutim*, were remarkable for their intense religious fervour and rich, often extremely difficult, language, spiced with recondite literary allusions in the taste of the time. Many *piyyutim* are still used in the synagogue services to-day. Some of these are sung, and it is likely that special melodies went with the various poems from the outset, though many *piyyutim* are not sufficiently rhythmical for this purpose.

The most important *paytanim* were Yose ben Yose, Hannai, and Eleazar ha-Kalir. We know nothing of their date or circumstances of life, but it is agreed to-day that they all worked in Palestine before 800 C.E. In the tenth and eleventh centuries, the *piyyut* flourished again in Italy and Germany, to some extent also in France (where Rashi was no mean *paytan*) and Spain. In the latter country, outstanding poetry in this genre was composed by Isaac Ibn Gayyat (1038-89) and Solomon Ibn Gabirol (1020-57). The latter, however, is much more remembered for his poems in Arabic metre and manner and pure Biblical language. This latter genre was introduced to Spain by Dunash ben Labrat (about 1000 C.E.), who may actually have been its inventor, and within a short time it displaced the *piyyut* altogether, even in the synagogue. A late representative of the *paytanim* was Israel Najara (1542-1619) in Palestine and Syria, who wrote poems of deep religious fervour to worldly, often non-Jewish, melodies.

---

[1] Poytan is the Palestinian pronunciation. The word is derived from the Greek *poietes*, or ' poet.'

His song *Yah Ribbon* is still sung during Sabbath meals. It is written in Aramaic, and its language and subject matter stem from the great Kabbalistic mystical movement initiated by Isaac Luria (1534-72). This intense emotional tendency produced a revival of Jewish song, the last echoes of which can be discerned in the chasidic *nigunim* of the eighteenth and nineteenth centuries.

At the beginning of the fourth century Constantine the Great elevated Christianity to the status of a state religion, with the result that the Christian church was able to assert its viewpoint in every sphere, including that of culture, with all the resources of state power, and could suppress all opposition by resort to force. As the Jews were dependent on their rulers and governors in the matter of religious practice, and those rulers were now rarely able to oppose the demands of the church, they were allowed no freedom of worship. Meanwhile, the Jewish community in Babylon was under Persian rule, and enjoyed extensive autonomy in many respects, so that it now acquired especial importance, producing a version of the Talmud much fuller than that of Jerusalem.

However, the Christian Church dominated Palestine for only some three hundred years. In 638 the Arabs captured Jerusalem, and the country remained in the hands of the Mohammedans until 1099, when the Crusaders took the city. During this period all Persia, Syria, Palestine, Egypt, and the Byzantine provinces of Africa, all the lands in which there were considerable Jewish communities, were united under the rule of the Caliphate. This comparatively peaceful era was very favourable to the development of industries, art, and science ; and the Arab culture greatly influenced the Jews. Indeed, Jews gradually adopted Arabic, employing it in their literature instead of the Aramaic which had been the everyday language. With the slow dissolution of the Caliphate of Bagdad the Jewish community in Babylon also declined in power. Towards the end of this period, as the ' oriental period of Jewish history' was drawing to its close, important Jewish communities were already emerging in Western Europe, first in Spain and then in France and Germany. These centres took over the task of carrying on the spiritual and cultural heritage of their forefathers.

Mediæval Judaeo-Arabic literature includes a number of treatises on music. This was largely due to the influence of Arabic philosophers and writers. In these treatises the Jewish scholars not only sought to throw new light on the old temple music by fresh exegesis, but, in harmony with contemporary thought, in their philosophical writings they inquired into music's various psychic, as well as æsthetic and ethical effects. As we know, these discussions did not stimulate fresh musical creation at the time. None the less, they did influence musical practice, though perhaps only later, centuries after, could it have any effect. The renowned Jewish scholar Saadiah ben Joseph ha-Pitomi, known as Saadiah Gaon, who was born in Dilaz, Fayyum, Lower Egypt, in 892, and died at Sura, Mesopotamia, in 942, wrote in 933 his 'Book of Beliefs and Opinions.'[1] In its tenth chapter he investigated the influence of music on the human soul. Saadiah, who is recognised as one of the leading Judaeo-Arabic writers, may have been influenced in his thinking by the Arabic philosopher Al-Kindi, who lived before him. The discussion of music continued in later Judaeo-Arabic writings.[2] For instance, *Sefer ha-Emunot*, the Hebrew translation of Saadiah's work, written by Berakyah ha-Nakdan in the last quarter of the twelfth century; and Yuhanan ibn al-Bitriq's 'Kitab al-Siyasah.'

There is a document dating from the twelfth century which is interesting because of its references to contemporary Jewish musical practices. This is the polemical *Ifham al-Yahud*, written by Samuel ben Yehuda ibn Abun, of Fez, a convert to Islam, who had the pen-name of Samau'al ibn Yahya al-Maghribi. He wrote that Islam had placed the Jews under the rule of the Persians, and that the Persians had frequently forbidden the Jews to practise their forms of devotion. 'But when the Jews saw that the Persians were in earnest in regard to the interdiction of their worship, they drew up prayers into which they intercalated parts of the customary prayers, and called them *al-hizana (chazzanut)*.

---

[1] In Arabic *Kitab al-i'tiqadat wal-amanat*; in Hebrew *Emunot we-De'ot*.
[2] *Vide* Farmer, Henry George: 'The Jewish Debt to Arabic Writers on Music'; 'Islamic Culture,' No. XV, January, 1942, pp. 59-63. Hyderabad. Also Werner, Eric, and Sonne, Isaiah; 'The Philosophy and Theory of Music in Judaeo-Arabic Literature.' Hebrew Union College Annual, Cincinnati, XVI, 1941, pp. 251-319 and XVII, 1942/3, pp. 511-72.

They composed many tunes to these, and they bound themselves to come together at prayer-times, to sing and read them. The difference between the *hizana* and the enjoined prayer (*salat*) is that the enjoined prayer is rendered without a tune ; it is read by the synagogue reader alone and no one accompanies him ; but during the *hizana* many accompany him with shouting and singing, and help him in the tune.'[1] This relation, which has more than a touch of malice in it and at times is self-contradictory, none the less clearly shows that at this time singing was an essential part of the service. Much earlier St. Hieronymus (circa 330-420), who knew the Jewish service of Palestine, relates that in their worship the Jews have a solemn singing of psalms, namely, the group of the ' Songs of Praise ' (*Hallel*—Psalms 113-118). Singing was a prominent feature of other ceremonies of a religious nature, as we learn from Nathan ha-Babli, a Babylonian Jewish savant who went to live in Africa about 950 C.E. On his arrival he reported to the local Jews on the practices of the Jews in Babylon, including the ceremony of ' institution ' into the office of Exilarch. The Exilarch, or, in Aramaic, *Resh Galuta*, was the head of the community in the Diaspora. He relates that in this ceremony ' a choir, of noble youngsters, endowed with musical voices,' took their places, ' the *chazzan* (cantor) of the synagogue struck up the devotional hymn, and the choir of youngsters joined in, accompanying him. . . . The *chazzan*, dressed in his prayer vestments, with his face turned to the podium, said special forms of prayer appointed for the initiation of the Exilarch, and the choir of youngsters joined in with a loud Amen. . . . When the Exilarch left the synagogue the people went before and behind him, extolling him in songs of praise, conducting him to his house.'

Without going into the question further, we can accept that throughout the period immediately following the destruction of the Temple there was a continuous tradition of vocal music as a prominent feature of the synagogue service, and that in particular many of the traditional tunes for the Psalms and prayers and reading of the Torah were passed down from generation to

---

[1] Elbogen, Ismar: ' Der jüdische Gottesdienst in seiner geschichtlichen Entwicklung,' p. 283, Leipzig, 1913.

generation of worshippers in the synagogues and religious students in *Chedarim* and *Yeshivot*. But the ban on instrumental music meant that the then existing musical tradition was lost for the Jews. The vocal tradition alone remained. It represented the only form of musical expression in the service, and we can assume that it gained in importance and was further developed.

CHAPTER IX

THE BIBLICAL ACCENTS

(The *Teamim* [Accents] and *Neginot* [Tropes])

THE text of the Jewish Scriptures is annotated with signs known as the biblical accents. In Hebrew they are called *teamim*. These signs indicate the accent of the words, the manner of rendering the word or phrase, and the tune to which the passage in question is to be cantillated. We must explain that from very early times it has been the tradition not simply to read the Jewish Scriptures, but to render them with 'high, pausing, vibrating, rising and falling tones.'[1] It is impossible to say when this manner of reading the Scriptures first came into use. The tunes or melodic phrases which these *teamim* designate are customarily called *neginot* (=melodies) or 'tropes' (from the Greek *tropos*, a turn, or figure). It is generally accepted by authorities that the original and primary function of the biblical accents consisted in ordering single words or phrases in the scriptural passage according to their grammatical and syntactic homogeneity. It is also thought that they may have indicated the manner of interpretation of the text (hermeneutics). At some stage in Jewish musical development these accents came to be used as expression marks in the musical sense, as well as for the functions just mentioned; but there is no means of telling whether this was prior to, simultaneously with, or later than their original and primary functions. The use of the Greek term, *trope*, for the neginot might indicate that the accents denoted the musical and declamatory rendering. But the term could also have been adopted from the punctuation and neume notation of the Greek gospels, as one authority suggests.[2]

Nor do we know exactly when the biblical accents the

---

[1] Aaron ben Moses ben Asher (cir. 10th century), the inventor of the Tiberian accent-system, in *Diqduqe ha-Teamim*, 1st ed., 1515; new ed. Leipzig, 1879.
[2] Praetorius, Franz: 'Über die Herkunft der hebräischen Akzente,' Berlin, Reuther und Reichard, 1901.

teamim, were first brought into use, though it is believed to have been during the period 500-800 C.E.[1] The first known system of Hebrew musical accentuation is developed in Asher's *Diqduqe ha-Teamim.*[2] Before the days of modern research the introduction of *teamim* was ascribed to Ezra and his contemporaries. The stimulus to the use of biblical accents, as well as the actual signs and their signification came from the philologists of the Mediterranean culture. But the signs had to be adapted to the special requirements of Hebrew, and so were altered or reformed. To-day it is no longer considered that they were of Jewish origin; but what they indicate, namely, the manner of rendering and the tune to be used, was almost exclusively specific to the Torah, and so is peculiar to the Jews.

עֵשָׂו: 23וְלֹא הִכִּירוֹ כִּי־הָיוּ יָדָיו כִּידֵי עֵשָׂו אָחִיו שְׂעִרֹת וַיְבָרֲכֵהוּ׃
24וַיֹּאמֶר אַתָּה זֶה בְּנִי עֵשָׂו וַיֹּאמֶר אָנִי׃ 25וַיֹּאמֶר הַגִּשָׁה לִּי וְאֹכְלָה
מִצֵּיד בְּנִי לְמַעַן תְּבָרֶכְךָ נַפְשִׁי וַיַּגֶּשׁ־לוֹ וַיֹּאכַל וַיָּבֵא לוֹ יַיִן וַיֵּשְׁתְּ׃
26וַיֹּאמֶר אֵלָיו יִצְחָק אָבִיו גְּשָׁה־נָּא וּשְׁקָה־לִּי בְּנִי׃ 27וַיִּגַּשׁ וַיִּשַּׁק־לוֹ
וַיָּרַח אֶת־רֵיחַ בְּגָדָיו וַיְבָרֲכֵהוּ וַיֹּאמֶר
רְאֵה רֵיחַ בְּנִי כְּרֵיחַ שָׂדֶה אֲשֶׁר בֵּרֲכוֹ יְהֹוָה׃

Example of teamim, *from Professor R. Kittel, Liber Genesis, Ch. 27, v. 23-27. Leipzig, 1909.*

The biblical accents have been classified in three systems:

1. The Tiberian system, in which the signs used are dots, strokes, and segments of circles, placed sometimes above, sometimes below the consonants.

2. The Babylonian system, in which the signs consist mainly of Hebrew letters, set above the consonants.

3. The Palestinian system, in which the sign is usually a dot set by the upper or lower part of a consonant.

---

[1] In the 'Zeitschrift der Deutschen Morgenländischen Gesellschaft,' vol. 5, Petermann states that the Armenians sing their church songs in accordance with signs similar to the *teamim,* and that these have been handed down unaltered since the fifth century.

[2] Sendrey, Alfred: 'Bibliography of Jewish Music,' p. 30, New York and London, 1951.

In addition there are two kinds of accents, one for the Books of Psalms, Proverbs, and Job, and the other for all the other books. Accentuation marks were also often employed in non-biblical Jewish writings. From earliest days there were separating accents, indicating a break, or caesura in the passage, and conjunctive accents, binding two words or a group of words together. All these characteristic features make for easier understanding and greater clarification of the text. Many of the accents are interdependent: certain accents can follow only certain other accents; and so accents often logically interlock in entire groups. All the accents have names, some of them have several, and the majority of these names are Aramaic in origin.

As we have said, besides possessing grammatical, syntactic, and hermeneutic functions, the accents determine the nature of the musical rendering. So they have always been of supreme importance in the preservation of the Jewish musical manner of execution. Without discussing their other functions, we must explain that they indicate how the recitative or melody to which the words are set is to be rendered. Each accent has its traditional musical rendering, without precisely establishing the melody in its rhythm or its tonal intervals. Like the mediæval neumes, the accents indicate musical motifs or phrases; but, unlike the neumes, they do not represent the melody in any way graphically. As they provide no graphic aid to the rendering, the executant has always had to learn by heart the traditional neginot, or tropes. But as the melodic line is not precisely fixed, the executant has always been free to introduce variations and to adapt the rendering to the musical language of his particular environment. We know that the custom of reading the Torah to neginot melodies is very ancient, but we cannot have any precise idea of how these neginot sounded in former times, for many centuries of foreign influence have left their mark on all these melodies.

Johann Reuchlin, the German fifteenth-century humanist, published a tablature, 'De Accentibus,' at Hanau in 1518, which contained the first musical notation of the biblical accents. It includes a transcription of the melody in the tenor, as was customary at the time. It is here reproduced (notation runs from right to left) and is followed by a transcription into modern notation.

Motifs of the Pentateuch-Modes according to Böschenstein, in
Reuchlin's ' De Accentibus'

To-day we customarily distinguish two separate groups of
neginot—the oriental and the European. The neginot sung by
the oriental Jews have always retained more peculiarities of the

82

oriental peoples, above all, of the Arabs; whereas the neginot of the European Jews have been modified in many respects in accordance with European musical tastes. We are unable to say which of these two groups is the more ancient, and which has departed less from the originals. But the neginot are properly the oldest existing melodies and groups of motifs in notation form, even if the form is only that of *teamim*. Undoubtedly the neginot, which perhaps convey to us some idea of what the temple music sounded like, originally differed very little from the music of their environment. And although in the course of the centuries they have necessarily undergone many changes— adaptations to the new times and the temporary environmental conditions, adaptations to foreign tonal systems, embellishment or simplification—they have always reflected Jewish experience first and foremost, and above all have conveyed the musical expression peculiar to the Jews, simply because of the fact that they are used only in association with the Hebrew text. The constant Jewish conservatism in regard to the liturgy hindered development of the neginot and ensured that the rendering of the Torah should always appear traditional, and archaic, even when it revealed traces of assimilation influences.

The majority of the neginot are restricted to a narrow tonal range and consist of short phrases, frequently reminiscent of the pentatonic scales of the ancient Chinese, Irish, Scottish, and other peoples. It will be remembered that the ancient Greeks also based their melodic system on a pentatonic whole-tone scale. Recognising that the biblical accents are of exceptional significance to Jewish music, both in the past and in the future, the Jewish musicologist, Idelsohn, studied the various melodies of the accents as they have survived till modern times, and compared them, drawing on the main Jewish centres of Europe, Asia Minor, and Egypt for his material. The comparative tables reproduced on the two following pages are taken from his 'Thesaurus of Hebrew-Oriental Melodies,' vol. 2, pp. 44-45. They clearly show the affinity of the accents and neginot used in the various centres, and that in each case the pentatonic character of the tunes is either partly or wholly retained.

These tables justify two deductions: first, that the majority of the accents known to us to-day from various Jewish centres are

Sof pasuq at - nah se - gol zaqef qaton rebi'a tebir geresin
Babylonian

Bokharian

Persian

Syrian

Moroccan

Gibraltarian

Italian

Sephardi (France)

Sephardi (Amsterdam)

Sephardi (Egypt and Palestine)

Ashkenazi — azla geres gersajim, tebir merha kefulla

Reuchlin's

for Canticles — munah z - qaton

[1] The signs above the first stave are the Biblical *Teamim*, as used in *i*

84

MOTIFS IN THE PENTATEUCH[1]

the Hebrew biblical text ; their names are given below the first stave.

musically related to one another, and so they must stem from a single prototype. Secondly, that their present-day differences can be ascribed to the variations in development arising from differing environments. It must also be accepted that in their musical aspect the biblical accents originally differed little or not at all from the music of the surrounding world ; yet, as they developed in conjunction with the Hebrew texts, they gradually acquired a characteristically Jewish expression. As the Jews always strove to retain the original, the traditional nature and form, the neginot melodies also retained their Jewish musical characteristics. It is noteworthy that the music of the surrounding world had a more circumscribed influence on the neginot of the biblical accents than on the melos of Jewish folksong, and even on the religious songs. One has only to listen to the reading of the *Torah* (the ' leinen,' as Ashkenazi Jews call it) in the synagogal service to have this impression confirmed ; the ' leinen ' unquestionably consists of musical phrases derived from the distant past. An example is given on page 87.

In modern times various transcriptions have been made of the neginot into modern notation. But in all such cases we have to remember that present-day notation is concerned only with the music and its performance, without being able to lay down precisely the interpretation, and often not even the exact rhythm. But that is precisely what the neginot achieve. So it is true that we can get some idea of them through their transcription into modern notation, but the only way to learn thoroughly the neginot in use to-day is to listen to the skilled interpreters.

A great deal of research has been done on the Biblical accents of recent years, the best known being that of Abraham Zvi Idelsohn, who devoted many years to collecting examples and investigating and elucidating the entire subject. Another name that should be mentioned in this connection is Salomon Rosowsky. He drew up tables which should give an idea of the course of assimilation of various tropes, in the hope of purifying the neginot from alien influences, and restoring them to their original form for Jewish use everywhere.

As a large number of neginot have been notated of recent years, we give only a few examples. There are innumerable variations.

After Idelsohn : 'Jewish Music in its Historical Development,' p. 41.

Comparative studies with Gregorian Chant have revealed many interesting facts. As in the musical example on page 70, so in many other cases, the musical motifs can be recognised as very similar or, at least, related to each other. It must be pointed out, however, that even where the Gregorian Chant might in musical respects appear similar to a Jewish melody or cantilation, the effect varies according to the different

87

tradition and interpretation. Comparative research is thus of great value for musicologists ; but for the creation of true Jewish music only those neginot can be used which are preserved by Jewish tradition.

The great value of the neginot as material for musical motifs and musical elaboration has been fully realised by modern Jewish composers, and they frequently draw upon them for both religious and secular compositions.

CHAPTER X

DURING THE DISPERSAL IN EUROPE
(Twelfth to eighteenth centuries)

BETWEEN the twelfth and eighteenth centuries the Jews living in Europe experienced many vicissitudes. They knew periods of peace and happiness, but far more often they had to suffer persecution. Yet during these many years they absorbed first the highly developed Arab, and then European culture, so enriching their spiritual perceptions. And they carried through a revolution in their manner of expression, for they adapted all their receptive and expressive powers in literature and music to the tradition of the European countries in which they resided. This adaptation could be only partially successful, for their own specific culture and sensibilities were still too highly charged to allow them to take over essentially alien forms of expression without modification. On the other hand, this different, European form of culture provided fresh stimulus to their oriental imagination. With the aid of these stimuli, in time they developed a new form of expression which was similar to that of Europe. On the other hand, during these six centuries European music was slowly evolving, and so the Jews in Europe had comparatively little difficulty in acclimatising themselves to the musical atmosphere. As one would expect, it was the neginot that suffered least adaptation, and so it was in this sphere that the original Jewish style was most retained.

Whenever the Jews were allowed to live in peaceable, satisfactory relations with their milieu, in Spain, Turkey, Poland, Germany, Austria, Holland, or anywhere else, they opened their eyes and ears to the arts and science of the land of their sojourn. Even Jewish conservative circles were not proof against the influence of non-Jewish culture, in so far as it affected them through their fellow Jews who concerned themselves with that culture. It must have left even stronger traces and influenced their cultural development in every respect when they were compulsorily converted to Christianity, for this necessarily involved contact with the Christian religion and its religious ceremonial, and their acceptance as a rule of the speech and non-religious culture of their environment. In fact, all the Jewish melodies that have survived reveal the influence of alien musical tastes, and, of course, especially those of the peoples among whom they have lived.

All musical taste, Jewish or non-Jewish, is continually subjected to the modifications resulting from musical developments. There is a class of Spanish song which is still sung to-day by the descendants of the Jews who were expelled from Spain at the end of the fifteenth century, and in fact is only preserved by them. Yet even these songs are sung in different versions in the various centres of these 'Sefardic' or Spanish Jews, and this applies to songs which they adapted from their Spanish environment. How much more must this have applied to the truly Jewish songs, songs which they themselves composed and sang in a manner of expression in genuine conformity with the times. Even the Jewish songs were always modified by the taste of the age, though as a rule the adaptation was too slow. On the other hand, it seems that Jewish music developed simultaneously with that of the environment, keeping pace with the general evolution of the tonal structure ; in Germanic and Slavonic countries especially the Jews gradually modified their songs as they, like their milieu, carried through the development from the old tonal systems to the modern major and minor modes, from homophony to polyphony, and so on to the modern chord and harmonic system.

A significant and typical phenomenon of these times was that of the Christian crypto-Jews, called Marranos in Spain, who were forced to renounce their Jewish faith. These compulsorily converted Jews continued to observe Jewish religious practices in secret and took the first opportunity to renew their open confession of Jewry, and they must have brought alien elements into the secret Jewish religious assemblies and even the synagogue service. As their Jewish service was mercilessly suppressed by the Christians, they tried to avoid offending their persecutors by employing well-known non-Jewish tunes, so that at least their singing would not betray them. It is impossible to estimate the extent to which these often popular and banal tunes were introduced into and preserved in the Jewish sacred service. But in this and other ways, from the eleventh century onward

Jewry was continually absorbing new, European musical elements, faithfully preserving them, and through habituation coming at last to regard them as its own. This, of course, is not a unique phenomenon ; it is found wherever cultural peoples come into contact with one another.

In those difficult times the synagogue service must have been extremely simple. The singing of psalms was an important component of the service, indeed of all religious and other communal occasions. They occupied much of the time ; in the Orient it is recorded that their rendering lasted more than an hour (this was *circa* 1200). Prayers for special occasions, or relating to the unhappy contemporary national history, were the most important innovations in the liturgy. These prayers and lamentations, usually written in poetic form, and frequently sung, varied from one Jewish community to another, since they were usually related to the experience of the community. We do not know the origin of the new tunes to which they were set ; we have to assume that, in so far as new prayers were not sung to old tunes, but to new ones specially composed, these new tunes were borrowed from the non-Jewish environment or at least were strongly influenced by it. In the course of time these circumstances brought about great variations in the rites of the various communities, especially as they each had their own traditions and had little contact with one another, and also as in each community it was the teacher and the community head who decided the choice of tunes for the services. Two main groups are to be distinguished in the Jewish rite: the Oriental and Spanish, called Sefardic, and the Palestinian and Germanic, called Ashkenazi. The territorial area of the first group covered Spain and the Islamic countries, that of the second covered the other Christian countries, especially those with Teutonic and later with Slavonic populations.

Despite the comparative simplicity of the synagogue service singing played an increasingly important part in it. The precentor's task was by his emotional singing to maintain the community in piety and devotion, or to stimulate these feelings. Often he exploited his customary liberty in order to give public performances of his own skill, to demonstrate his vocal power or his gift for composition. That such performances were not always called for we can tell from the frequent complaints about such practices. But even the various religious trends and groups that sprang up among the Jews, such as the German mystics of the thirteenth century, the Cabbalistic movement initiated by Isaac Luria (1534-72), the *Chasidim* of the eighteenth and nineteenth century, etc., did a great deal to further Jewish religious song by their intensive practice of hymn- and psalm-singing. Judah the Pious, in the thirteenth century, recommended the use of pleasing and well-sounding tunes in prayers, tunes that contributed to the concentration and exaltation of devotion, tunes that moved the heart to tears or to outbursts of joy. Imanuel Romi, who lived about 1300 C.E., thus extolled his own gift of song: 'When I say the great *Kedushah*, a *Yotzer*, or the *Kerobah*, then the hardest will be melted ; when I pray on *Yom Kippur* (the Day of Atonement) or read the *Megillah* during *Purim*, execute an *En Kamochah* for the pilgrimage festival, or a psalm, then the mighty tremble at my voice ; and when I bring the laments to the ear, then not one eye is left without tears.'[1]

The tunes to which the various prayers were to be sung were handed down at first in script, but later frequently in printed prayer-books as well. Though we cannot be specific in regard to any individual tune, we know that they originated from various sources, for the comparative method of research has revealed traces of the folk song and *minnelieder* of many lands. Christian church music also appears to have been drawn upon. The synagogue precentors, the ' cantors,' made use of any tune that suited them, without reference to its source and character. Complaints were openly made that profane tunes were being used in the Jewish sacred service, just as we find complaints in ecclesiastical writers in regard to Christian church music. But, generally speaking, the tunes adopted were either used in conjunction with new prayers, or certain of their motifs were employed in the creation of new tunes. Each community had a permanent repertoire of old and new tunes, clearly distinguished from that of every other community. Of course, the recommendation of Rabbi

---

[1] Elbogen, op cit. *Kedushah, Yotzer, Kerobah,* and *En Kamochah* are prayers in the liturgy ; *Megillah* is the designation for the Book of Esther, which is read during *Purim,* the festival in memory of the Jewish salvation through Queen Esther.

Jacob Levi Mölln (called *Maharil*), who lived 1356-1427 C.E., that a community should care for its customary tunes and not drop them in favour of new ones was often followed ; but as such calls were frequent, obviously they must have been ignored frequently. Apparently in Germany and Portugal the Jews were strict in regard to this question, but in Poland the cantors gave free reign to their imagination, and were allowed to improvise. Not seldom the cantor developed his vocal performance greatly to the detriment of the prayers, for, especially if he was untrained, he sang without regard to the meaning of the words, only in order to demonstrate his vocal powers. Here one may also mention Israel Najara (1542-1619), who is the best example of the tendency to employ popular tunes.

With few exceptions, singing in the synagogue was originally confined to soloists. As time passed the custom grew of reinforcing the cantor with other singers, usually not more than two, one with a high, the other with a low voice ; these two partly accompanied the cantor and partly sang the responses. So far as we know, the first synagogue singing which made use of a number of voices, singing with some pretensions to artistry, was in Italy. We do not know how far this artistic manner of singing spread, but in any case the innovation, which clearly was a pure imitation of contemporary non-Jewish music, met with energetic opposition. We possess a collection of works written for such part-singing, composed by Salomone Rossi, called ' Il Ebreo,' who was born in Mantua about 1570 and died in 1628. He published music for thirty pieces taken from the Jewish prayer-book ; the translation of the Hebrew title of the book reads : ' Solomon's Songs, Psalms, Hymns, and Temple-songs, composed in accordance with the rules of music for three, four, five, six, seven, and eight voices by Salomon Mehaadumin, a citizen of Mantua.' The work was printed by Pietro and Lorenzo Bragadini in the Printing Office of Giovanni Caliumi, in Venice, in 1623 (1620 ?) and bore the following dedication :

' To the noble, magnanimous, Moses Sullam of Mantua, who conjoins erudition with greatness :

' Since that day when the Lord granted me the favour of opening my ear to music, the first and noblest of the arts, and permitted me to understand and to learn it, I have made a firm resolution and have been fortunate in devoting the first-born of my songs to the glory of the Lord, to praise him with hymns of joy and thanks and to do him honour for the many gifts which he has bestowed upon me. God has been my aid. He set my lips to sing new songs which have been written in accordance with the rules of the art, in conformity with the spirit with which he inspired me; songs suited to the days of festival and joy. I have subjected a large number of the Psalms of David to the laws of music, in order to make them more attractive. After I had finished my work I was of the opinion that it would be well to make a selection and to publish these, not to my own glory, but to the glory of the Lord, who of His grace gave me this life and whom I shall always praise. . . .'

The introduction was written by Leone da Modena, at whose instance the work was published. It reads:

'Judah Aryeh (Leone) da Modena, son of Isaac, to all whose ears can understand the truth:

'One knows the words of the poet: "The Lip of Truth shall be established for ever." Music speaks to the non-Jews: "I was stolen away from the land of the Hebrews." The savants have flourished like grass and have disseminated knowledge, and have been admired by all other nations, for they have mounted up like eagles into immeasurable heights with wings. From the Hebrews is the music of other nations borrowed. Who could forget King David, who, as it is written, instructed the sons of Asaph, Heman, and Jeduthun in music? He made them understand singing and the playing of instruments during the periods of the first and second Temple.

'But our exile, our dispersion over the earth, our troubles and persecutions have made them forget knowledge and lose understanding of art. The wrath of God descended upon the people and he cast them into a pit void of all knowledge. We had to borrow our wisdom from other nations, until now Salomon alone is excellent in this science and wiser than any man of our own people, through which he was taken into the service of the Dukes of Mantua. Nay, his musical works, printed in a foreign language, meet with appreciation, as they were liked by non-Jews. The Lord opened the eyes of the blind. Despite the opposition of his brethren, he sought to perfect the work. His power is unto his God. He added every day to the psalms, hymns, and Temple-songs till he brought them together in one volume. Now the people sang his compositions ; they were pleased by their excellence and their ears were delighted by them.

'The leaders of the community, headed by the most reverend and virtuous Moses Sullam (whom may God guard), urged the author and persuaded him to publish his compositions. I, too, who am proud to be reckoned among his admirers, brought all my influence to bear to persuade him to occasion this publication. Finally, he submitted to our requests and gave his collection to be printed. He commissioned me to supervise the printing of the book, to see it through the press and to eliminate errors. . . . The reader will see that the author preferred the words to be written from left to right, contrary to our Hebrew custom, rather than change the musical notation. He did not consider it necessary to print the vowel signs, since our singers know the text by heart and read correctly without them, which does them great honour.[1]

'Ye are blessed, my brethren, because we have begun the publication of the work of the outstanding musician who composed songs in his sanctuaries on holy-days. Teach them to your children, that they may be instructed in music, as was the custom among the Levites. I am convinced that from the moment of its appearance this work will spread the taste for good music in Israel, to praise the Lord. Among us people were to be found—of this there is no doubt—those

---

[1] This touches on a problem which still exists, namely, how to print a Hebrew text, running from right to left, to fit notation running from left to right. Rossi sacrificed the Hebrew text, for indeed the singers knew the text perfectly. He did not even punctuate the texts. (In Hebrew the vowel signs are set below the consonants, but educated people do not need them, and they are seldom printed.) The modern solution to the right-left problem is to transliterate the Hebrew into Latin script and print left to right ; or to set each Hebrew syllable separately under the notes.

who infallibly resist all progress and who will also resist these songs which are beyond their understanding. I therefore consider it advisable to refer to the answer to a question put to me when I was still Rabbi at Ferrara; all the great scholars of Venice agreed with me. I demonstrated that there is nothing in the Talmud which can be cited against the introduction of choir-singing into our Temples; and that was sufficient to close the malevolent mouths of the opponents. Despite all they can say, I put all my trust in the honour and nurture of song and music in our synagogues, to extend these things and to make use of them, until the wrath of God is turned away from us and He builds His Temple again in Zion, and commands the Levites to perform their music, and all singing will be happy and joyful again, not as it is to-day, when we sing with heavy hearts and in anguish of spirit for the pain of our dispersion.'

In this introduction we have a clear picture of the status and conditions of the contemporary synagogal vocal music. It is obvious that in Italy there was a group of Jews who either as composers or as musically trained amateurs knew the well-developed art of Italian music and desired to raise synagogue music to the same level. But there were two conflicting parties: one seeking the introduction of choral singing in the developed style of contemporary secular madrigals (Rossi was a composer of madrigals) and an opposition group which resisted such an alien modification of synagogal singing. Moreover, it appears that Rossi did not make use of any traditional melodies in his compositions, but composed quite freely; though, as his religious songs were clearly differentiated from his madrigals, this may not be so. In any case it is clear that his synagogal compositions made no appeal to the simple, musically uneducated Jews, and did not achieve great popularity. A new edition of Rossi's works was edited by Samuel Naumbourg, senior cantor of Paris (who is also known for his own synagogal compositions), together with Vincent d'Indy.[1]

We shall understand why Rossi's synagogal works were not

---

[1] Cantiques de Salomone Rossi, Ebreo; two vols., Paris, 1877. Vol. 1, Chants, Psaumes et Hymnes; vol. 2, Choix de Madrigaux.

generally taken up, and met with no response among the main body of Jews, if we consider the following facts. When he was writing these religious works, which undoubtedly were modelled on the style and nature of contemporary church compositions, the Jews had not yet experienced the spiritual and intellectual reformation which came in the days of the Emancipation in nineteenth-century Germany. We know that church vocal music had followed a very different line of development from that of synagogue vocal music, in each case the reasons being due solely to the constitution of the service. In Rossi's day synagogal singing still consisted usually of a solo performance on the part of the cantor, with the congregation singing in unison ; where there was a choir it sang the responses or accompanied the cantor. But the church already possessed a highly developed choral music, together with independent instrumental works (Ricercares, preludes, etc.). The church had gradually developed first its homophonous and then its polyphonous choral music, but all this was still unknown to the synagogue and Jews could not but regard this kind of music as completely alien.

In his ' Jüdische Merkwürdigkeiten,' published at Frankfurt in 1714-17,[1] Johann Jacob Schudt has given details of synagogal music in Prague which indicate the high standard it had reached. Although he was not a Jew and not accustomed to synagogal music, he was greatly impressed by it in Prague, and especially by comparison with the singing in the Frankfurt synagogue (which apparently he knew), finding the Prague singing much more progressive. He writes: ' In Prague there are thirteen synagogues or Jewish schools, the smallest of which is larger than the largest in Frankfurt. In the " Alt-Neu-Schul " in Prague they have an organ, which is rather rare among Jews, so it is only played on Friday evening shortly before the Sabbath, since the approaching Sabbath has to be welcomed as " kallah " or bride, with the song: " Legah[2] Dodi Likrat Kallah " (Come, my friend, to meet the bride).'[3] We have no information concerning the nature of this organ playing. Nor do we know whether it was

---

[1] New ed. Berlin, 1922.
[2] Correctly: *Lechah Dodi* . . .
[3] Op. cit., vol. IV, chap. 34.

really only an organ accompaniment to the *Lechah Dodi* song, which is a regular part of the Sabbath eve service.

Arno Nadel has given details of a collection of synagogal tunes issued in 1744, which he possessed.[1] It was called ' Hannoversches Kompendium,' and, according to his statement, contained 302 written melodies, without text, but provided with superscriptions. This must have been one of the oldest surviving memorials of Jewish liturgical music.

Some fragmentary details can be given of the participation of Jewish musicians in European non-Jewish music. In Germany the minnesinger Süsskind von Trimberg, who was born *circa* 1220 at Trimberg, near Schweinfurt, Bavaria, was a well-known character, and the ' Mannessische Liederhandschrift,' preserved in Heidelberg University library, includes a picture in which he is depicted. We know nothing of the kind of music he sang in his *minnelieder*, but from the texts of his six lieder which have come down to us it is clear that he was consciously a Jew, at least in his old age, for the texts are based entirely on Jewish literature. There are records of a number of Jewish musicians in Italy, especially in the sixteenth and seventeenth centuries, at the court of the Gonzagas in Mantua. The most famous of these was Salomone Rossi, already mentioned, who wrote madrigals and instrumental works. But he is chiefly known to musical history for his introduction of the monodic style into instrumental music. Some information concerning Jewish players in Prague in the sixteenth century is given in a description of the wedding of Peter Wok von Rosenberg in 1580, at which a Jewish orchestra played.[2] In fact, Jewish musicians were active in Bohemia in the fourteenth century, but only in the seventeenth century did they form a musical guild of their own, playing at markets and non-Jewish weddings. At times they were very popular, so much so that non-Jewish musicians often objected to this Jewish competition, and at times they succeeded in getting a ban imposed on Jews playing at non-Jewish functions. The ' Jewish dance' tunes accepted as such in Christian gatherings of this period appear to be renderings

---

[1] Musica Hebraica, I-II, 1938, pp. 28-31.
[2] 'Zivot Petra W. z. Rozemberka' (Life of Peter of Rozemberk), edited by Mares, and quoted in Bondy Dvorsky, II, p. 1024.

of the common dance tunes of non-Jewish folk music. Thus, one example given in Heckel's *Lautenbuch* in 1562 runs:

Although these Jewish players, who were known to the Jews of their time as *Letzim* (jokers), also played for Jewish secular functions, at weddings, for instance, no notation of the music they used has survived. So we cannot say whether it differed from the pieces played at non-Jewish functions. From the text and illustrations to Schudt's 'Jüdische Merkwürdigkeiten' we know that Jewish bridal processions of his time, in both Frankfurt and Prague, included musicians—wind, percussion, and even drummers. In his smaller work, telling how the Jews of Frankfurt and Prague celebrated the birth of the Imperial Crown Prince, Schudt relates: 'and by the tower were nineteen trumpeters, eight fiddles, four French horns, and four kettle-drums.'[1]

---

[1] Jüdisches Franckfurter und Prager Freuden-Fest wegen der höchst-glücklichen Geburth des Durchläuchtigsten Kayserlichen Erb-Printzens ... Frankfurt-on-Main, 1716.

CHAPTER XI

THE DAYS OF ENLIGHTENMENT, EMANCIPATION, AND REFORM

(Nineteenth Century)

TOWARDS the end of the eighteenth century a movement began among the Jews in many parts of Europe which very quickly brought about great changes in their spiritual, intellectual, and material affairs. It was the direct consequence of changes in their living conditions, especially in France, Germany, and Austria, in which countries they were given emancipation and granted either equality of legal rights or at least the right of entry into the various professions, and the right to reside outside the ghettoes or their special urban districts. The greater freedom this involved brought the progressive and the wealthy Jews especially into closer social relations with their Christian neighbours.

At first their one desire was to acquire the speech and the culture of the land in which they were resident. But this led to their mastering European science and knowledge, of which the inevitable concomitant was the immersion of many of the assimilated Jews in the culture of the country. Whereas in past times the cultural tastes of the non-Jewish environment had affected the Jewish cultural productions against their own will, the time now arrived, especially in Germany, when Jews concerned with specifically Jewish forms of creative activity readily tried to imitate the products of non-Jewish culture. The emancipation of the Jews in Germany brought them into direct contact with German culture; they took particular interest in German literature, philosophy, and music, and before long were active in all the German intellectual spheres. Although the non-Jews displayed a constant aversion from these Jewish newcomers, the latter, thanks to their adaptability, were highly successful with their productions. In their desire for complete adaptation and assimilation many of the German Jews were not content with imitating non-Jewish culture; they believed that baptism into Christianity would enable them to become wholly German in their cultural tastes, and so to cut all spiritual and intellectual ties with their former brethren. We shall have something to say about this in the next chapter, which deals with Jews in music. For the moment we propose to discuss only the development that occurred in Jewish music as the result of the Enlightenment and Emancipation.

The changes that occurred in Jewish music during the nineteenth century were so great that one would hardly have thought them possible of achievement in so short a time. The Jewish Reform Movement which started early in the century not only introduced elements of non-Jewish religious and secular song into German synagogal vocal music, but even attempted to refashion it as far as possible on the model of church music. Four reforms which were bound to have very considerable effects on synagogue singing were the introduction of the organ ; the refashioning of traditional synagogue song on the lines of church singing, where possible in four-part choral style ; the composition of new songs in this ecclesiastical style ; and singing in the language of the country, e.g., German. It is typical of the Jewish attitude that the newly introduced style of singing, based on Christian models, was greatly disliked at first, but then, when it was better known, was generally accepted. But the reforms were not carried through and accepted without considerable opposition. Israel Jacobsohn, an energetic reformer who went from Kassel to live in Berlin in 1815, had great difficulty in instituting his innovations, which included an organ accompaniment to the Sabbath and holy-day services, a choir singing in German, and regular sermons in German. The conflict that resulted within the Jewish community led to a Prussian Cabinet Decree, issued in the reign of Friedrich Wilhelm III, on December 9, 1823, which prohibited all changes in the Jewish religious service. This order read: ' Occasioned by the attached representation of a part of the local (Berlin) Jewish community, I once more determine hereby that the Jewish religious service shall be conducted only in the local synagogues and only according to the rite previously in use, without the least innovation in language or ceremonial, in prayers or in singing, and wholly in accordance with the ancient ordinances. I hold you (the competent officials) under obligation to adhere strictly to this order and to tolerate no sects whatever among the Jews in my state.' On the other hand, the reformist attempts of the 'Neuer Israelitischer Tempelverein' (New Israelite Temple-Society) in Hamburg came up against the resistance of the rabbis. None the less, as time passed the innovations, including four-part choral singing, and the use of the organ, made their way in various places, though often they were allowed only temporarily, then were rejected again. However, they corresponded increasingly with the demands of the progressive, educated section of the community. Very often the reformation of the ritual and the modernisation of the synagogue service, its adaptation to the Christian environment, especially in regard to choral singing and organ-playing, were adopted in order to keep the youth within the community. The youth, who, indeed, were already partly assimilated, were to find in the Jewish service what they admired in the Christian service.

In 1837 the entire rabbinate of the city were present at the consecration of a synagogue in Prague, although the ceremony included choral singing and organ-playing. In Prussia as time passed the ban of 1823 was forgotten, and sermons in German became common. The reform movement, which advocated a policy of embellishment of the synagogue service and its modification to accord with the times, gained steadily in influence everywhere. The reforms of the German synagogue services also influenced those of other countries. Of all the reforms, it was the introduction of the organ that was least acceptable to the conservative Jews; Israel Jacobsohn had been the first to use it, at Wesen in 1810, at Berlin in 1815, and at Hamburg in 1818. A violent agitation both for and against its use was the result; rabbis entered the fray on both sides, and a large amount of writing was devoted to discussing whether the organ and organ music in the service was permitted or forbidden by Jewish religious law. The fact that the Prague synagogues were reported to have had organs a hundred years before did not ease the task or those who wished to introduce it in Germany. The resulting 'organ-battle' went on for years; and even to-day it is not entirely decided, for the question is raised from time to time, when some conservatively-minded Jewish community bans organ accompaniments in the service, or at least is forced to discuss the problem.

Of recent times the reforms in the musical aspect of the synagogue service, as we know them especially through the compositions of Sulzer and Lewandowski, have been attacked on the ground that wherever they were introduced they eliminated the characteristically Jewish qualities. But, viewed historically, the innovations must be recognised as in conformity with the Jewish cultural tastes of the time. These reformers did not feel that they were neglecting the Jewish element; their greatest desire was that the spirit of the Enlightenment and the Emancipation, which had definitely improved the Jews' social position and tended to dominate their lives, should find formal expression in the service. Thus the reforms were a concomitant of the Jewish spiritual and intellectual trend in the nineteenth century, of their new, freer manner of living; they were the consequence of their intellectual assimilation and their improved living conditions.

As time passed, the reformation in the Jewish services, especially in regard to synagogue music, caused an increasing differentiation between the Jewish cultural sphere of Germany and Austro-Hungary and those of other lands. The Polish-Russian cultural group continued to practise the simple synagogue vocal music described in the previous chapter, in which the cantor's improvisation and the traditional melodies played a great part; whereas in Germany and Austro-Hungary the trend was to make the Jewish service as musically like the Christian as possible.

An outstanding representative of the reformist trends in synagogue music was Salomon Sulzer. He was born at Hohenems, in Voralberg, on March 30, 1804; it is told of him that when he was quite young his life was miraculously saved from a mountain torrent in spate, and that this decided him to enter the Jewish religious ministry. He attended a Talmudic academy at Endigen, Switzerland, and afterward had music lessons at Karlsruhe, where he decided to become a cantor. He was chosen as cantor in his native town at the youthful age of thirteen, but first began to practise it when he was sixteen. He studied the *chazzanut* under a well-known cantor named Lippmann, in Switzerland. He acted as Chazzan (cantor) at Hohenems for five years, and completely rearranged the local synagogue service on reformist lines. One of his innovations was four-part choral singing; as he had no music of this nature available, he either arranged existing music for four-part choir or composed entirely new synagogal music for the purpose. Although he was more ready than many another reformer of his day to take the traditional melodies into account, he tended to fall in with reforming tastes. Having had a general musical education, he did not regard organ-playing and choral singing wholly in the Christian contemporary manner as at all in conflict with his Jewish spirit. On the Emperor's birthday he even allowed a string quartet to play during the synagogue service. When he was only twenty-one he was called (1826) to the office of Chazzan of the synagogue in the Seitenstettengasse, at Vienna. There he continued his organising activities, working in collaboration with the local Jewish preacher and reformer, Mannheimer.

In many respects the reformist movement in Vienna was less drastic than those in Hamburg and Berlin, for the local Jews held more closely to the traditional observances and to Hebrew as the liturgical language. Even so, as Sulzer continued his own musical development and sought to assimilate the contemporary non-Jewish musical style he widened the breach between himself and those Jews who in their musical tastes held fast to the traditional manner of singing. In 1838 he published his first book of compositions for the synagogue, giving it the title ' *Shir Zion,* songs for the Israelite religious service.' This volume contained works in which such motifs were so seldom employed that the compositions could have been taken as Christian. It is noteworthy that it included contributions by his non-Jewish friends Schubert, Seyfried, Volkert, Würfel, and Haslinger, and that in their style and content these display many points of similarity with those of Sulzer. His own compositions were widely approved in his day, not least because he possessed outstanding talent as a cantor and put special expression into the music he sang; because of his training that expression could not but sound Jewish. In addition, in his cantillation he frequently kept to the traditional melodies. As the senior cantor of the synagogue he enchanted all who heard him, and exerted a great force of attraction; many non-Jews, including musicians and even royalty, were among his audiences. Through his acquaintance with great musicians like Schubert and Liszt he was continually adding to his musical knowledge. Yet it would seem that as he grew older he felt the need to hold fast to the traditional forms and spirit of Jewish religious vocal music, for the second volume of *Shir Zion*, published in 1865, includes a number of pieces in the traditional style. In 1860 he published a liturgical song-book, *Duda'im*, for the purpose, *inter alia*, of regulating and facilitating ' the training of Israelite schoolchildren in liturgical singing.'

Sulzer had a greater influence than any previous synagogue reformer in the musical sphere. His work was followed by the composition and publication of a large quantity of synagogue music for which it set the pattern. Many of his songs were widely circulated, and were, and still are, sung even in communities which rejected many of the reforms. In his lifetime he was accorded an honour shown to no other Jewish cantor : on his seventieth birthday he was made a freeman of the City of Vienna. He was awarded several orders, was professor of the Vienna Conservatoire, an honorary member of the Academy of Arts in Rome, etc. After fifty-six years of official activity he retired in 1881 ; he died in Vienna on January 17, 1890, and his funeral was an occasion of public honour to himself and his work. His son, Joseph, published a posthumous volume of his music in 1891, and his works have had several further editions. ' *Shir Zion,* songs for the Israelite religious service,' was revised and republished by Joseph Sulzer in 1905, and a fourth edition, with an introduction by Arno Nadel, was issued at Frankfurt-on-Main in 1929. The 1905 revised edition had some minor changes and improvements ; Joseph Sulzer added a fourth part to a number of compositions originally written for three-part singing, and wrote in a line for harp to many of the festival songs. He also rearranged the Psalms of Affliction, which his father had set for four-part singing, allotting the soprano and alto lines to boys' voices ; Joseph Sulzer arranged them for male voice choir.

A number of cantors and synagogue choirmasters declared themselves in favour of synagogue music as Sulzer conceived it. But it was Louis Lewandowski who followed him most closely, continuing his style of compositional writing. Lewandowski was born at Wreszen, near Poznan, on April 3, 1821 ; when quite a child he showed a bent for religious music. On high holy-days his father acted in an honorary capacity as cantor for many of the prayers in the local synagogue, and he brought all his five sons, including Louis, into service to help him. Old Lewandowski, who came of a long line of rabbinical and learned ancestors, gave Louis instruction in the Talmud; but after his mother's death the boy went to Berlin, where he attended the high school and studied the violin and piano. The Berlin cantor, Ascher Lion, took him on as singer in the synagogue when he was twelve, and as he had a fine soprano voice and musical gifts he quickly made his mark. Many of the synagogue congregation took an interest in him, among them being Salomon Plessner, who taught him Hebrew. Plessner introduced him to the home of Alexander Mendelssohn, a grandson of Moses Mendelssohn. Alexander was a well-known philanthropist, and his house was frequented by many artists; so Lewandowski, who became a regular visitor, was able to mix in musical circles and to listen to intellectual conversation. About this time he decided to devote himself entirely to the study of music. He spent two years at Berlin University, attending lectures by Adolphe Marx, Dove, and Gans. As a protegé of Alexander Mendelssohn, after a strict entrance examination, he was accepted as the first Jewish student at the Academy of Arts, where Rungenhagen and Grell were his teachers. While at the Academy he was awarded prizes for two works: his Cantata for soli, chorus, and orchestra, and a symphony; they both had a very successful first performance with himself as conductor.

There followed a period of four years' continual illness, during which he had to give up all his activities. On his recovery he turned to the field of synagogue music. In 1840 he was appointed choirmaster at the Old Synagogue in the Heidereutergasse; a four-part choir had recently been instituted there; he was placed in charge of it, and entrusted with the arrangement of the services in conformity with the new tastes. Under his influence the obsolescent liturgical music performed by a *chazzan*, a bass, and a 'singer,' in other words, a cantor, bass, and a boy soprano, was to be replaced by music suited to the times. But before undertaking the task he went to Vienna, to get thoroughly acquainted with the synagogue services as arranged by Sulzer. His first step on his return to Berlin was to attempt to introduce Sulzer's *Shir Zion*, but this led to a conflict between him and the old cantor of the synagogue, Ascher Lion. Not until a young cantor named Lichtenstein was engaged did Lewandowski make any progress with his reforms. Moreover, Lichtenstein had an extensive knowledge of *chazzanut*, and so made a valuable collaborator for Lewandowski, whose thorough musical training had been entirely on non-Jewish lines and was influenced by nineteenth-century musical tastes. His synagogal works, *Kol Rinnoh utefilloh* (The voice of praise and prayer) and *Todo v'Zimroh* (Praise and Song) clearly reveal this influence ; while using the traditional melodies he tried to adapt their ornamentation and coloratura to contemporary tastes, and to bring them into conformity with the nineteenth-century conception of form by arranging and harmonising them. It is not surprising that he frequently seemed to be even more advanced than Sulzer, for he had had a longer and more thorough musical training, so that his outlook was even more closely in harmony with the European music of his day.

In 1886 he was called to the New Synagogue in Oranienburgerstrasse, and here he went even further in modernising the liturgy. The Old Synagogue did not possess an organ, and his works for its choir had been composed for two-part singing *a capella* (the *Kol Rinnoh utefilloh*, 1871). But now he added an organ accompaniment both to works for the choir and to certain compositions for the cantor, though he still used the instrument chiefly to support the vocal line. In 1876 he published his ' *Todo v'Zimroh*, first part, Songs for the Sabbath ' ; the second part, ' Songs for Festivals,' was published in 1882. Others of his works included a collected Hebrew liturgy for the Nuremburg community, and music for over forty psalms with German text ; he also wrote a number of secular compositions. In the Berlin Jewish teachers' training college he took a very active part in the training of cantors, and at the Jewish community boys' and girls' school as singing-master. He died on February 3, 1894. He received various marks of distinction in his lifetime ; on the occasion of his official silver jubilee he was appointed Imperial Director of Music, and on the occasion of his golden jubilee the title of Professor of Music was conferred on him by the senate of the musical section of the Academy of Arts.

Lewandowski's synagogue compositions published in the first part of *Todo v'Zimroh* are striking by reason of the fact that almost throughout he wrote in major keys, only a few being written in the minor. This is not so noticeable in the second part; for, as he said in his foreword to the first part, in 'Songs for Festivals,' he was more concerned to make use of the traditional melodies, and so 'to mitigate the alien effect for the synagogue congregation.' This also applies to his first volume of synagogue compositions, the *Kol Rinnoh utefilloh*, in which the minor is used for some songs, as it contains many traditional melodies. As a composer he had a more perfect technique than Sulzer. He came strongly under the influence of the German romantics, but elements of Italian music and especially Italian coloratura are discernible in his work. He often made use of canon and imitation; his compositions reveal some affinity with Mendelssohn. His recitatives, especially in the first part of *Todo v'Zimroh*, mostly in major keys and based on the triad, are frequently of a secular character. The second part, as we have said, has songs and recitatives based more on traditional material. Sulzer was responsible for the beginnings of all this development in synagogue music; but he was more deeply rooted than Lewandowski in the traditional song, and Lewandowski, naturally enough, usually tried to avoid melodies Sulzer had already laid under contribution. So most of his work consists of original compositions that are independent of traditional song. His work, like Sulzer's has remained in favour for synagogal and other use; a new edition of *Kol Rinnoh utefilloh* was published by J. Kaufmann Verlag, Frankfurt-on-Main, in 1921; the first part of *Todo v'Zimroh* went into a sixth edition from the same publisher, and the second part has had several editions under its original publisher, Bote and Bock, of Berlin. Arrangements of *Kol Rinnoh utefilloh* have been published in America.

One other name has to be mentioned together with those of Sulzer and Lewandowski, for Samuel Naumbourg also had a share in the development of synagogal musical style during the nineteenth century. He came of a family of cantors, and was born at Donaulohe in 1816. At quite an early age he became a member of the Munich synagogue choir, while receiving tuition in musical theory. Later he acted as choirmaster in Strasbourg and then as cantor in Besançon, whence in 1845, on the recommendation of the famous composer Halévy, he was called to the post of Senior Cantor at Paris. Here he worked very intensively in the field of

Jewish religious music. Like Sulzer and Lewandowski, he was on intimate terms with the leading musicians of his time, so his collections of composed music included not only his own works, of which three were dedicated to Rossini, but synagogue songs written by Halévy and Meyerbeer. Among the works he wrote during his years at Munich must be mentioned the manuscript collection: 'Complete year of the old original melodies of the synagogue, with recitative tonic accents for the public rendering of all prayers and tablatures of the Torah and Megillot for the Sabbath, Holy Days, and the Day of Atonement, set to music in accordance with the rendering of Cantor L. Sänger at Munich, by S. Naumbourg; Munich, January 3, 1840.' This collection, together with his extremely extensive knowledge of traditional synagogue melodies, enabled him to exploit these melodies and to put them on permanent record for future generations.

However, his greatest work was the *Zemirot Yisrael*, three volumes of which were published in 1847. A second edition was published at Paris in 1863. On the title-page he describes it as 'religious songs of the Israelites, containing hymns, psalms, and the complete liturgy of the synagogue from the most ancient times down to our days, with organ or piano accompaniment *ad libitum.*' In this work he had regard to the old, traditional tunes, especially in the songs for festivals. He was reverent in his attitude to the old synagogue melodies, but often he treats them, in regard both to style and to melodic phrasing, in the manner of the Italian and French composers. This is so, for instance, in the case of *Etz Chayim,* in the second part, a work dedicated to Rossini. The simplicity and integrity of his compositions, their excellent and clear harmony, and fidelity to the melody, resulted in their having wide circulation, and in most Jewish communities they rank with the songs of Sulzer and Lewandowski. A selection of *Zemirot Yisrael* was published under the title of *Aguddat Shirim,* and this also contains an historical study of the music of the Hebrews. We must mention his editing, together with Vincent d'Indy, of the synagogal compositions and madrigals of Salomone Rossi. This new edition, published in 1877, constitutes a lasting service to music. Naumbourg died in 1880.

Sulzer, Lewandowski, and Naumbourg were the three

founders of nineteenth-century synagogal music, and their work has been taken as a starting point for most synagogal compositions ever since. From their time onward great advances were made in synagogal music, for every choirmaster and every cantor of any prominence composed works for the service. The best of them were dominated by the endeavour to preserve and arrange the melodies that had been handed down in their various communities. But these synagogal composers did not always have sufficient theoretical training to be capable of producing technically unobjectionable works, quite apart from the many quite untalented individuals who occupied themselves with similar activities. Even so, an extensive synagogal music came into being, consisting partly of arrangements of traditional melodies and partly of original compositions. In addition there was a continual influx of religious song from Eastern Europe, where there had been no reform at all. The western synagogal composers readily made use of these songs, because they seemed old or traditional, since the *chazzanim* of Eastern Europe, especially Poland and Russia, frequently composed their own melodies in the style of the traditional *nigunim*, the age-old synagogal tunes. The result was that these same melodies from Eastern Europe quite often were incorporated in the new synagogal works of western composers, especially of those who had themselves originated from the East or at least were under its influence.

The collecting of traditional synagogue tunes, which formed a great part of the activities of nineteenth-century synagogal composers, was furthered by Abraham Baer, who was born on December 26, 1834, at Filehne, and died at Gothenburg in 1894. His *Baal tefilloh*, or ' The Practical Cantor,' was based specifically on the model of Lewandowski's *Kol Rinnoh utefilloh*. It was first published at Gothenburg in 1877, had a second edition in 1883, and a third, enlarged and improved edition was published in 1901 at Frankfurt-on-Main. A new edition was published by J. Bulka at Nuremberg in 1930. In his youth Baer had travelled a great deal and had collected many synagogal tunes, and in this work he frequently noted several melodies for the one text. When notating the tunes he distinguished them as ' old,' ' new,' ' German,' ' Polish,' or ' Portuguese ' (Sefardic). A few of them are arranged for a two or more part choir, or are provided with organ accompaniment. In a foreword he gave certain details of research into synagogue vocal music which were intended to help to a better understanding of the work. The book as a whole contains valuable material for the cantor, and it gives an excellent notation of the neginot.

Lewandowski had an outstanding pupil in Aron Friedmann, who was born at Szaki, in Poland, on August 22, 1855, and died at Berlin on June 9, 1936. He held the post of cantor to the Berlin Jewish community for over forty years, from 1882 to 1923. His studies at the *Meisterschule* of the Academy of Arts gave him a knowledge of music outside the *chazzanut*, of which he was complete master. His works consisted of musical compositions, as well as literary writings on synagogue music and its history. His *Shir Lishlomo* (The Song of Solomon) 'chazzanut for the entire liturgical year,' which was published in 1901, contains traditional melodies which are not to be found in earlier collections. His most important literary works were 'Der Synagogale Gesang' (Synagogue Song), published in 1908, an outstanding study and analysis of the subject; and the 'Lebensbilder berühmter Kantoren' (Life Stories of Famous Cantors), a valuable collection of biographies, in three parts published in 1918, 1921, and 1927. He also issued a 'Liturgisches Gesangbuch für die jüdischen Religionsschulen Deutschlands' (Liturgical songbook for German Jewish religious schools).

One other German collector of synagogal songs must be mentioned. Hirsch Weintraub, who was born at Dubno in 1811, and died at Königsberg, East Prussia, in 1881, published his *Shire Bet Adonaj* (Songs of the House of the Lord) in 1859. In this collection he made it his task to notate traditional melodies most of which had been passed on to him by his father, Salomon Kashtan (1781-1829). Salomon was a famous chazzan of Dubno who travelled from town to town in Lithuania, Poland, Hungary, and Prussia. According to Weintraub's statement the third part, *Shire Shelomo* (Songs of Solomon), contains very ancient melodies in the Phrygian, Mixolydian, and Aeolian modes.

Hungary also had a collector of Jewish songs in Moritz Friedmann, who was born at Hrabòcz on March 7, 1823, and died at Budapest on August 29, 1891. He was a member of Sulzer's choir in Vienna for a time, then became senior cantor in Budapest.

His songbook, 'Israelita Vallasos Enekék,' was used in most of the Hungarian communities.

Frederico Consolo, a well-known Italian violinist and composer who studied under Liszt, and was born at Ancona in 1841 (1840 ?) and died at Florence on December 14, 1906, made an important collection of Sefardic synagogue songs according to the rite of the Jewish community at Leghorn. He called it *Sefer Shire Yisrael* (Book of the Songs of Israel) and published it at Florence in 1890. It contained 445 tunes for solo voice, without accompaniment. He later published an appendix to this work, in which he arranged eighteen Sefardic synagogue tunes, seven of them as solo songs, with piano accompaniment; six as preludes for organ; four as preludes for piano; and a duo for two violas. He wrote an historical survey of Jewish music, 'Cenni sull' origine e sul progresso della musica liturgica,' with an appendix on the introduction of the organ.

That the reform movement did not leave Eastern Europe entirely unaffected is shown by the publication at Moscow in 1884, of Jacob Bachmann's *Shirat Jacob* (Songs for the Israelite religious service, for solo and choir, with and without organ accompaniment). These were chiefly for tenor cantor and four-part mixed choir *a capella*. A note in the introduction says the work is 'chiefly for use in the synagogues in Russia.'

Since those days, music for synagogue use has grown steadily in volume, and has been progressively enriched. All this great development was rendered possible only as the result of the nineteenth-century Reform, and especially the work of the composers we have mentioned. At a later stage it was carried to the concert platform. But from the middle of the nineteenth century music that observed the modern rules of the art became a regular feature of synagogue services.

CHAPTER XII

'JUDAISM IN MUSIC'

THE emancipation of the Jews and the assimilation movement that followed during the nineteenth century brought Jews right into European, and especially German, French, and Russian musical life. But despite the predominantly liberal trend of the age, there were many people in Europe who took a hostile attitude to Jews and regarded musicians who belonged to, or originated from, Jewry as intruders. The 'Jewish musicians' had hardly escaped their former restrictions when they found themselves involved in a bitter struggle for existence. It was not long before the opposition to 'Judaism in Music' began to exert pressure, and the entire question was brought to the forefront of discussion. Thus, under Franz Brendel's editorship the 'Neue Zeitschrift für Musik,' which Schumann had founded, opened its pages to a discussion on 'Hebrew Artistic Taste.' The article which made most stir was that of Richard Wagner who, under the pseudonym 'Karl Freigedenk,' contributed his 'Das Judentum in der Musik' ('Jewry in Music') to the 'Neue Zeitschrift' in 1850. In 1869 he published an extended version of this article under his own name,[1] being moved by the belief that the original article had incurred for him the enmity of the Jews and their friends and sympathisers.

In the revised version Wagner maintained that it was because of his persecution by the Jews that his works and those of his followers had met with a hostile reception, especially in Paris and his own native land. We shall not discuss this question, especially as neither his original article nor the revision provides any objective consideration of the problem, but simply attributes his failures to Jewish influence. He did not trouble to investigate the part Jews had played in shaping Western music, a subject that would have been of great interest, for through the Catholic church the West had borrowed many melodies from the Jews.

---

[1] 'Das Judentum in der Musik,' Gesammelte Schriften, Vol. V, Leipzig, 1869. Also: 'Neue Zeitschrift für Musik,' Vol. XXXIII, September 3, 1850.

If he had argued that the Jewish entry into German music consequent on the Emancipation was detrimental to, or had a bad influence on, that music, there would have been matter for a discussion, coming, to some extent, within the sphere of musical æsthetics. But he was concerned only with his own work, and simply attributed the difficulties attending his struggle for success to Jewish hostility, which in fact did not generally exist. He made disparaging references to Jewish religious music, though he had no close acquaintance with it. And he asserted: 'What the educated Jew with his distinctive disposition had to say when he wished to express himself artistically could naturally only be indifferent and trivial, since all his bent for art was only something of a luxury, and unnecessary.' On Mendelssohn he delivered the following judgment: 'He has shown us that a Jew can be of the richest individual talent, can have had the finest and most varied of education, can possess the most exalted, delicately perceptive sense of honour, yet with all these merits he can never, not even once, have that profound, heart- and soul-stirring effect upon us which we expect of art, though we are susceptible to that effect, for we have experienced it times out of number immediately a hero of our art, so to speak, simply opened his mouth to speak to us.' And he goes on: 'In listening to a work by this composer we feel captivated only when nothing but our imagination, avid for amusement, is moved by the production, ordering, and interweaving of the finest, most polished and skilled of figures in the changing colours and formal charms of the kaleidoscope; but not when these figures are intended to take on the shape of the more profound and fundamental feelings of the human heart.' Wagner's view of Mendelssohn was that despite the inadequacy of the musical heritage which was obviously his as a Jew, its influence had been mitigated to some extent because of his own extraordinary talent, and he had produced something apparently respectable. On the other hand, without mentioning his name, Wagner attacked Meyerbeer, whom he disliked, declaring that he was what he was because he was a Jew. And here he took the opportunity to refer to the undisciplined service of the synagogue. He explained Meyerbeer's success as being due to his ability to amuse his audiences in their boredom, and to gratify their artistic demands by a great expenditure of artistic resources which were concerned chiefly with trivialities and banalities. We do not intend to discuss these side issues, but it seems desirable to adduce his statements, since they were made by an outstanding non-Jewish musician, and have frequently served as a basis of discussion. We put them on record also because later on we shall be quoting statements from the Jewish side in regard to the value of composers, Jewish in origin, who had an important share in the music of non-Jewish cultural groups.

Wagner's article provoked a great deal of discussion, and there were a number of replies to it. One of these, published anonymously in 1869, is particularly interesting because of its objective treatment of the subject. The standard adopted in 'Richard Wagner and Jewry, a Contribution to present-day cultural history, by a Non-partisan,'[1] is very different from that of Wagner's article, and the arguments used in it are much more interesting. The anonymous author, a non-Jew, calls Wagner's article 'a pamphlet soaked in poison,' and truly remarks: 'The second, newly published part argues that the practical consequences of the article were a general Jewish conspiracy against the author; by his lachrymose tone and shamelessly revealed self-infatuation and self-idolatry he falls so irrevocably into the ludicrous that one must be content to leave it, with our tacit commiseration, to Wagner's tendentious opponents as an object of their cheap derision.' However, 'Non-partisan' was chiefly concerned with investigating the Jewish quality in Jewish musicians; and we may well consider his opinions on this question, not only because he strives to be impartial, but even more because his views are interesting and are the product of fundamental thinking. He wrote:

'More than any other production, a work of art is a product of the whole, completely distinctive individuality, and of inexorable necessity it bears that individual's signature. A Jewish child will always be a Jew; and, unless it is produced in a retort as an unviable homunculus, a Jewish artistic product will have a Jewish character.' And going on to discuss what is the 'Jewish' characteristic, he says: 'Already, when we have contact with

[1] 'Richard Wagner und das Judentum, ein Beitrag zur Kulturgeschichte unserer Zeit, von einem Unparteiischen'; Sam. Lucas, Elberfeld, 1869

Jewish artists and virtuosos actually engaged in direct reproduction of art, we experience something which to our perception is an alien, prickling, restless element, a straining after effect; and this is characteristic; and we can just as little mistake their characteristic qualities, their disposition to cling so tenaciously to nationality, in their greater intellectual creations. It is simply that they lack that deeper passion which sets the heart aglow, and that peace which comes of conflict resolved, that they lack the true pathos and heroic exaltation . . .' On which we may remark that this author was too close to the works and the spiritual and intellectual currents of his day. He did not realise that in his estimation of what he found or missed in Jewish creations he was basing himself solely on the ideals which governed him or his cultural circle. His observations are shackled to the demands made on art in his time. So he remarks:

'It is these characteristics which we have recognised as Jewish, the hurried, the restless, the unstable elements, which have made it impossible for him to achieve in any form of art that which one may call the gently vibrating line of beauty. Mendelssohn, and Meyerbeer himself, can be cited as brilliant examples of the fact that the gift of original melodic invention is not dependent on nationality; but a musical work of art does not consist simply of melody, rhythm, harmony in isolation or separately, it is not the effluence of one or another special talent, of the gift of melodic invention, of the active soul life, and so on, but is the product of the whole man, the emanation and expression of the entire personality. And so there will always be something Jewish about it, so long as the Jew in the composer is not completely eliminated. . . . Speaking generally, if, out of all the arts, the Jew favours mostly, or indeed, only music, the reason is first that he lacks feeling for plastic form, and secondly the strong sensuous attraction of his character; correspondingly, his productions are either of a sensuously stimulating (Meyerbeer, Offenbach, etc.) or a sentimental nature. . . .' The foregoing passage reveals how much the author's arguments are grounded in and relate only to the nineteenth century, when the Jews had not yet entered any other sphere of art except music, and when 'Non-partisan' had only Mendelssohn, Meyerbeer, Halévy, and Offenbach to generalise from.

This cannot be said of a much later attempt to get to the bottom of and isolate the ' Jewish' element in European music, made by Heinrich Berl in 1926.[1] Although not himself a Jew, he did much research into the question of Jewish music, and absorbed a perceptible Jewish background and training, so that he was equipped to consider the problem fundamentally. However, his observations tend to be of a ' musico-psychological,' not to say ' musico-metaphysical ' character, which tends to depreciate their value from the historical aspect, interesting as they may be to anyone concerned with these problems from the psychological aspect, as psychological factors of cultural development. None the less, even though one cannot agree with many of his views, it is noticeable that he did make a thorough investigation into what passes current as the ' Jewish' musical quality, and which is regarded as having found entry into European music through Jews, among whom he includes all who originate from Jewry. For instance, among modern Jewish composers he includes Adolf Schreiber, Gustav Mahler, Arnold Schönberg, and Erich Wolfgang Korngold.

According to Berl, Jewish music is typically the music of an Oriental. Incidentally, here he commits the fundamental error of lumping Indian, Chinese, Arabic and other ' Eastern ' music together, and then of contrasting all these various forms of primitive, original music with European art-music[2]; although in fact each of these musical cultures has its own specific features, its own rules and desiderata, which are not susceptible of comparison with those of European music. According to Berl, since the Jews who have contributed to European music are Orientals, they have

---

[1] ' Das Judentum in der Musik.' Deutsche Verlagsanstalt, Stuttgart, 1926.
[2] I hope that readers will forgive me for using this literal translation of the German, ' Kunstmusik.' In effect, ' Kunstmusik ' means music created by musicians trained in modern musical techniques, and so is itself rather a misnomer, since ' art ' is not primarily a matter of technique. In German, as in English, it is the secondary meaning of the word that is indicated here ; if we can say that folk music is ' artless,' then the compositions of composers trained in modern musical techniques may, perhaps, be called ' art-music,' without begging the question whether all such compositions are really in the category of ' art.' The alternative suggested translation, ' classic music,' is obviously misleading. So I have used ' art-music ' (art-song) here and later, in default of any better English term.—H.C.S.

different musical desiderata from the Europeans ; and the Jewish triviality and sentimentality is the result of their orientalism. In distinction from the European, who is harmonic in his perceptions, the Oriental perceives melodically and rhythmically and so forth. ' Owing to his remarkable concatenation of blood the Jew is the " unplastic " man *par excellence*. He does not see things as shapes, he perceives them only in their essence. . . . If the Jew is necessarily an unplastic type, he must also necessarily be the opposite (of the plastic), i.e., the most musical.' This is how Berl explains the executant, the player in the Jew, the Jewish talent for virtuosity ; and he holds that the reproductive cannot in the least be regarded as uncreative. In an examination of Schreiber, Mahler, Schönberg, and Korngold he discovers their ' racial ' points of contact, though often there is very little of these. The fact that this manner of classifying composers makes it quite possible to say that any non-Jewish composer exhibiting these characteristics is Jewish reveals the inadequacy, not to say danger, of such a method. Moreover, all the composers under discussion have been uprooted from the Jewish community and have got far away from it, and the consequences of this on their musical expression remain uninvestigated.

If Berl's arguments had been of any practical importance they would have had some influence on later Jewish musical development. But, apart from provoking certain replies, by Arno Nadel, Paul Nettl, etc., the book has had no consequences whatever. It was for Berl ' to show Jewry's share in Western musical development '[1] ; we shall not go further into analysis of his assertions and arguments. We may simply remark that his views on the ' trivial, banal, a-harmonic, melodic, etc.,' elements in Jewish music have been rejected by modern Jewish musicians and composers and controverted by the music which Jewish composers have written. Later on he proceeds to discuss ' Hebrew ' music, which he distinguishes from ' Jewish ' music, by which he means the music of Mendelssohn, Mahler, Schönberg, etc. And then— like many others, for that matter—he commits the error of attempting to describe, or at least to conjecture the music of the

---

[1] Vincent D'Indy went so far as to distinguish a ' Jewish or Semitic school ' in French music, including in it Meyerbeer, Auber, Hérold, Halévy, Adam, David, and Offenbach.

ancient Jews, in the days of David and Solomon. But we cannot express any satisfactory opinion as to the original character of the Jewish music which has survived till to-day, since we do not know its original form. Such studies and opinions may have some scientific value, e.g., in helping to classify present-day traditional Jewish music according to its authenticity and age ; but they are of doubtful significance for the history of music.

Although we have discussed certain non-Jewish views on the subject of ' Jewry in Music,' it has lost most of the actuality it had in the middle of the nineteenth century, when it really did seem, to some, a ' burning question.' In fact, the question has been disposed of in the most satisfactory way possible by Jewish composers who set out deliberately to create Jewish music—by their achievement of the object they set themselves.

Before we turn to a discussion of the new Jewish music, we may put the case of the Jew himself on the question of ' Jewry in Music' as Wagner and others argued it. To begin with, it must be made perfectly clear that most Jews do not accept and recognise the music of Mendelssohn, Meyerbeer, Halévy, Offenbach, Rubinstein, Goldmark, Mahler, Schönberg, and so on as specifically Jewish. All these composers were or are subjected to the tendency to be submerged in the cultural sphere of their non-Jewish milieu, and to develop a form of artistic expression arising from and corresponding to the spirit of that sphere. Some achieved this more, some less; but all achieved it in great measure. Even so, not one of them escaped being regarded as a Jew and treated inimically on that account, at some time in his life. Consequently they could not achieve a harmonious development of their artistic personality from the social aspect, as a member of the community. This was bound to be a main cause of the dichotomy in their artistic means of expression and in all their musical creation. It was natural enough that anyone who decided to discuss the problem of ' Jewry in Music,' i.e., in Western music, should take into his purview everything that Jews had achieved in the musical sphere since their emancipation. But one cannot find the clue to the characteristic quality of Jewish musicians by so doing, since those Jews who played a part in Western music had psychologically, and often even physically, unhealthy relations with their milieu. In those early days they could not properly function either as Jew or as non-Jew; they lived in an artificially 'normalised' atmosphere, and that was bound to influence their artistic creation to a great extent. Even when one can distinguish Jewish characteristics in their works, those characteristics essentially find expression not in the form of a positive interpretation, but only indirectly, as some of the factors moulding and shaping their work. For the artistic personality is shaped not only by his racial, national, and individual idiosyncrasies, but also by the taste and perceptions of his time, through his environment, education, language, training, experience, social relations, and so on. If any of the composers we have mentioned had been moved by the desire and fundamental necessity to create works of art expressive of their Jewish feelings, reflecting the Jewish spiritual and intellectual world, then undoubtedly their works would have been impressed with a deliberately expressed Jewish quality. But it so happens that in every case this was impossible. Some of them had had no Jewish education or training whatever, and had grown up in a non-Jewish environment; certain of them had never belonged to the Jewish community; others deliberately cut themselves off from that community, because they felt they had no ties with it. Even those who remained consciously Jewish felt no call towards the expression or employment of Jewish elements in their music; on the contrary, every one of them felt the urge, in accordance with the trend of the time, to identify their perceptions and experience with those of the non-Jews. In these circumstances, we are completely justified in refusing to regard their music as the music of Jews and in classifying it with the music of their non-Jewish cultural world.

We shall be discussing the concept 'Jewish music' in our final chapter, so here we may briefly add that as the modern Zionist movement developed, partly out of the Emancipation and Assimilation movements of Central Europe, but even more out of the more conservative and less emancipated, more persecuted and less assimilated, Jewish communities of Eastern Europe, so a new urge towards Jewish expression in music began. We shall see in a later chapter how the new Jewish national consciousness, which found expression in the Zionist movement, led by a Central European (Dr. Herzl) and in the trend towards emigration to Palestine, which was almost wholly Eastern European in its earlier phases, also found expression in the work of new Eastern European and, later, Central European and American Jewish composers. From the beginning these later composers aimed consciously at developing a new Jewish music as a form of national artistic expression. And it is this music which present-day Jews regard as their specific cultural expression, and as being on the same plane, though still young and comparatively inchoate, as that of the art-music of other cultural peoples.

It must be added that not all the Jews who have interested themselves in this question share this standpoint. There are still Jews who consider that the music of Mendelssohn, Mahler, and similar composers of Jewish origin is to be regarded as Jewish, or that it possesses many Jewish characteristics. Such views are found particularly among Jews who have come from the countries of Central Europe which have had cultural contacts with Germany. Even to-day, though the question can now be discussed with a considerable degree of clarity, there are certain prominent advocates of Israeli music who cannot turn their backs on the idea, but return to it again and again. So we must take up a little space in discussing it.

Max Brod was greatly interested in the subject in his earlier days, and now that he is living in Israel he still believes that Mendelssohn's and Mahler's music is to be regarded as characteristic of the Jews. He even goes so far as to place Mahler above Bloch in this respect.

Of Mendelssohn's music Brod has written:

'Outstanding among Mendelssohn's work is his violin concerto, which by its profound passion belongs among his most moving and beautiful creations. And it is just in this concerto that the Jewish note—albeit unconsciously used—can most clearly be heard, pervading the essence of the work rather than its details. Yet it is possible to trace it in details, too. In the first bars of the concerto, the intensity achieved by the manifold repetitions of the shortest melodic phrases (a repetition recalling the cantillations and later employed by Mahler) has something of the irresistible and urgent. Here, in the dark and sad musical configurations, is a most intense impulsive movement like an involuntary gesticulation of the soul, a hidden recollection that breaks the bonds of discipline and will.'[1]

This example can easily be put to the proof. Has anyone else obtained such an impression from listening to this popular concerto? Max Brod's reactions seem to us highly individual and personal. In Mendelssohn's case judgment of the question is rendered more difficult because his work is often presented as that of a 'Jewish' composer. Both in concerts and in synagogues it was customary for decades to present his work as Jewish music, partly because they did not know of anything better, and partly because it passed current as the 'Jewish music' of a prominent but really non-Jewish composer, which music, however, was very suitable. Mendelssohn's compositions were performed in many synagogues, either as instrumental works, or in arrangements adapted to the singing of various prayers. This very often happened to certain of his melodies (his 'Songs without Words' and themes or sections of symphonies, etc.) which could not in any way be regarded as Jewish. The Jews of Central Europe especially were accustomed to hearing these 'Jewish' melodies from their childhood, at Jewish functions and in the synagogue. Here the association can be traced easily enough; since they had accepted these melodies as Jewish in their childhood, when they heard them again in later life they could not but regard them as Jewish. Those who had not had this experience as children had a different reaction. We have already pointed out such influences in the cases of Sulzer and Lewandowski and, so far as the latter composer is concerned, we have expressly mentioned the kinship between his music and that of Mendelssohn.[2] No wonder that to many Jews the music of Mendelssohn as well as that of Sulzer and Lewandowski strikes a traditional and intimate note.

Now let us consider the case of Gustav Mahler. Max Brod finds a common characteristic in the circumstance that march rhythms occur so frequently in Mahler's music, as they do also in the songs of the Chasidim. This proves nothing. But where would deductions of this nature lead us to? March rhythms are to be found at least as much in the music of other peoples, especially

---

[1] Israel's Music, by Max Brod. Translated by Toni Volcani, WIZO, Tel Aviv, 1951, p. 27.   [2] Supra, p. 108.

of those among whom Mahler lived, and this would rather seem to indicate the source of his inspiration. Referring to an earlier article of his,[1] Brod says: 'There are other features which Chasidic folk songs and Mahler's "Melodik" have in common: a melodic line fluctuating between major and minor; a slow beginning, in which the same note is repeated several times—in a way that may sound too persistent to Western ears—before the melody begins to progress in short but ever-lengthening arcs.'[2] This may be true or not; to our way of thinking it does not affect the issue. In any case we know that Mahler's musical imagination was trained and nourished in a similar atmosphere to that of many Jewish songs, geographically speaking: i.e., in the area of the former Austro-Hungarian monarchy. So whether he was stimulated by the same phenomena, or whether in his case these specific qualities were crystallised out of his 'sub-conscious' is very difficult to investigate and determine. Brod also says, in similar strain to our own view above: 'It may be that Mahler's music, though apparently German, is instinctively recognised as being non-German—which is indeed the case. From the German viewpoint his work seems to be incoherent, without style or form; bizarre and cynical; alternately too soft and too harsh. From this viewpoint, it appears lacking in unity.'[3] So if this is perceived by the Germans, how should it be otherwise with the Jews? Except that Jews find still less of the Jewish in it—even those who do find it—than Germans find of the German, since the other, non-Jewish element is the consciously shaped and clearly impressed part of his composition.

So what is left to us of the music of the Jews in these composers? Even such advocates of this viewpoint as Brod find in such works nothing of the art of the Jews, nothing that can be regarded as the expression of their Jewish spiritual life. In the best case this music lies spiritually between the Jews and the non-Jews; but not in the form of a bridge. It is unsuitable for that if only because to neither party can it be presented as the pure product of the other party, and interesting as such. So it remains generally alien to both parties.

---

[1] 'Der Jude,' Vol. 5, No. 1.
[2] Israel's Music, p. 31.
[3] Op. cit., p. 31.

Before finally leaving the question of 'Jewry in (Western) Music,' we must add a few words on the penetration of 'Jewry into Music,' in the form of the employment of Jewish songs in that music. Western composers have been in the habit of employing and arranging Jewish melodies for centuries. The Italian, non-Jewish maestro, Benedetto Marcello (1686-1739), used Hebrew melodies in his psalms ;[1] he went so far as to adapt his notation to the Hebrew text, making it read from right to left. But the idea of using a 'Hebrew' colouring when biblical material was used was usually applied in opera music. Meyerbeer (1791-1864) ; Halévy (1799-1862) ; Anton Rubinstein (1829-1894) ; and Goldmark (1832-1915) all of Jewish origin, introduced Jewish melodies into their works, but in general did not aim at achieving any strong Jewish 'atmosphere.' Saint-Saëns (1835-1921) who is said to have been of Jewish origin through his mother, incorporated Jewish musical motifs in his opera 'Samson and Delilah,' especially in the choruses, and in the ballet music of the last act ; the effect was attractive and of a characteristic quality. Even greater success in this respect has been achieved by the Italian composer, Lodovico Rocca (1895-   ). Though not Jewish himself, he undertook to turn Ansky's play *Dybuk* into an opera. The play, which dramatised the old Jewish tradition that the earthbound soul (the *dybuk*) of a dead person can take refuge in a living human being, was popular among the Chasidim of Eastern Europe, and won international fame when performed by the Habima Players. It is strongly mystical in mood, incorporates many folk customs, and has strongly individualised Jewish types. For his operatic version Rocca made use of Chasidic folk tunes, and although his work was not free of Italian operatic conventions he achieved the authentic mood and atmosphere of Eastern European Jewry.

The same subject is treated in David Tamkin's opera 'The Dybuk,' written in 1931, to a libretto by his brother, Alex Tamkin, which is based on Ansky's story. But the effect achieved is very different from that of Rocca's work. The opera opens well, but falls away as it proceeds. It contains very little folk-music, and fails to capture the true atmosphere. Where folk or traditional

---

[1] Estro poetico-armonico, Venice, 1724-27.

tunes are used the treatment is so bizarre that they are almost unrecognisable. Tamkin's opera had its first performance on November 4, 1951, by the New York City Opera Company, with Joseph Rosenstock conducting.

If we also mention Arnold Schönberg (born in Vienna on September 13, 1874, died July 13, 1951, in Los Angeles, California), the founder and chief practitioner of the twelve-tone technique, it is because—unless the future decides otherwise—we have to reckon him as a member of the German, or at least of a non-Jewish cultural group. Yet it is true that, especially toward the end of his life, he attempted to give some of his compositions a Jewish content and expression. The cantata 'A Survivor from Warsaw,' op. 46, composed in 1947 to his own text, for perform-ance by a 'reader,' male voice choir, and orchestra, closes with a traditional melody for the Jewish Sabbath morning prayer, *Shema Israel*. Though a very impressive piece of work, it is not greatly different from others of his works which we do not regard as Jewish. So far as its Jewish expression is concerned, this cantata, and the 'Kol Nidre' for rabbi, mixed chorus, and small orchestra, written in 1938, do little more than make use of Jewish motifs and so they are of no special significance for Jewish music. Schönberg also wrote an opera on a biblical theme, 'Moses and Aaron.'

Of the many non-Jewish composers who have made use of Jewish melodies we may mention Mussorgsky (1839-1881) in for instance his 'Joshua,' a chorus for mixed voices, on a Hebrew theme ; Rimsky-Korsakov (1844-1908) ; Prokofiev (1891-1953) with an 'Overture on Jewish Themes' ; and Ravel (1875-1937). It can certainly be said that they revealed special interest in, and understanding for, the Jewish melos.

PART THREE

THE NEW JEWISH MUSIC
NINETEENTH AND TWENTIETH CENTURIES

CHAPTER XIII

JEWISH FOLK-SONG

FOLK-SONG is a descriptive rather than a definitive term, and we shall use it broadly to cover the various kinds of song sung by the people and expressing the characteristics of the people. It is admitted that as a rule these songs, too. have been composed by individuals ; but in the course of time the people who sing them have modified, simplified, or embellished them according to their taste, and they have acquired the characteristics of communal expression, they have become truly songs of the people. Modern research into folk-song, especially thorough since the end of the eighteenth century, early recognised that the material, the content, and even the form of a folk-song are often passed from one people to another. But the manner of expression always remains distinctive, and in conformity with the specific popular taste. Consequently, the question to be applied to folk-song is not so much the what as the how ; the result is that language and melody are of enhanced importance and in turn become the subjects of a specific and characteristic manner of performance.

In this chapter we shall confine our remarks chiefly to the secular folk-song of the Jews in Europe and Palestine. But we must make it clear that religious folk-song is popular among Jews all over the world, being especially rich among oriental Jews, as Idelsohn, the famous investigator of Jewish folk-song, has shown. And at times there cannot be said to be any dividing line between the religious and the secular in Jewish folk-song.

It is, of course, possible to treat European folk-song as a single group, as distinct from the Asiatic, the North or South American, and other geographical divisions. On this basis, we then proceed to investigate the differences in the folk-songs and the folk-song types of the various European peoples. As has been established by investigators in this field, these differentiations are due to differing racial development, to the nature of the folk community, the racial branch, the cultural group, national history, geographical situation and, by no means least, the language. Needless to say, there are no rigid bounds to any folk-song group ; the contiguous folk-groups come into active contact with one another, exerting reciprocal influence, so that there is a resulting affinity in the character of their folk-song. Regarded from this standpoint, the folk-song of the East European Jews can certainly be classified as European.

The Jewish differs from other folk-song primarily by its language, which is Hebrew or Yiddish, and by its mood. Melodically it took over a great deal from Jewish religious song. The songs usually have a simple melody, with a plain harmonic foundation, not particularly rich in modulations, and clear, definite rhythm. Some songs are set to a form of recitative. From the tonal aspect, we find that the great majority, in fact almost all the songs are written in the modern minor mode, only a few being in the major. Frequently the seventh note is not sharpened ; and the Dorian (d, e, f, g, a, b, c, d, with the variants B flat and C sharp) and the Phrygian (e, f, g, a, b, c, d, e, with the variant G sharp) modes are often found.

It has been said again and again that the minor mode of the Jewish folk-songs is due to their mournful character. This is by no means the case. As we know from the ancient melodies that have come down to us (the *Neginot*, for instance), in antiquity the Jews sang in modes that we know to-day as the Greek and ecclesiastical modes, or, at least, in modes similar to these. Originally, perhaps, the melodies consisted of only a few notes, and this view is supported by the pentatonic nature of many of the traditional tunes. It is well known that this transformation of the old tonal systems into the modern minor mode, with some modification has occurred in the secular song of other peoples besides the Jews. For that matter, the Slavonic peoples of Eastern Europe still often sing in the old modes ; and this fact has helped to preserve the style of singing of the Jews living among them, and has facilitated, if not actually brought about, the creation of new songs of this kind. Music written in minor keys need not necessarily be of a mournful nature, nor must the note of ' laughter mingled with tears,' as is often said, be sounded in these songs. The view that a minor key gives a sorrowful, gloomy effect and the major a joyful, bright one is not invariably correct. The well-known rondo movement, the 'Alla Turca' of Mozart's A major sonata has minor sections which no one ever thinks of as mournful. The truth is rather that the minor confers a dark subdued effect, while the major is light and clear ; and, so far as it relates to Jewish song, this opinion is supported by Idelsohn in the ninth volume of his 'Thesaurus of Hebrew-Oriental Melodies,' in which he deals with the folk-song of East European Jewry. It is true that the Jews of those parts experienced little brightness or lightness in their life, for most of them lived in the unhealthy, gloomy conditions of the ghetto. In Israeli folk-song, on the other hand, the minor mode is in conformity with the style of singing which is common and natural there as the tradition reaching back to antiquity. It must be added that customarily Jewish folk-song is sung in unison. It is not possible to decide what relationship exists between the original melodies and those that have been passed down to our day, or have been written in imitation ; various opinions have been expressed on the question. The influence of Russian, and especially Ukrainian, as well as Polish, Czech, Roumanian, German, and Hungarian song on Eastern Jewish folk-song can be traced very clearly. But these influences have been so far modified by the manner of performance characteristic of the East European Jews, and by adaptation, that the songs are to be regarded as Jewish, regardless of the fact that in general only songs that have an essential affinity with the Jewish song have been taken over.

Folk-song can thrive and be practised only in a folk-community, where there is a vigorous communal life. There have been two large Jewish cultural centres possessing characteristic Jewish folk-song—in Eastern Europe and in Palestine.

The folk-song of East European Jewry is especially rich, and through emigration it has a flourishing offshoot in North America, where Jews from Eastern Europe live in large communities. It reflects all the life and conditions of the Jews in those parts, and it is generally accepted that it came into being and began to develop at the beginning of the nineteenth century. The songs still sung to-day may have come into existence at any time since the middle of the nineteenth century. The language is Yiddish, which is based on old, preponderantly middle-high

German, with an admixture of Slavonic and Hebrew elements. It is a developed language, having various dialects of its own, and an extensive literature. Under the influence of Zionism and the movement back to Palestine, many of the East European folk-songs have now been translated into Hebrew. Certain students and collectors of folk-song have divided the East European Jewish songs into the genuine and the spurious. Among the pseudo-folk-songs they reckon all the popular songs and couplets from Jewish operettas and folk-plays, two genres very popular among the East European Jews, and the so-called *Badchen* songs.

Badchen is the Yiddish name for the folk-singer, the entertainer, and wag who was always present at merry-makings, weddings, and many family celebrations. His songs consisted as a rule of an interminable series of couplets on events and topics of the day, entertaining and amusing by their witty treatment. Many of these folk-singers became famous and published collected editions of their own songs; they included Wölwil Zbaraschher Ehrenkranz (1826-1883), Eliakum Zunser (1838 or 1840-1913), also Abraham Goldfaden (originally Goldenfodim, 1840-1908), who wrote several operettas still performed in Yiddish theatres; and Mark Warschawsky (1845-1907), who wrote, *inter alia,* the well-known folk-songs: *Hecher, besser,* and *Af'n pripitchok.* Music to match the *badchen* songs was produced by the *klezmer* (plural, *klezmorim*),[1] bands of musicians who were hired especially for weddings. Usually the band of *klezmorim* consisted of a violinist, a double bass, a clarinettist, a drummer, and additional instruments according to the pretensions of the particular group. They played the dance music and accompaniments, etc., for the singing, and their repertoire included songs which had widespread popularity as folk-songs.

There are also religious songs, often based on Biblical texts, and sung on the Sabbath, or the Sabbath eve in the home, or on holy-days, on occasions of marriages or deaths, also as table-songs or mealtime prayers. The great majority of these are sung in Hebrew, only a few being in Yiddish or other languages. In Europe they are known as *Zemirot* (from *zamer,* to sing) and in the Orient as *pizmonim* (from *pizmon,* refrain).

---

[1] From Hebrew *Kele-zemer,* 'musical instruments.'

As the Jews of Eastern Europe lived in more or less self-contained communities they possessed a much greater variety of folk-song than other Jewish communities. In content and mood, most of the songs correspond with their manner of life and their customs. There are many collections of these songs, and each tends to classify them in its own manner, to accord with the aim and idea of the publication. But if we keep strictly to their classification by content and mood, we can distinguish the following groups:

Children's songs, sung by children and with words and music adapted to their needs.

Marching songs, most of which have come into being of recent years. They consist partly of non-Jewish songs of this kind, translated into Yiddish or Hebrew, and are generally sung by the youth.

Love songs, telling of the troubles and longings of lovers. Together with the cradle-songs they are the most moving of all the Eastern Jewish songs.

Wedding songs, conforming in mood and content to the occasion.

Cradle-songs, in which the mother expresses her hopes for her child's future, and often tells of her everyday troubles and cares. They are the finest and most moving of all the folk-songs; melodically they are extremely clear and are strictly lyrical in style.

Dance songs and wordless dance tunes, often of Chasidic origin, and very rhythmic, frequently beginning in slow tempo and working up to a climax.

Humorous and satirical songs, often telling of the deficiencies of living conditions, of poverty, etc., and making merry over these and similar trials. Some of these have macabre humour.

Religious and mystical songs, which also form a bridge between religious and secular song, deal with various religious problems outside and apart from the synagogue service, and often take the form of an adjuration to God or a duologue with God.

Sometimes the tune, or part of the tune, is taken directly from the synagogue service. Part of the tune may therefore be in recitative, or cantillated, and, in conformity with the style of the East European religious service, there is frequent resort to coloratura.

Nature songs, which include those which depict nature and man's relations with it. These were the latest of the Jewish folksongs to be developed in Eastern Europe, and many of them have been taken to Palestine, where they were popular especially among the Zionist pioneers, known as *Chalutzim*. If not written in Hebrew, they are usually translated into Hebrew.

Soldiers' songs tell of the cares and plagues of the young recruits who were compelled to serve as conscripts in a non-Jewish environment, with no possibility of observing Jewish holy days and the ritual prescriptions. Many of these derive from conditions in Tsarist times.

Workers' and chalutzim songs are concerned with labour and the workers' problems. They include socialist songs borrowed from other peoples, the text being translated into Yiddish, and later into Hebrew.

Like most classifications, the foregoing is only rough, and must not be regarded as exhaustive. Quite a number of songs could be allocated to more than one of these categories. It is striking that the ' drinking song,' a class of folk-song which occupies an important place in other communities, is not to be found in Jewish folk-song.

A very distinctive, and highly tense and expressive kind of folk-song was sung by the Chasidim. The Chasidim (the plural of *chasid* or *chosid*, literally meaning ' devout') are a Jewish sect which came into existence in Eastern Europe, originally in the Eastern Carpathians, in the middle of the eighteenth century. They give free rein to the expression of their religious feelings, and singing plays an important part in that expression. Like the Biblical prophets, the Chasidim resort to singing to exalt their mood to the state of ecstasy. Many of their songs are without words. The Jewish poet, Peretz, has described their views on the melody which alone speaks to God: 'There are many degrees of melody . . . there is a melody to which words belong, that is a very low degree. A melody that allows itself to be sung entirely without words is a purer melody. Yet it still needs the voice . . . and the lips, through which the voice proceeds. And lips—you understand—are still corporeal. And the voice is, truly, of noble corporeality, but it still remains corporeal. . . . So far as I am concerned the voice is on the confines between spirit and body. Yet, no matter what the melody, if a man hears it through the voice, if it is tied to the lips, it is not yet perfectly clean . . . not yet true spirit. True melody can be sung entirely without voice, it is sung within the heart, within the bowels. That is the secret sense of king David's words: *kol atzmotai tomarna* (all my bones speak). In the marrow of his bones must man sing; there must the melody reside, that highest praise of God, may He be praised! That is no longer the melody of a man of flesh and blood, it is not excogitated melody! It is already a part of that melody with which God created the world . . . and of the soul that He has set in it. And that is the singing of the *pamalya shel ma'alah* (the immediate surroundings of God).'[1]

Sussman Kisseloff, who was an expert on Jewish folk-song, and made a collection which originally was published by the St. Petersburg Society for Jewish Folk Song, has said of the Chasidic songs: 'They are the most original in form and character of all the Jewish folk-songs, and they are richest, too, in regard to the form and variety of the musical coloration. They are entirely without words, and the people regard them as the "highest" of all songs. They are usually expressive of a prayerful mood, or of religious exaltation, and they are generally mystical in character. The Chasidic song, this highest wordless melody, is a conversation, a communion with God. In it the singer asks God questions, and is answered; he gives expression to supplications and hopes, his sorrow and his profound belief in God. To the Chasid, God is simultaneously both near and far; He is everywhere, and the song regards its partial appearance in man as being associated with the great God. The Chasid sings his song in the middle of or before prayer, in order to put himself in a prayerful mood, and during the singing of this song-prayer he

---

[1] From *Mequbbolim* (Cabbalists). Quoted in Kisseloff's 'Das Jüdische Volkslied,' Jüdischer Verlag, Berlin, 1913, p. 9.

lives so profoundly that he passes into ecstasy. His profound perception, his fulness of mood and feeling, demand a materialisation of the sound, its consummation in a swaying movement of the body and in exaggerated gesticulation. In executing the song the most important thing is the sincerity of the feelings.'[1]

When emigration into Palestine, and especially that of the *Chalutzim*, or pioneer workers, developed on a larger scale and a strong Jewish community was built up in that country, i.e., after the First World War, there was a great increase in the singing of folk-songs. Actuated by the spirit of the ' regeneration of the nation,' the Jews of Palestine and later of Israel took to singing their songs only in Hebrew. So the Israeli folk-song differs from that of Eastern Europe principally by its language. In musical regards the Palestinian and Israeli songs, and to some extent even those which have been taken over from Eastern Europe, have been influenced by the Palestinian Arab and the Yemenite Jewish songs. These influences are perceptible in the melody and the rhythm. The songs imitating Arab songs, chiefly of a pastoral nature, are written in a free metre and so are not easily fitted to European measures. Adopting the same classification for the Palestinian as for the East European folk-songs, we have the following classes:

Children's songs, which in Israel are sung in the highly developed kindergartens and schools. *Marching songs. Love songs,* which often have a strong oriental strain. *Cradle songs,* most of them taken over from Eastern Europe, the text being translated into Hebrew. *Dance songs and tunes,* including many wordless Chasidic songs from Eastern Europe, and sung for the Israeli *Hora* dance. *Religious songs,* with religious texts but non-religious in mood, and often used as marching and dance songs. *Nature songs,* which here have a closer association with nature and are more developed than in Eastern Europe ; often they are adapted Arab and Bedouin songs. Also *workers'* and *Chalutzim songs,* which naturally have had their true development only in Palestine. As time passes the Palestinian-Israeli folk-songs, which exhibit very different characteristics from those of Eastern Europe, are steadily superseding the old ghetto songs for the

---

[1] Op. cit. Kisselhoff, p. 18.

purpose of arrangement and exploitation in works by Jewish composers.[1]

The Spanish ballads which are still sung by the Sefardic Jews scattered round the shores of the Eastern Mediterranean are in a separate category, and are not accepted as Jewish folk-songs. Many of them are known only to these, the so-called *Spanioli* Jews. They have an easily recognisable Romance character with a mingling of Moorish melodic elements. They are known as Ladino (from ' Latin ') songs ; the language employed is the old Castilian dialect.

As we shall see in the next chapter, the revival of Jewish music began with the collection and then the arrangement of Jewish folk-songs, approximately at the opening of the present century. In this field the publications of the Petersburg ' Society for Jewish Folk Music,' which had the support of some of the leading Russian composers, blazed a pioneer trail. It was not long before Jewish composers, both minor and major, were arranging folk-songs for part singing, as well as with piano accompaniment. Then, as the Zionist movement developed and especially after the First World War, Jewish choral societies were formed in many towns in Europe and both North and South America. This in turn led to a demand for arrangements of Jewish folk-songs for choral singing *a capella* and with instrumental accompaniment, and Jewish choirmasters, cantors, and concert artists set to work to meet this demand. In this field the work of Samuel Alman, Abraham Wolf Binder, Israel Brandmann, Julius Chajes, Joel Engel, Max Ettinger, Ziga Hirschler. Leo Kopf, Leo Low, Aron Marko Rothmüller, Erich Elisha Samlaich, Lazare Saminsky, E. W. Sternberg, Jacob Weinberg, and many others has been very productive. Most of these composers will be discussed separately in a later chapter.

The final step was the employment of folk-songs in purely instrumental works for concert performance. In this field there has been a great variety of achievement, from works with the simplest of harmonic accompaniments, to complex arrangements, such as those of Dessau and Rothmüller. Often, too, the melody is ' modernised,' in other words, freed from its Jewish melodic

---

[1] Many collections have been made of Jewish folk-songs of all these classes.

embellishments or typical Jewish turns, in order to bring it more into line with European non-Jewish musical tastes. But this tendency has died out of recent times, partly through the influence of modern non-Jewish treatment of folk-song, e.g., that of Bartók. On the other hand, modern Jewish composers draw a distinction between the simple harmonisation of folk-song and its treatment. Thus, arrangements have been made in which the folk-song—viewed strictly from the compositional aspect—is raised to the status of an art song, following the example of Brahms, Dvorák, Smetana, Bartók, Kodály, Vaughan Williams, and others, while every care is taken to retain and preserve the character of the melody, and of the folk-song as such. Then, out of such arrangements, a Jewish art song emerges as a further stage of development. But the folk-songs retain their significance as a form and expression of Jewish musical taste and qualities.

CHAPTER XIV

THE TWENTIETH CENTURY

THE great revival in Jewish music which has marked the first fifty years of the present century was initiated by Jewish composers in Russia, who devoted their lives to the cultivation of Jewish folk-song. At that time the Jews in Russia and Russian Poland were aggregated in such large communities that they could develop their own cultural life to the full. In every respect they were fitted to be the foremost Jewish cultural group, at least for the first twenty-five years of the century; they were intensely Jewish by training and upbringing, by all their manner of thinking and feeling; their chief, indeed their only, concern was to maintain and continue their exclusively Jewish tradition and life; and they spoke their own Jewish (Yiddish) speech. Moreover, in that area was then concentrated almost seventy per cent of the world's Jewish population. True, Russia was a country with a number of provincial cultural centres, so that there were also a number of Jewish cultural centres; but, so far as music was concerned, they hardly differed from one another. So we are fully justified in speaking of a single Eastern European Jewish musical group, in which the Russian and Polish Jews were overwhelmingly preponderant.

Leading Russian composers had been interested in Jewish folk-song, making various arrangements of them, from the time of Glinka onward; in the latter part of the nineteenth century Mussorgsky and Rimsky-Korsakov were especially prominent in this activity. The Russian nationalist trend in music also led to Russian composers paying much attention to folk-song and dance, and introducing them into their own compositions. All this was bound to stimulate Jewish musicians to do the same, collecting their own (Jewish) folk-songs and arranging them for concert performance. The official inauguration of this movement can be ascribed to a lecture by Joel Engel, a leading Russian-Jewish composer, in 1900. In that year he gave a talk on Jewish folk music to a meeting of the Imperial Ethnographical Society in Petersburg; besides communicating his own observations he had a number of Jewish folk-songs performed in his own arrangements.

Two years later a further lecture on the subject was given by the well-known collector of Jewish folk-song, P. S. Marek, to the Moscow 'Society for Natural Science and Anthropology.' Marek dealt with the specific poetic qualities of Jewish folk-song, while Engel provided the musical illustrations, and briefly analysed them. Engel spent the next few years diligently collecting Jewish folk-songs, in the course of which he gradually gathered a group of young Jewish musicians around him. In 1908 the 'Society for Jewish Folk Music' was founded in Petersburg; in it collaborated such well-known Jewish musicians as Joseph Achron (who joined the Society three years after its foundation), Michael Gnessin, Alexander Krein, Moses Milner, Salomon Rosovsky, Lazare Saminsky, Leo Nesviszky, and Arie Abileah, while it was actively supported by prominent Russian composers. It is an interesting commentary on the difficulties which Jewish composers had to face in the Russia of that time that originally the society proposed to call itself the 'Society for Jewish Music,' but for the forming of such a society the permission and confirmation of the authorities had to be obtained. The city's Chief of Police, Drotchevsky, took it upon himself to decide what was to be the object of the proposed society, and, as he considered it was only a matter of folk-tunes, he ordered the name to be changed to 'Society for Jewish Folk Music.' The society at once set to work to organise the collection of Jewish folk-songs, their arrangement, performance, and publication, and formed branches in other large cities: at Moscow in 1913, and at Kiev and Kharkov later. Others who took up the work were J. Kaplan, H. Kopit, P. Lwow, M. Shalit, A. Zhitomirsky, and Leon Zaitlin. In due course the first satisfactory collection of East European Jewish folk-song was published by the society.

However, from the beginning the society had a hard struggle for existence. The assimilated Jews, and especially the intellectuals, refused to have anything to do with it, and even the Orthodox were against it, reproaching the society with neglect of Jewish religious song, and declaring that any kind of arrangement was detrimental to and a distortion of folk-song. They supported their arguments by reference to the religious melodies, such as the *Kaddish* and the *Kol Nidrei*, which the reforming cantors of Germany had arranged so thoroughly that they had turned them into Protestant chorales. Many Jewish musicians who were outside the movement regarded its work as being only of scientific and ethnographical value. Even the leading East European Jewish poet and author, J. L. Peretz, was distrustful at first, and had no understanding of the value of the society, which for the first time was working in the field not only of religious but of all folk-song. But it was not long before he linked up with it, becoming a zealous collaborator and leader. Despite enormous difficulties, including its interdiction during the years of Tsarist reaction about 1911, in the first ten years of its existence the society arranged over a thousand concerts, thus improving musical taste and reviving folk-song in many places where it was tending to die out.

At first the members of the society, with the support of their teachers, Rimsky-Korsakov, Liadov, and Glazunov, set themselves the task of ' clothing the old song in new forms '; they did not start with the object of creating Jewish music, but simply of harmonising and arranging folk-song. They were alienated by the style of the German reformers' synagogal music, and ignored this ' cantoral-music,' turning rather to the Chasidic melos. But, later, many of them turned back to the religious motifs, and composed religious works which in style and content were fundamentally different from those of the Emancipation and Reform period. There followed a time of ideological and æsthetic analysis and discussion, in which Saminsky, Engel, Schorr, and Alexander Krein, among others, took part, and the society's composers turned to a modernistic manner of writing, without necessarily employing Jewish folklore material.

As soon as Jewish musicians began to display activity in this field they produced considerable quantities of this kind of music. Now they began to arrange folk-songs and tunes for instrumental performance, taking European virtuoso works as the prototype. But a formidable opposition arose to this development. Various arguments were adduced against it, the weightiest coming from Jews who were already associated with non-Jewish musical groups or regarded such association as their goal. They, rather than the non-Jewish circles themselves, altogether denied that there was such a thing as a distinctively Jewish musical expression. From the opposite aspect, it was also argued that the Jewish folk-songs had lost all their Jewish qualities in the course of being arranged or harmonised. Although a host of able Jewish musicians was now working for Jewish music and was actively creating it, there were many who preferred not to believe in it. They were not content simply to distrust the trend, but fought the movement vigorously, with voice and pen. But it was too vital to be suppressed ; it was its own justification and, being on right lines, was bound to develop. The pioneers of the new Jewish music had rather an instinctive feeling than an intellectual perception that they were right ; they felt that they were calling a Jewish music into existence. No one to-day disputes the respectable quantity and quality of Jewish music ; it is a fact that an interesting, vital, artistically distinguished programme can be composed entirely of Jewish music written by present-day composers. The pioneers who devoted themselves to the service of Jewish music forty to fifty years ago were primarily responsible for this swift development.

Jewish music since the beginning of the century has passed through three phases. The first phase began with the collection of Jewish folk-song and dance melodies, and their simple arrangement, going no farther than straightforward harmonisation ; it ended when composers began to employ folk-song as thematic material in the writing of free compositions, chiefly simple pianoforte works, or works for violin or other instrument and piano, or small chamber pieces. In the second phase, which followed immediately on the first, composers wrote works in which they attempted to transform the folk-music material into something new, often in the form of ' rhapsodies,' ' paraphrases,' ' kleine stücke,' ' sketches,' suites, dances, etc., or sought to clothe the folk-song in a distinctive tonal colouring. In the third phase, which in turn followed immediately out of the second, there is strong emphasis on elaboration that shall be artistically unobjectionable, both in the form of arrangements and in the composer's own freely invented composition ; now, too, the Palestinian folk-song, its melody and rhythm, has the primacy, and from the formal aspect all the large-scale concert instrumentation and compositional forms exploited by the musicians of other nations are adopted.

The chief representatives of the first generation of Jewish national composers were Joel Engel, Michael Gnessin, M. Shalit, Ephraim Skliar, Lazare Saminsky, Salomon Rosowsky, Joseph Achron, Moses Milner, H. Kopit, and Leon Zaitlin. Some of these perhaps belong more truly to the composers of the second phase. Joel Engel dominated the early period. The trend which these composers represented grew very popular shortly before the First World War, during that war, and especially after it ; their works were performed and widely disseminated not only in Russia but in Europe and America, and publishing companies for Jewish compositions were organised, primarily in Warsaw, Berlin, and Vienna, though their activities were rather indiscriminate. The tasks which fell to this first group of Jewish composers were difficult, and they could not be precisely laid down. They began with the object of collecting and arranging Jewish folk-music, but they were quickly faced with the question whether they should take religious song into their purview. However, they soon recognised the great importance of Jewish religious song, for instance, the *Neginot,* to the new Jewish music. This section of Jewish traditional music had been kept freest of all from foreign influences, for in the sphere of religious music the process of isolation and conservation had been carried as far as possible. It was here that the new composers most clearly found what they were seeking: the traditional Jewish melos and the Jewish typical expression. As they studied this religious music they found a treasury of melody which in many respects provided a guiding principle. Enormous possibilities were opened up for Jewish composers through the publication of Idelsohn's ten-volume ' Thesaurus of Hebrew-Oriental Melodies,' the result of a lifetime of study and collection of all the kinds of Jewish music. His work was all the more valuable because in the ' Thesaurus ' and elsewhere he theoretically discussed and analysed the music peculiar to the Jews. Nor was he alone in this field: Arno Nadel, and, later, Salomon Rosowsky, also added to the wealth of music thus made available.[1]

The composers chiefly concerned with achieving the transition

---

[1] Idelsohn's work is further discussed in Chapter XVI.

from the first to the second phase were Juliusz Wolfsohn, Alexander Krein, Alexander Veprik, Samuel Alman, Ernest Bloch, and Joachim Stutschewsky, some of whom can be included in the earlier group, or had direct contact with the composers of that group. Most of them began their activity with the ideal of collecting and arranging Jewish folk-music ; but in the course of their development they reached the point in which they employed folk-music elements freely, and so created their own, original compositions. They made use of folk tunes either in the writing of rhapsodies and ' Paraphrases,' really representing the instrumental arrangement of folk-music (e.g., Wolfsohn) or in smaller musical forms (Stutschewsky) ; and then, in larger forms, such as sonatas, quartets, oratorios, symphonies, concertos, etc. (Bloch, Alman, Krein, Veprik, etc.). True, Ernest Bloch deliberately rejected the direct utilisation of folk-music and created his works out of his own Jewish perceptions ; none the less, in his Jewish works the Jewish musical motifs, as we know them especially in the synagogue service, are easily recognised. But he shaped these musical ideas quite freely, making them his own and giving them his own manner of expression.

These composers were followed by the latest generation of Jewish musicians, who represent the third phase. They consist partly of composers who were born or grew up in Israel (Palestine) or who emigrated there in mature years, and partly of a number who have an idealistic association with the Jewish homeland. As we have said, this group has as its characteristics a recognition of the primacy of the form of musical perception found in Israel, and, above all, a positive striving to create music of the highest quality, which will stand the test even in a non-Jewish environment. They have composed songs with various types of accompaniment, choral works, much chamber music, and orchestral works ; and in this respect the group is in close affinity with the previous group (especially with Alexander Krein, Ernest Bloch, and Joachim Stutschewsky), with whom they have many points of artistic contact. For that matter, it is quite obvious that the third is a logical development out of the second group. Its most prominent representatives to-day include Menachem Avidom, Paul Ben-Haim, Leonard Bernstein, Ernest Bloch, Alexander Uria Boscovich, Israel Brandmann, Julius Chajes, Shula Doniach, Marc

Lavry, Oedön Partos, Aron Marko Rothmüller, Karl Salomon, Verdina Shlonsky, Erich Walter Sternberg, and Joachim Stutschewsky.

The works of these composers reveal the clear impress of melodic elements derived from Israel, and, to a lesser extent, of Arab or Yemenite-Jewish motifs. Frequently they handle Palestinian folk-song and dance in the manner customary in Western music (variation form, style of harmonisation, choral suites, etc.). But in their chamber music also they often make use of melodic elements drawn from Israel, frequently in association with elements drawn from the Diaspora.

Naturally, it is impossible to draw a clear line of demarcation between these three groups. Because of their nature, certain later works of composers in the first group have to be assigned to the music of the second or third phase, while certain works of the second group come more naturally into the third phase. We have simply attempted to distinguish the three phases of Jewish music of the national school, so far as those phases are discernible in the course of its development.

Treated in chronological order, the next period of Jewish musical development after that of the early East and Central European composers occurred in the United States. There the first phase was represented mainly by musicians from Eastern Europe.

Like those of Israel, the Jewish composers in America have certain features, in addition to their Jewish quality, which determine or influence their musical character. Like their colleagues in Israel, almost all of them are either immigrant Jews, or at the most are only second-generation Americans. So they, too, are faced with the problems that arise from being uprooted on the one hand, and from being grafted into the developing culture of their new homeland on the other. The Jewish elements of their culture and musical perceptions are part of themselves, and they attempt to express these elements. But they practise their art, especially when it is not directed to the functional purposes of the religious service, in a different cultural atmosphere from that of Israel, where the composers live and are active in a purely Jewish milieu and a Jewish country.

Music-writing for the synagogal service has come to be of

great importance to American Jewish composers. In this connection many are exposed to the same danger that faced the Reforming Jews (see Chapter XI) with their close approach to Christian religious music. Now, as then, one can detect the note of admiration, and can tell that Christian religious music has been regarded as the model to be followed. Owing to the modern understanding of these matters, and especially the fact that to-day the fight for the preservation of Jewish musical elements is waged with other means than those of the beginning of the nineteenth century, and that the decisive rôle falls to Israel, this time the danger may well be less. And, finally, the lessons drawn from the time of the Emancipation in the nineteenth century will also help to ensure greater prudence. A return to the melodic characteristics of traditional religious song is frequently to be noted in America.

An interesting experiment, reminiscent of the one made by Salomon Sulzer, is the collection that Cantor David J. Putterman, of the Park Avenue Synagogue, New York, edited for the publishing house of Schirmer, in 1951. It is entitled 'Synagogue Music by Contemporary Composers,' and all the contents are intended for synagogal use. Among the contributors are Jews who hitherto have had little connection with Jewish music, such as Lukas Foss, Paul A. Pisk, and Kurt Weill. It also contains works by non-Jews ; the *Adonoy Moloch* (Psalm 27), by Alexander Gretchaninoff, who has used some traditional material as his prototype, must be particularly mentioned.

Yet another problem arises from the fact that in America there are Jewish composers who were born in that country and have forgotten their European or the influential East European Jewish culture, and so have no satisfying musical or intellectual connection with that culture. Consequently, they have no East European Jewish orientation, yet on the other hand they have no more than an ideological and sentimental link with the Land of Israel. So they must be classified simply as American Jewish composers (as proposed by Reuven Kosakoff) and they seek a corresponding cultural expression. Further, it must be remarked that the East European Jews and the Israelis consider that their music is based on old traditional, mostly religious, music or chants. Naturally, this attitude has the effect of placing beyond discussion certain problems that only the future can pose as serious issues.

As there is a very active life among the Jews of America, there is a good deal of 'utility' or functional music, consisting of works with a very easily absorbed arrangement of usually East European, but of latter years also Israeli, songs. To this category must be referred many of the pieces composed for the Sabbath Morning or Evening Service, and Alfred Pochon's 'Fantasie Hébraïque' for string quartet, George Perlman's 'Ghetto Sketches' and 'Suite Hébraïque' for violin and piano.

The influx of musicians from Europe has continued right down to the present time, so assisting in the continuity of development. In addition, a younger, native generation of composers has come into being, fostered by and organised in many societies for the cultivation of Jewish music. One of the most notable and active of these organisations is the New York 'Jewish Music Forum, Society for the Advancement of Jewish Musical Culture.' These younger composers have already written many interesting works, and undoubtedly the Jewish music being written in America will form an important contribution to the Jewish musical heritage. The overwhelming majority even of this generation have origins in Eastern Europe, and many of them have spent some time in Palestine. Most of them look musically to Palestine, and so their works often present a happy blend of East European Jewish with Palestinian musical elements. Their harmonisation and arrangements of Palestinian folk-songs especially reveal a greater integrity than is found in many other Jewish composers. The American sacred service figures largely in their compositional activity, and music written for the service is often on a concert scale. In their synagogal works the American Jewish composers seek to integrate the traditional melodies with those of the new times. Their harmonic treatment is in conformity with modern tendencies, and astringent harmonies are often employed even in the works written for the sacred service. As a rule the melodies are simplified, in the spirit of modern composition, and are stripped of exaggerated or excessive coloratura, etc. It is striking that in the United States synagogal music is continually being enriched and advanced not only within the synagogue walls but also in public, concert performance.

This activity is much stimulated by a regular annual event throughout the United States and Canada, known as 'A Month of Jewish Music.' During a whole month, usually February, Jewish organisations, musical and non-musical, perform and discuss Jewish music, many radio stations and non-Jewish organisations also taking part. The Jewish Music Council of the National Jewish Welfare Board is mainly responsible for this important institution.

✿   ✿   ✿   ✿

Now we must return to the area with which this book began, and to the Jews of the Orient ; we take another look at the Land of Israel. The reconstruction of the country and of its people's life has taken quite a different course from that after the return from the Babylonian exile. In the field of music the difference is even greater, and it is quite impossible to draw any comparison with the problems of those early times. Then the emphasis of the musical renaissance was on religion ; to-day it is on secular music, so far as the Land of Israel is concerned.

The people of Israel went all out to make their country once more a Jewish State and a cultural centre for all Jews the world over. And this applied in the sphere of music. The musicians of Israel, most of whom had been born elsewhere and had had their education and training elsewhere, set themselves the objective of creating a new, and, indeed, their own distinct forms of musical expression.

However, they have various ways of approach to this problem. The outstanding composers are linked in various groupings. There are those who originate from Eastern Europe, and had their general musical education and training in that area ; others came from Central Europe, with Germany and Austria as their musical centres ; a few were either born in Israel, or entered it when very young, and so have been educated in the country itself, or have gone abroad specifically for educational purposes. Naturally, in these various groups there are composers who occupied themselves with the problem of Jewish musical expression even before they settled in Israel, while others have been stimulated into consideration of the problem only through going to live there.

However, these are simply superficial points of contact in their careers. Yet each composer reveals an intellectual and spiritual perception that differentiates him from the others. There are, too, certain opinions and ideas which are generally accepted by Israeli musicians, as well as the people generally. Thus the new spiritual mood of the country, the note of optimism, hope, and confidence, is regarded as valid for music, as it is for other spiritual and intellectual spheres and trends. A further feature of this mood, so far as music is concerned, is that the new musical speech is to be based on what remains of the Jewish heritage from ancient times. In fact to-day it is the song of the immigrant into Israel from the Yemen that is inspiring most of the composers in the country, since it is regarded as of very ancient origin.

The songs and folk-songs of the Yemenite Jews are continually being noted down and treated by most of the musicians in Israel. It is worth mentioning that among these songs are some that have already been transcribed before, by Idelsohn or others. But in the new transcriptions many of them differ from the former versions. This does not justify the deduction (at least, not in all cases) that either the earlier or the later transcription is faulty. It is far more likely that these songs have been passed down in various settings, or that even in the brief interval between the two transcriptions they have suffered modification.

One feature of the music that has been produced in Israel of recent years is very striking. In the Diaspora, where Jewish life is always intensive, that life finds expression particularly in the development of religious music. This is remarkably true of America, where in recent years an enormous number of compositions have been written for the synagogue service. In Israel, on the contrary, Jewish life finds expression in everything with which it comes into contact, so the necessity to occupy oneself with works for the religious service, and on the other hand the demand for such works, is not so great as elsewhere. In consequence the Israeli composers are devoting themselves to the creation of ' secular,' general music, or works which, though based on religious themes, are not thought of as specifically for the religious service but for general musical performance.

This relaxation of the tension in Jewish life, and in the spiritual and intellectual currents in Israel, finds expression in yet another respect. In his choice and treatment of the musical material the Israeli composer is often much less restricted than is his colleague in the Diaspora. He believes himself to be less dependent on the traditional melodies with their Jewish treatment, since such melodies can now be drawn from contemplation of the everyday Jewish life. This allows him to search for freer development, even when he is planning a composition with some folk connection. In Israel the concept of 'nationality' has a rather different quality from that which it implies for other Jews. This is natural enough. In the Land of Israel the creative artist is creating the national culture out of the Jewish life in a Jewish land. We shall return to this question in chapter sixteen.

A very striking phenomenon in Israel is the creation of modern folk-song. Many composers have written popular songs which have already to some extent become folk-songs; in writing their songs these composers have made such natural use of various musical elements that are part of the Israeli people's cultural background that their songs have come to be regarded as true folk-songs. It is interesting to note that composers of the Diaspora have frequently arranged or utilised these very songs in the belief that they were making use of anonymous folk-songs. For the present it is the creation of these Israeli folk-songs that one must regard as the most positive success of the Israeli musicians.

To-day the cultivation and arrangement of such songs is very extensively practised, both in Israel and elsewhere. Moreover, a number of musicians are occupied in collecting, transcribing, and arranging the songs of the Jews from the Yemen, who have come into Israel in large numbers, especially of recent years, and now form an important part of the population. Other composers are employing these melodies in their own works.

These songs of the Yemenite Jews have a special attraction for the Israeli musicians because it is generally accepted that they have come down from comparatively ancient times, and in many respects are much closer to ancient Jewish song than those of other Jewish communities. This view is supported by the fact that they have an oriental character, though, of course, this is quite understandable, as the Yemenite Jews lived in an Arab milieu. And no matter how secluded their life has been, and how great the cultural isolation imposed on them by the ghetto and guaranteed by the fence of tradition as well as that of primitive conservatism, it seems unlikely that the Jews in the Yemen were not, like other Jewish groupings, submitted to a certain degree of enforced assimilation in their forms of musical expression. But since in the Arab world the key-structure (modes, etc.) has been modified, so far as song is concerned, only to a relatively small extent, whereas in any case those employed by the Jews of over a thousand years ago must also have suffered modification, it can be accepted in principle that these songs of the Yemenite Jews are closer to ancient Jewish song than are most of the songs sung by European Jews.

For this very reason the Israeli musician who has been trained in Europe has difficulty in adapting himself to the spirit of these songs. Even more than when arranging and treating the folk-songs of the European Jews the composer is faced with the problem of an arrangement that shall form an organic unity with the basic song. This difficulty can be more simply and easily overcome if these folk melodies are not treated by way of arrangement or harmonisation, but are drawn upon in the creation of free compositions, for instance, the utilisation of single motifs from such songs.

At the moment, for understandable reasons, the people of Israel are opposed to anything originating from the Arab world. So it is rather convenient that the songs of the Yemenite Jews make use of type-motifs which in former times would have sounded to our ears as Palestinian-Arab or Palestinian-Bedouin. To some extent these Yemenite motifs are similar to those which one formerly bore in mind when seeking to give a Palestinian colour to music.

The European training and the resulting compositional style of certain Israeli composers are still very perceptible, and they impose definite constraints on the creation of a purely Palestinian musical style. Yet already it is possible to note certain melodic and rhythmic phrasings that pass as typical. Of course, this is especially the case with regard to the popular songs we have already mentioned. Such phenomena are to be found in the music of almost all Israeli composers ; in dependence on the composer's own character and personality one can find in his music more or fewer such musical ideas, and these can in turn be regarded as

THE MUSIC OF THE JEWS

more or less good and characteristic. Only as music develops
further in the country will it be possible to pass a more definite
judgment on this trend.

The foundation of a first-class symphony orchestra, the
Philharmonic Orchestra, by Bronislaw Hubermann in 1936,
together with the existence of a number of distinguished composers in Israel, has proved a great stimulus to the advancement
of music. The orchestra gave its first concert on December 26th
of that year, with Toscanini conducting. As the Israel Philharmonic Orchestra it has recently paid a successful visit to the
United States. In 1936, too, the Jerusalem radio station was
brought into operation, transmitting in English, Hebrew, and
Arabic; the music department was headed by Karl Salomon. It
has played a great part in encouraging the creation and
performance of Jewish music.

As early as 1923 Mordecai Golinkin founded the 'Palestine
Opera'; the opening performance consisted of Verdi's
'Traviata.' In 1941 the 'Palestine People's Opera' was founded
by Georg Singer, Lav Mirski, Mordecai Golinkin, Wolfgang
Friedländer, and Marc Lavry. Lavry wrote an opera, 'Dan the
Guard,' for this opera company; the libretto, by Sh. Shalom and
Max Brod, was based on a Palestinian story.

The Joel Engel Prize, instituted in 1945, and awarded by the
Tel Aviv municipal authorities to Jewish musicians, has had a
very stimulating effect. The Labour Federation, too, promotes
concerts and presentations, especially in the settlements and
colonies, this work being done by its Cultural Department. There
are a large number of choirs in Israel, and most of them confine
their activities to the performance of Jewish music.

The Jewish interest in music in Palestine and Israel has been
revealed in many other ways. The business of publishing books
and sheet music is extraordinarily developed for the size of the
country. Several music schools, conservatoires, and academies
have also contributed greatly to the country's musical life. Now
that Israel is a sovereign state the country has its Ministry for
Education and Culture, which has set up a special department for
music, with the well-known pianist, Frank Pelleg (Pollak) in charge

We have already mentioned some of the composers now
working in Israel, and a fuller list will be found in the following

chapter. In the new music of Israel it is above all the landscape, the sun, the climate, the speech, and not least the tremendous will to build up the country, and the indomitable optimism of its people which have most influenced the Israeli composer. To-day he is seeking new, sunny, optimistic means of musical expression, he is endeavouring to replace the gloom and oppression of the Diaspora by the brightness and hope of the old yet new homeland, and to create and shape his works in this spirit. As the majority of the present-day composers in Israel have come from abroad, their first problem is to get acclimatised and to adapt themselves to this new spirit. Some of them call their new style the Eastern Mediterranean style. Many of their works have been played with success in various countries abroad, and great interest has been shown in their compositions in America, France, Czechoslovakia, Italy, Switzerland, Austria, and elsewhere.

All the tendency of Jewish culture to-day is to be focused on Israel, and that is also true of modern Jewish music. As soon as the centre of gravity of Jewish art music becomes established in Israel a new era begins for it. The country will not merely be an ideal in the Jewish struggle for a cultural centre, but will become the real, existing and active cultural centre of the Jewish people, and of their music.

CHAPTER XV

JEWISH COMPOSERS IN THE
TWENTIETH CENTURY

IN the previous chapter we have sketched the general development of the new Jewish music of the national school, from its origins at the beginning of the century down to its consummation in the two main centres of the United States and Israel. In the course of that sketch we mentioned the names of a number of Jewish composers who were prominent in the movement from its earliest days, and perhaps there could be no better way of illustrating, and filling in the details of that movement, than by giving brief biographies of these and other outstanding Jewish composers, both of the older and the younger generation, who have contributed to the general stream of Jewish national music. That this may be achieved the more effectively, we not merely give the bare details of their life and work,[1] but attempt to appraise their vital contribution, their interconnection with one another, and their position in the world of Jewish music. In doing so we follow the plan adopted in the previous chapter, so far as possible: i.e., we begin with the Russian Jewish composers of the early years of the century, and then, by way of Central and Western European, and American composers, come finally to those who are active in Israel to-day.

It is fitting that we should begin with JOEL (Julius Dimitrievich) ENGEL, for, as we have said, he must be regarded as the earliest pioneer of all modern Jewish music. He was born on April 16, 1868, at Berdiansk, in the Tauride province of Southern Russia, and began by studying law at the universities of Kharkov and Kiev. But from 1893 to 1897 he studied composition under Taneiev and Ippolitov-Ivanov at the Moscow Conservatoire, and from 1897 down to 1919 he was the senior music critic of the

---

[1] It is unavoidable that throughout this chapter titles of compositions should appear in several languages. The situation would only be further confused if they were all translated into English, since many of the works mentioned are not known, or have not been published, in English-speaking countries and so are without accepted English titles.

leading Russian newspaper 'Russkaya Viedomosti' (Russian News). As one of the foremost Russian writers on music, he was placed in charge of the Russian edition of Riemann's 'Musik-lexikon,' and also published a pocket music-dictionary and several guides to opera. His first important work on behalf of Jewish folk-song was his lecture, in December 1900, to the Imperial Russian Society for Natural Science, Anthropology, and Ethnography, which he accompanied with the performance of songs he himself had collected and arranged. The lecture aroused great interest in the subject, and from then on he made it his life work to collect and arrange Jewish folk-song, and to work for the development of a new Jewish music. He organised concerts of and lectures on Jewish music in most of the large towns of Russia ; at that time Jewish published music hardly existed at all, and the fundamental task was rather to make propaganda on its behalf, in order to stimulate interest in and demand for such publications. Engel had a great gift for organisation, as he demonstrated in his work to found two Jewish publishing companies : the 'Society for Jewish Folk Music' in Russia, and the 'Juwal-Verlag' in Berlin. Like certain other pioneers whom he inspired by his example, he usually had to neglect his gifts as a composer in favour of his propagandist and organising work, with the result that he never really succeeded in developing an individual style.

His creative activities were in complete conformity with his life work. He began by noting down Eastern European Jewish folk-songs and providing them with a pianoforte accompaniment ; they were published with the original Yiddish text and with Russian, German, and Hebrew translations. He also wrote original songs to Yiddish and Hebrew texts from the poets Bialik, Peretz, and Tchernikovsky, and together with his folk-song collections these songs are still among the best items in the repertoire of singers presenting Jewish music. His songs are distinguished by their melodic beauty and strong harmonic and formal construction. Another well-known work of his was his incidental music to Ansky's play 'The Dybuk,' in which he employed mainly old Chasidic tunes. When the Moscow Habima Theatre, for which the music was written, went on tour in the 'twenties this incidental music became known all over the world. The work was published

(By courtesy of Mr. A. Friedmann-Lewow, Haifa)

Facsimile of an original manuscript by Joel Engel

by the Jibneh-Juwal-Verlag, of Berlin, as a 'Suite aus der Legende Hadibuk' (op. 35) for string quartet, clarinet, double-bass (*ad lib.*) and percussion (which can be played by the 'cellist; the writing is for triangle and tambourine). It has also been arranged for piano solo. Owing to its very simple, occasionally primitive compositional technique, its conformity to true folk-song style, and its use of corresponding characteristic dance rhythms. this music sounds particularly authentic, and it achieves a deeply mystical mood. Others of his works included 'Fünf Klavier-stücke' (op. 19); 'Volksweisenkranz' (op. 41), for piano, also arranged for four hands; 'Chabader Nigun' (Melody) and 'Frejlachs' (Dance) (op 20, Nos. 1 and 2), for violin and piano. Lesser-known works include the 'Adagio Misterioso' (op. 22), for violin, violoncello, harp (or pianoforte) and organ (or harmonium); and his few choral works, e.g., his *Adonai Ori* for male voice choir and piano. Although his many other activities prevented Engel from achieving the full promise of his talents as a composer, his works were of great importance as examples to his own and later generations of Jewish musicians.

Engel left Russia and went to Berlin in 1922; there he founded the Juwal-Verlag for the publication of Jewish music, which published all the works he had brought with him, as well as many others. In Berlin he organised concerts and lectures on Jewish music. In the autumn of 1924 he went to Palestine, and lived in Tel Aviv for the rest of his life, concentrating chiefly on activities as a teacher of composition and pianoforte at the music school. He became greatly interested in songs for children to sing at home and at school, and wrote a number of such songs to Hebrew texts. He died on February 12, 1927, leaving much of the work he had planned still unaccomplished. But before his death he had the undeniable satisfaction of seeing that a large number of composers were following in his steps, taking up his ideas and developing them, and promising to achieve the creation of the Jewish music which had been his lifelong dream.

The group which Joel Engel built up around himself gave us the first of the compositions or arrangements which to-day are performed as 'Jewish,' or, as they are often called, 'Hebrew' music. In musical expression, however, they still clung to the Russian idiom. The ideological programme, and, at the most, the employment of Jewish traditional melodies, especially the neginot or biblical tropes, had to serve as substitute for a specific and original Jewish musical expression, and, perhaps, to prepare the way for that expression. When Achron hoped to create a Jewish atmosphere by employing tropes in his ' Children's Suite ' (op. 57) he had to resort to this method because there was none other at his disposal. In Achron more than in any other of the earliest group of Jewish national composers we can trace the search for his own, specifically Jewish musical expression. His activities as a composer were controlled and influenced by his occupation as an outstanding violin virtuoso and teacher. Naturally enough, most of his earliest works consist of pieces for virtuoso and concert performance, and it may be added that they were in due course performed by violin virtuosos in the concert halls of the world, as the first works of the first Jewish national composer.

JOSEPH ACHRON was born on May 1, 1886, in the town of Lezdzeye, Suwalki province, which was then in Russia, but after 1917 was part of Lithuania. Even at the age of two he displayed a strong musical sense and a fine ear. His father made him a violin, and he soon became perfectly accustomed to playing it. His first advanced training on the instrument was given him by Professor Michailowicz in Warsaw, to which city his family had removed ; here he gave his first public performance in a concert, at the age of eight. After a concert tour through Russia in 1897 he continued his violin studies at Warsaw under Professor Lotto, and at the age of thirteen he went to the Petersburg Conservatoire, where he studied under the famous Leopold Auer, and took harmony under Liadov. He left the Conservatoire in 1904, being awarded the gold medal and a court award. After three years of concert activity, with headquarters at Berlin, he worked to complete his studies in composition, especially counterpoint, fugue, and form and analysis, and took a course of instrumentation under Steinberg. He continued his concert tours and took up teaching, but grew more and more occupied with composition. From 1913 to 1916 he was leader of the violin and chamber music class at the music school of the Imperial Russian Music Society at Kharkov, and from 1916 to 1918 he served in the Russian army. After 1918 he again engaged in concert tours and in 1921 was

leader of the master-classes for violin and chamber music of
the Artists' Union in Petersburg. For a short period (1922-24) he
lived in Berlin ; in 1924 he gave a number of concerts in Palestine,
and in 1925 he went to the United States. There he was professor
of the State Conservatoire in Chicago, and later conducted his
own master-class for violin in New York and then Los Angeles,
where he died on April 29, 1943.

Unlike Engel, Achron did not devote himself to propaganda
activities, so he was able to develop his musical personality on
the one hand as a virtuoso violinist and teacher, and on the other
as a composer. He is of importance not simply as a Jewish composer but as a modern composer generally. His earliest works
tended to conform to his interpretative requirements, for he was
chiefly concerned to write compositions suitable for virtuoso
performance. But his gift for writing poetic musical works came
more and more to the forefront. His works are distinctive for their
formal construction, and as time passed he reached out to the
larger instrumental forms. One of his later works, the ' Evening
Service for the Sabbath,' (1932) which he wrote for the Temple
Emanu-El in New York, reveals all his profound poetic power, his
depth of feeling and gift for musical representation. Despite the
use of modern harmonies which, however, are never dry, these
vocal pieces for the sacred service make a powerful effect. And
they might well serve as an example to the many compositions
which other composers were to write for the Sabbath service.

Achron wrote over sixty works of various kinds. His smaller
compositions, which constitute the bulk of his pieces for virtuoso
performance, include for violin and piano the ' Hebrew Melody,'
composed in 1911 ; a ' Hebrew Dance ' ; op. 35, a ' Hebrew
Cradlesong ' ; op. 37, ' Improvisation on a Hebrew Folk-song ' ;
op. 42, ' Sher ' (a Hebrew dance) ; op. 46, *Agadah* (Legends) ;
op. 52 No. 2, ' Canzonetta ' (this is his song, ' Licht so träumend,'
transcribed both for violin and piano, and also for 'cello and
piano) ; his op. 42, ' Sher,' and op. 43, ' Fragment mystique
sur un thème hébraïque,' are for 'cello and piano, while for
pianoforte he wrote his op. 56 No. 1, ' Traum,' and No. 2,
' Begrüssung.' His op. 57, ' Children's Suite,' for two violins, viola,
violoncello, clarinet, and piano, composed in 1925, consists of
short character-pieces, linked together with musical motifs drawn

chiefly from the 'tropes.' This suite was also arranged for the piano.

All the foregoing pieces certainly added to the general virtuoso literature, but they differed to a large extent from the ordinary pieces in that style since in most cases their folk-lore material was allowed to convey a poetic mood that reflected the specific Jewish manner of expression. The same is true of Achron's songs (op. 52-55) for voice and piano, to texts by Fichmann, Ben-Izchak, Frischmann, Schneur, and others. (Op. 55 also has an orchestral accompaniment.) His 'Symphonic Variations and Sonata on a Hebrew theme, El Yivneh Hagalil, for pianoforte (op. 39) composed in 1915, showed that he had now perfected his compositional technique, especially in regard to works for pianoforte. This piece also reveals his gift for the variation form ; one of his earliest Jewish compositions was his ' Jewish Variation ' on the ' Kamarinskaya ' dance, which he had written in 1904. In form and content these symphonic variations are very representative of his work. Of his violin concertos we must also mention his op. 60, composed in 1925; its second movement is titled: ' Improvisations sur deux thèmes yéméniques.' He also wrote two sonatas for violin and piano; a 'Chromatic String Quartet'; four 'Tableaux fantastiques'; 'To the Jewess,' for orchestra and declamation (op. 40); also music for a number of plays. These include his op. 49, to Waiter's 'Fartog'; op. 50, to Peretz's 'The Fiddle's Soul'; music to Sholem Aleichem's 'Mazeltov'; to Goldfaden's M'chashefa (The Witch); and to Maeterlinck's ' Die Blinden,' and ' Belshazar.' His orchestral suite ' Golem ' (1931) was performed at the second international festival of music at Venice in 1932. His work as a violin teacher had fruit in his essay on 'Fundamentals of Violin and Bow Technique.'

The above summary of Achron's best-known compositions shows how varied was his musical imagination and how wide his culture. He still ranks among the outstanding Jewish composers of this century, though it must be added that his work is not to be judged exclusively by that standard, for he won general recognition.

Other better-known members and composers of the Russian ' Society for Jewish Folk Music ' were Michael Gnessin, Alexander and Grigory Krein, Michael Milner, Salomon Rosowsky, Lazare

Saminsky, Ephraim Skliar, Alexander Veprik, and Leon Zaitlin. Certain of these played a considerable part in the later development of Jewish music.

MICHAEL FABIANOVICH GNESSIN (GNIESSIN) was born at Rostov-on-Don on January 23, 1883 ; he was the son of the local rabbi. He was given instruction in music by Cantor Gerovitz and the pianist Oscar Fritsche at Rostov, and in 1899 by Konuz in Moscow ; in 1901 he studied at the Petersburg Conservatoire under Liadov, Glazunov, and especially Rimsky-Korsakov. In 1911 he paid a visit to Germany, after which he settled in Rostov, where he taught composition in the State Music School. Later he was made director of the school, and he was active in the organisation of musical life in the town. In 1921 he toured Palestine, and in 1923 he settled in Moscow, where he taught composition in the music school which his sister had started, but which had been taken over by the State. Gnessin became one of the most prominent composers of the Jewish national school. In his style (especially in his earlier works) he remained far more under the influence of the Russian composers, Liadov, Rimsky-Korsakov, etc., than either Engel or Achron ; the fact that he wrote three Hebrew songs to words by the Russian poets Bunin, Maikoff, and Shurilin is indicative. His works were of importance to modern Jewish music above all because of his taste in choosing characteristic and pregnant musical themes, and because of his fine compositional technique. His op. 34, ' Song of the Wandering Knight,' for violoncello (or violin) and piano ; his op. 24, ' Variations on a Jewish Folk Theme,' for string quartet ; and op. 35, *Hora* (Dance of Galilee Workers) for four-hand piano, made a strong impression by their high qualities and interesting musical form. He has also written an opera in oratorio style, ' The Youth of Abraham ' ; further, a piece for orchestra, ' The Jewish Orchestra at the Mayor's Ball ' for a scene in Gogol's ' Inspector-General ' ; also ' Danses funèbres,' op. 22 ; a ' sonata-ballade,' op. 7, for violoncello and piano ; a piano quintet, ' Requiem,' op. 11 ; a ' Symphonic Fragment, after Shelley,' op. 4 ; Music to Greek Tragedies,' op. 13, 17, 19 ; music to ' Dichtung vom Roten Mottele,' to words by Joseph Utkin, op. 44 ; and many songs, choral works, etc.

ALEXANDER VEPRIK (WEPRIK) was much more progressive in

the choice of thematic material and in regard to his style as a composer. His themes are almost ascetically simple, and melodically and rhythmically are restricted to the most fundamental of Jewish thematic material. His style and harmonisation are in close affinity with modern music and, like Alexander Krein, he is in the line of Debussy-Scriabin-Stravinsky. Born at Lodz on July 23, 1899, in 1909 he went with his mother to Leipzig and studied at the Conservatoire there until 1914. Then he continued his studies at the Petersburg Conservatoire under Kalafati and Zhitomirsky, completing them under Myaskovsky at the Moscow Conservatoire, of which he has been on the teaching staff since 1923. Among his more notable works are ' Songs and Dances of the Ghetto,' for orchestra ; *Kaddish*[1] for violin (or viola, or flute, or oboe, or wordless voice) and piano ; two piano sonatas ; an ' Heroic Poem ' for orchestra ; songs, etc.

MOSES (MICHAEL) MILNER is distinguished by his sensitive employment of traditional Jewish, mainly religious melodies in vocal compositions, such as his ' Psalm 13 ' for voice and piano, ' An den Vogel ' to a poem by Bialik, *Aggadah* for piano, ' Baim Reb'n zu Mlave-Malke ' ; the synagogal work *Un'sanneh Toiqef* for choir *a capella*, etc. He also wrote incidental music for several plays produced by the Habima Theatre, e.g., ' Jacob's Dream ' and ' The Golem.' More than any other Jewish composer Milner has rooted his thematic material in the simple Jewish folk-melos.

LEON MOISIEVICH ZAITLIN, who was born in Memel on March 14, 1881, was a violinist who studied under Leopold Auer at the Petersburg Conservatoire in 1901. Until 1910 he was a member of the Orchestre Colonne, in Paris, and the first violinist of the Zaitlin Quartet ; he then went to the Zimin Opera House in Moscow as orchestral leader, and later was leader of Koussevitsky's orchestra. He became a teacher at the Music School of the Moscow Philharmonic Society and at the Moscow Conservatoire, and in 1922 was chairman of the ' First Symphonic Ensemble ' in Moscow (a conductorless symphony orchestra). Later, he went to the United States, where he died in 1931. His best-known works are *Eli Zion*, for violoncello and piano, which

---

[1] The *Kaddish* is a prayer, written in Aramaic, in praise of God ; it is also the prayer to be said in memory of the dead.

Achron arranged for violin ; and 'Reb Nachmann's Nigun,' for string quartet.

Although GRIGORY ABRAMOVICH KREIN, who was born at Nizhni-Novgorod on July 4, 1880, and studied under Paul Juon and Glière, has achieved some success as a composer, he is not so important from our standpoint as his brother, Alexander. His works include a string quartet, a piano quartet, a piano sonata, violin and piano sonata, songs, a violin concerto, and three symphonies.

ALEXANDER ABRAMOVICH KREIN must be regarded as among the foremost Jewish composers of the past fifty years. His compositions range from operatic and full orchestral works down to settings of folk-songs, etc. Much of his later work is unknown to us, owing to the difficulty of obtaining sheet music from the U.S.S.R. ; but his earlier compositions reveal his vigorous personality, and a modern and daring style that stems from Grieg, Debussy, Ravel, Scriabin, Mussorgsky, Stravinsky, and modern German composers. But it is in his exploitation of Jewish thematic material that he clearly reveals his gifts as a composer. His themes are taken from Jewish folk-lore, and consist mostly of brief melodies or outline motifs, and although he retains their original style they are developed and intensified musically and poetically. In all his work he identifies himself so completely with his theme that he unfolds it as something quite original, shapes it magnificently and builds up the whole work into a natural unity. Rich in his harmonisation, and gifted in his instrumental combinations, he does not regard this technique as an end in itself, but uses it only to give the strongest and truest significance to the character of the melody. The Chasidic and synagogal melodies which he often uses retain their note of exaltation, which springs from the Jewish religious spirit, and the compositional writing intensifies their mood, conveying their ardent emotional expression. The motifs are frequently interwoven into a sumptuous outburst of sound. His work is rich in melodic ornamentation and copious in ecstatic exaltation, both specifically oriental features.

Alexander Krein was one of the nine sons of Abraham Krein, seven of whom became musicians. Abraham Krein was himself a good violinist, and also composed. In his youth he played a great deal at weddings, and he collected folk and synagogue melodies.

So Alexander, who was born at Nizhni-Novgorod on October 20, 1883, was familiar with the Jewish melos from his earliest days, and as soon as he devoted himself to Jewish compositions he was able to draw upon his memories. His father was his first music teacher, but at thirteen he began to study the violoncello under Professor von Glehn at the Moscow Conservatoire, and had private tuition in composition under Nikolayev and Yavorski. But as a composer he was really self-taught. During his earlier years he wrote no works with Jewish themes, but he was one of the many whom Joel Engel won over to recognition of the value of the Jewish melos. Now he wrote a number of compositions in which he sought to explore his Jewish musical imagination. As time passed he outgrew other stylistic influences and found his own form of expression. His first works employing Jewish melodic material were his 'Hebrew Sketches' for string quartet and clarinet (op. 12 and op. 13), which consisted mainly of the harmonisation of folk-songs taken from his father's collection. These he wrote at Engel's instigation. The symphonic poem 'Salome' for large orchestra, composed in 1913, was on an altogether bigger scale ; in this work he gave the thematic material artistic formulation and attempted to give it characteristic design by the use of Jewish ornamentation. His op. 23, 'Three Songs of the Ghetto,' set to poems by Bialik ; his op. 28, 'Fragments from the Song of Songs' (text by Efrat) ; his op. 29, No. 1, *Rakkim Me-Rokh Panayich* ('How fair and pleasant is thy countenance'), to a text by Jaffe ; op. 31, 'Ghaselen' (a song cycle to texts by Efrat), all reveal the stylistic features of the later Krein in their recitativo-melodic manner and their rich, saturated harmonisation. 'Ornaments,' op. 42, are three songs without words. He also tried his hand at setting the text of the *Kaddish,* composing the symphonic cantata *Kaddish* for tenor solo, mixed chorus, and orchestra. This work caused a sensation with its profound melodic invention and bold harmonic design. But it has to be admitted that this striking piece makes no ordinary demands on the performers. We must mention, too, his string quartet in C sharp minor, op. 9 ; his sonata for piano, op. 34 ; and his symphony, op. 35. He wrote music for plays, and this was afterwards arranged for performance as suites. In 1923 he composed music to David Pinski's 'The Eternal Jew,' for the Moscow Habima

Players; in 1924 to 'Sabbatai Zvi' for the Ukrainian State Jewish Theatre; in the same year to 'Ghett' and 'Die Nacht auf dem alten Markte,' by Peretz; in 1925 to 'Doctor' for the Moscow State Jewish Theatre; in 1912 to 'People'; and in 1925-26 to 'An der Busskette' for the White Russian State Jewish Theatre. In this incidental music for plays the folk-lore style had always to be followed, and he made skilful use of Jewish motifs. As in all his works, this music achieves an unusually clear and plastic effect through its richly coloured instrumentation. Alexander Krein died on April 20, 1951. In his own lifetime he was accepted as an outstanding composer not only of Jewish but of Russian status.

JACOB WEINBERG was born at Odessa in 1879. One of his uncles was married to a sister of Anton Rubinstein, and in their house he regularly heard good music. But his musical training did not begin until he was seventeen, after he had left High School and had entered the Moscow University as a student of law. Later he studied at the Imperial Conservatoire, Moscow, as a pupil of K. N. Igumnov and Sergei Taneiev. In 1906 he graduated as a pianist and composer. The years 1910 and 1911 he spent in Vienna, studying with Leschetitzky. On his return to Russia he met Joel Engel, and joined the Moscow section of the Society for Jewish Music. After the Russian revolution he and his family emigrated to Palestine and lived there for five years, writing the opera 'Hechalutz' (The Pioneer), etc. In 1928 he travelled to the United States, and since then he has lived in New York, working as a composer, pianist, and teacher. We can mention only a few of his numerous compositions: a fine arrangement of the Palestinian folk-song 'Reitiha' (the theme is Arabic in origin), for voice and piano (published 1929); various liturgical works, e.g., the 'Sabbath Eve Service' (Servizio Pentatonico), which is based on the pentatonic scale (1935). This is less successful than the 'Sabbath Morning Service' (1938-39), which rather proclaims his affinity with the sound traditions of his former Russian homeland. Although this service is written in free counterpoint it is very lucid in its settings of the liturgy and highly suitable for synagogal use. In addition, in 1942 he wrote a 'Sabbath Service for Congregational Singing,' and in 1947 he published a volume of 'Thirty Hymns and Songs with organ or piano accompaniment, for Congregation, School, or Home.'

Another interesting work is 'Chazak Veematz,' for mixed choir and piano.

SALOMO ROSOWSKY, one of the founders of the Petersburg 'Society for Jewish Folk Music' in 1908, was extremely fruitful in his work on behalf of the society, and has occupied himself with the advancement of Jewish music ever since. Born on March 4, 1878, he was the youngest son of the celebrated Riga Cantor Baruch Leb Rosowsky (1841-1919), who wrote *Shirei Tfilo* (Songs of Prayer), for solo, chorus, and piano ; and he was familiar with Jewish song from his earliest childhood. He studied law at the University of Kiev and music at the Imperial Conservatoire in Petersburg under Liadov, Rimsky-Korsakov, and Glazunov. In 1905 he studied conducting under Arthur Nikisch at Leipzig Conservatoire. In 1918 he became music director of the Jewish Art Theatre in Petersburg, composing incidental music to Sholem Asch's play, 'The Sinner,' to Gutskov's play, 'Uriel Acosta,' and his Biblical poem, 'Amnon and Tamar.' In 1920 he went to Riga, where he founded the first Jewish Conservatoire. In 1925 he emigrated to Palestine and spent 22 years there as composer and teacher and as director of the School for Cantors. He also worked in the field of musical research, notating and analysing versions of the biblical tropes (neginot), as sung by various interpreters. The results of this work are shortly to be published in volume form in New York, under the title: 'The Music of the Bible.' In Palestine he wrote incidental music for various plays performed at the Habima and Ohel Theatres in Tel Aviv. He went to New York in 1947, and now resides there.

Rosowsky's early works were born of the desire to arouse interest in Jewish folk-music, so he began by arranging folk-songs, and wrote small pieces for the piano (the 'Poeme') ; for violin and piano ('An der Wiege') ; a 'Fantastic Dance' for piano trio, in which he made use of Chasidic themes (later scored for orchestra) ; and a 'Trauerode' in memory of the poet Peretz, for voice, violin, and piano. More highly esteemed is his music for the plays: 'The Sinner,' by Sholem Asch ; 'Uriel Acosta,' by Gutskov ; 'Sabbatai Zvi,' by Bistrytsky ; 'Messiah, the Son of Joseph,' by Steinman ; 'Jacob and Rachel,' by Krasheninnikov ; 'The Crown of David,' by Calderon ; 'The Treasure,' by Sholom Aleichem ; and others.

One other of the Jewish composers who were active in the 'Society for Jewish Folk Music' requires consideration. LAZARE SAMINSKY was born on October 27, 1882, in Vale-Gotzulovo, not far from Odessa. In 1905 he studied composition under Boleslav Yavorski at the Moscow Philharmonic Society's Conservatoire, and in 1906 with Rimsky-Korsakov; then he took conducting under Tcherepnine, and finally was a pupil of Liadov's in the Petersburg Conservatoire, remaining there until 1910. Meanwhile he studied mathematics at Petersburg University (1906-1909) where he acted as conductor to the University choir, and also to an orchestra. In 1909 he conducted his 'Overture' with the Conservatoire orchestra. During this period he worked with his Jewish colleagues in Rimsky-Korsakov's composition class in the 'Society for Jewish Folk Music,' in which society he advocated the importance of the old synagogal motifs, whereas his friends were more interested in folk-song; he has remained faithful to this branch of Jewish music ever since. In 1913 his Poem for Orchestra, 'Vigiliae,' was performed in the Koussevitsky series of concerts in Moscow. Now he went as a member of an ethnological expedition to Georgia in the Caucasus. At this time he wrote an essay on historical and æsthetic problems of Jewish music and occupied himself with the problem of the cantillation of biblical passages, i.e., the biblical accents (neginot, or tropes). In 1951 he also published a 'Song Treasury of Old Israel,' arrangements for voice and organ or piano, with a few for cantor and choir. In this work he presented old cantoral and Chasidic songs of Eastern Europe, songs of the Georgian and Persian Jews, and those of the *Spagnioli* Jews of Turkey, as well as certain of the older canticles of Israel, and some of the new tradition. Part of this collection consists of songs which he collected in 1913. while taking part in Baron de Guenzburg's ethnological expedition to Caucasia and Turkey. Joel Engel and S. Ansky, the author of the Yiddish dramatic legend, 'Dybuk,' were also members of this expedition.

Saminsky's Biblical ballet, 'Lamentation de Rachel.' for speaker, dancer, female voice solo, a small female choir, and orchestra, was written in its first version in 1913, and was thoroughly revised in London during the summer of 1920. He completed his first symphony in 1914. During all these years he acted as conductor for various orchestras. In 1919 he spent three months in Palestine, and then travelled to England, where he founded the 'Hebrew Music Society.' In December, 1920, he went to New York, where he has lived ever since. In 1924 he was appointed director of music at the Temple Emanu-El in New York, and he has given many public concerts with the Temple choir. During his residence in New York he has made a number of journeys to Europe to conduct orchestras, to give lectures, and for purposes of study. He has also arranged for the performance of Jewish composers' works in various cities, including first performances of works by Joseph Achron, Ernest Bloch, Michael Gnessin, Alexander Krein, and himself, in Paris in 1925. He has always been ready to interest himself in the presentation of Russian and other contemporary music.

Saminsky, who had an unusually varied education, including the study of philosophy and mathematics, has not restricted his compositional activities to the writing of Jewish music. Even so, the themes of his symphonies and other works always reveal melodic and rhythmic elements in affinity with his Jewish musical thought. In the matter of harmonisation he takes his own path, and frequently breaks completely with accepted principles. A dissonance will be neither prepared (as in strict compositional writing) nor resolved, even when the manner of setting resembles strict style. In part-writing he seldom adheres strictly to the same number of voices ; four-part passages may be transiently resolved into unison, and unisons in turn resolved into multi-part passages without preparation. This comparative freedom in composing enables him to give free rein to his imagination, and confers on his work an originality which is not prejudiced even by the discernible extrinsic influences of chiefly Russian, French, and often German composers. We must add that no single school or trend of style is recognisable in his music ; he chooses the form of expression that he regards as exactly right for the formulation of his musical thought of the moment.

His fourth symphony, fifth symphony (' Jerusalem '), and the two operas, ' The Daughter of Jephtha ' and ' Julian, the Apostate Cæsar,' the latter a three-act work written 1933-38, are regarded as his most important creations. The characteristics mentioned above are also to be found in these works. His ' Daughter of

Jephtha' contains some of his finest music. He is one of the most prolific of Jewish composers. He has written many folk-song arrangements for voice and piano and for mixed choir, e.g.: *El Jibne Hagalil* and the Yemenite melody *Ani Hadal*; songs to Hebrew texts, e.g., to Psalm 137 ('By the Waters of Babylon'), and to the texts of non-Jewish poets, including, Pushkin, Verlaine, Gaston Dru, Baudelaire, and Cherubina de Gabriac; pianoforte compositions: 'Conte Hébraïque,' 'Deuxième Conte,' 'Danse rituelle du Sabbath,' etc.; pieces for violin and piano: 'Little Rhapsody,' 'Hebrew Rhapsody,' 'Chasidic Suite'; five symphonies for large orchestra: a 'Sabbath Evening Service,' songs for the Sabbath evening service and for holy-day services in the Temple Emanu-El at New York; an 'Anthology of Hebrew Sacred and Traditional Songs,' consisting of a selection of traditional melodies and his own compositions for cantor, choir, soli, and organ; an opera-ballet 'La Gaglairde d'une Peste joyeuse'; the cantata-pantomime 'The Daughter of Jephtha'; a 'Requiem' for soli, choir, and orchestra; and much else. In his opera-ballet 'The Vision of Ariel' (1950), which is set in Flanders during the Spanish domination in the latter part of the sixteenth century, he makes use of 'Ladino' and Sefardic songs. In every respect he is an outstanding, versatile musician, who has succeeded in maintaining his position in modern music and has had great influence on the development of the new Jewish music.

Of his many writings we must mention his 'Music of the Ghetto and the Bible' (Bloch Publishing Co., New York, 1934). This is a collection of various articles, all of them written very interestingly and collating many little-known historical facts. The information they contain on the Jews and their problems in Russia down to the First World War are of special value.

Although SAMUEL ALMAN spent most of his creative life in England, he was educated and had his early musical training in Russia, and so may well be considered at this point. He was born on September 20, 1879, in the little South Russian town of Sobolovka, in Podolia. Among his forebears, who were very devout, there were many Jewish scholars. He began to write songs at the early age of thirteen; at the age of eighteen he entered the Odessa Conservatoire, then he served four years in the Russian army as a musician, and afterwards returned to the

Conservatoire to complete his studies. After the great pogrom at Kishiniev in 1903 he fled to London in 1905, where he finished his studies by attending the Royal College of Music. He settled permanently in London, and was appointed choirmaster of the Great Synagogue. His compositional activities were extensive, and included many songs on religious texts, by the poets Tcherni-kovsky, Bialik, Heine (in Hebrew translations), Isaac Katznelson ; synagogal compositions for choir ; the big work *Shire Bet Hakneset* (synagogue songs) in East European Jewish style ; arrangements of Jewish folk-songs, in Yiddish and Hebrew, for voice and piano ; ' Two Piano Pieces ' ; ' Pilpul ' for piano ; a string quartet, ' Ebraica,' in three movements ; Three Small Pieces for string quartet or string orchestra ; eleven small pieces for organ ; the successfully produced opera *Melech Ahaz* (King Ahaz), for which he wrote the libretto in Yiddish (1912) ; and much else. His writing is solid, the composition clear, and his melodic fancy reveals the influence of traditional song. He did much to stimulate the development of Jewish secular choral singing among London Jewry, and his influence, unobtrusive and quiet, was greater than is realised. He died on July 20, 1947, in London.

The Jewish composers of Central Europe did not form such a distinct and homogeneous school as those who gathered round the Petersburg ' Society for Jewish Folk Song,' and in any case certain of them also originated from the same East European environment, and migrated to the musical centres at Berlin, Vienna, and elsewhere. Thus, we may regard JULIUSZ WOLFSOHN as forming a bridge between the East and Central European Jewish musical groups. He was born at Warsaw on January 7, 1880, but he spent his childhood in Moscow, where his father had a large soap and perfumery works. He displayed a strong musical talent from his earliest years, and in due course began to attend the Moscow Conservatoire. But as the result of a Tsarist ukaze his family had to leave Russia proper, and they returned to Warsaw, where he continued his studies. He took pianoforte lessons from the famous interpreter of Chopin, Alexander Michalowski, and composition from Noskowski. In 1903 he went to Paris to be trained by the famous pianist Raoul Pugno, then he went on to Leschetitzky in Vienna. After several concert tours in Europe and America he settled in Vienna. As soon as he had made his name as a pianist he devoted himself intensively to the cultivation of Jewish folk-song, with which he was thoroughly familiar, and advocated the cause of Jewish music in many lectures and articles. He wrote his 'Jewish Rhapsody' at the age of twenty. His works for the piano include twelve Paraphrases of Jewish Folk Melodies, a four-movement 'Hebrew Suite' (also arranged with orchestra), 'Fünf Stimmungsbilder aus der Kinderwelt,' an 'Album für die Jüdische Jugend.' and twenty 'Charakterstücke für Klavier,' intended for beginners. He is quite alone in his manner of arranging Jewish folk-song. His pianoforte compositions betray the hand of a distinguished interpreter of Chopin and Liszt, and this has had its influence on his general style of composition. As a rule his arrangements are in three-section form: an introduction is followed by statement of the folk-song theme, which is then worked up and treated in variation style in the manner of the romantics, and the work usually ends with a repetition of the introduction. Wolfsohn's arrangements could not have any great influence on the development of original Jewish composition, because of their stylistic peculiarities; he is too greatly influenced by Chopin and Liszt, and so his works tend to have a uniformity of treatment. But his tasteful selection and arrangement of the popular folk-songs and his distinguished pianoforte writing for these works, which of itself earns them the right to consideration, have won them wide distribution.

MAX (MARKUS WOLF) ETTINGER was born in Lemberg (Lwow) on December 27, 1874, and so within the then Austrian Empire. In this sense he came within the orbit of Central European Jewry; but Lemberg was also a centre of East European Jewry, and in his childhood Ettinger had a thoroughly Jewish education, including a course of Talmudic study. Even so, he began to take up the arrangement of Jewish folk-song and wrote his first compositions employing Jewish folk-music only after producing a large number of other works which have to be regarded as belonging to German musical culture. Owing to constant illness he was not able to take up the study of music in earnest until he was twenty-five, though he had been drawn to it earlier. In 1899 he went to Berlin, and in the following year to Munich, where he attended the Academy of Music under Rheinberger and Thuille. Because of his poor health he gave up his plans to become a theatre conductor and devoted himself entirely to composition. Down to 1930 he lived in Munich, and then at Ascona in Switzerland, where he died on July 19, 1951. He wrote a large number of vocal and instrumental works. His many songs include ' Schlaflied für Miriam ' to words by Richard Beer-Hoffman, songs to words by Else Lasker-Schüler, Heinrich Heine, and Jehuda Halevi, songs for voice and piano and for male voice choir, arrangements of Palestinian and East European folk-songs, and Psalm 130 for vocal solo and piano (1943). He also composed melodies for a singing-hour with refugee children (1943), concert-pieces on two Jewish folk-songs, for violin and piano (1940) ; ' Der ewige Weg ' (to words by Ilse Blumenthal-Weiss) for mixed choir *a capella* ; a string quartet on Chasidic melodies (1945) ; ' By the Waters of Babylon,' songs of the Babylonian Jews for small orchestra (also for piano), planned as a basis for a ballet (1936) ; ' Cantus Hebraicus,' variations on an old Hebrew melody, for small orchestra (1943) ; ' Queen Esther,' an oratorio on Biblical texts for four solo voices, choir, and orchestra (1945) ; ' Yiddish Lebn,' a cantata for tenor solo, male voice choir, and small orchestra, on poems by Frug, Reisin, and Bialik, and employing Chasidic melodies (1943) ; ' Das Lied von Moses,' an oratorio on Biblical texts for four solo voices, mixed choir, and orchestra (1934) ; the opera ' Judith,' a musical tragedy to a libretto from Hebbel (1920), which was played in several German theatres ; and other works.

In his oratorio ' Das Lied von Moses ' Ettinger used old Jewish religious songs or motifs, drawing on the collection of songs of the Yemenite Jews made by Idelsohn. In 1947 he wrote ' Zum Ondenk in di Gefallene vun Warschauer Ghetto ' (In memory of those who fell in the Warsaw Ghetto) for soprano, tenor, and baritone soli, male voice choir, and orchestra. This is a composition in oratorio style, setting Yiddish texts by Layzer Ajchenrand and Bialik. Those of Ettinger's works which utilise Jewish themes are built up on clear musical figures, usually of a simple folk tune nature. They express true East European moods.

Two other Jewish composers originating from Eastern Europe were to become well known in Germany through their activities as arrangers and popularisers of Jewish music. ARNO NADEL was born on October 3, 1878, at Vilna, which was then part of Russia ; but in 1890 he went to Königsberg in East Prussia, to study under Eduard Birnbaum and Robert Schwalm. In 1895 he went to Berlin, and lived there for the rest of his life. Until 1900 he was a pupil in the Jewish Teacher Training College and studied music under Ludwig Mendelssohn and Max Löwengard. From 1916 onward he was choirmaster to the Berlin Jewish community, and in 1923 the community commissioned him to arrange the music of the Jewish liturgy anew. In Germany he became known as a poet and dramatist and also as a painter, chiefly of portraits. But he was also known, both inside and outside Germany, as a writer on music, as an editorial collaborator in various works on music, and as an arranger of Jewish folk-songs. Among his works must be mentioned the ' Jontefflieder ' (twenty-two Jewish Festival songs, published in ten parts, 1919) and two volumes of Jewish folk-songs (1920 and 1923) both provided with simple pianoforte accompaniment. He wrote many articles embodying the results of his own studies of Jewish music, e.g., an essay on Jewish music in the volume ' Juderna ' of the ' Nationernas Bibliothek,' in 1920 ; and contributions to the journals, ' Der Jude,' ' Ost und West,' etc. He died in a German concentration camp.

JANOT SUSSIA ROSKIN was born in 1884, at Reshitsa, in the Vitebsk province of Russia. He travelled a great deal as a choir-singer and cantor, and later as a singer of folk-songs. In 1903 he settled in Berlin, where from 1911 to 1918 he was director of the Halenseer Conservatoire which he had founded. In 1916 he started the ' Musikverlag für nationale Volkskunst,' known from 1921 onward as ' Musikverlag Hatikvah,' a company specially concerned with the publication of Jewish music. At the same time he was acting as a choirmaster. He has published many arrangements of Jewish folk-songs, a number of songs in folk-song style, etc. His last years were spent in America, where he re-established his publishing company. He died at Indianapolis on August 5, 1946.

Of one European Jewish composer it cannot be said that he originates from Eastern Europe, and it is noteworthy that he holds a unique position among the Jewish composers of the national trend. The Jewish compositions written by ERNEST BLOCH have gained a wider and more enduring place in the international concert repertory than those of any other Jewish composer of the present century. He is accepted as one of the most interesting living composers and his works are played in Europe and America ; this applies equally to those based on Jewish thematic material and despite their Jewish titles (*Shelomo, Baal Shem,* 'Israel' Symphony, etc.). Taking his works as a whole, Bloch is a composer entirely in his own class, with a distinctive personality. As a man and as a musician he has a remarkable understanding of both the general and the Jewish manner of thought, and his life is striking for its spiritual struggle to bring these two intellectual currents into harmony with each other and with the surrounding world. He will make no concessions to either of these two spheres. He himself has known nothing of the struggle for a Jewish manner of expression. He listened in to his own manner of expression, and that also revealed to him the Jewish musical elements. He has had hardly any necessity to resort to the employment of Jewish folk-song melodies (the East European folksong in his *Simchat Torah* is an exception). In a kind of confession of faith he has said: 'It is not my purpose, not my desire, to attempt a "reconstruction" of Jewish music, or to base my work on melodies more or less authentic. I am not an archæologist. I hold it of first importance to write good, genuine music. It is the Jewish soul that interests me, the complex, glowing, agitated soul, that I feel vibrating throughout the Bible ; . . . the freshness and naïveté of the Patriarchs ; the violence of the Prophetic Books ; the Jew's savage love of justice ; the despair of Ecclesiastes ; the sorrow and the immensity of the Book of Job ; the sensuality of the Song of Songs. All this is in us, all this is in me, and it is the better part of me. It is all this that I endeavour to hear within myself, and to transcribe in my music: the time-honoured emotional urge of the race that slumbers deep down in my soul.' These words express a clear and definite attitude, based on Bloch's recognition and understanding that he is Jewish.

To date Bloch is the most outstanding composer of the Jewish national school that Western or Central Europe has produced. He is very different from those originating from Eastern Europe. He was born in Geneva on July 24, 1880. His paternal grandfather, who died before he was born, was President of the Jewish community of Lengnau in the Argau canton of Switzerland. His father studied for the rabbinate, but gave it up and became a bookseller. In his parents' house Ernest Bloch was a participant in many Jewish customs which left an abiding impression on him.

Facsimile of the original manuscript of the full score of Avodath Hakodesh *by Ernest Bloch*

At the age of six he was playing the flute, but his father was not exactly pleased to see his son's interest in music. None the less, he began to study the violin when he was nine, and soon he was writing small pieces for this instrument. After a long illness, he left school at the age of fourteen and went to Emile Jacques-Dalcroze to study harmony and counterpoint, and to Louis Rey, with whom he continued his violin studies (1894-1896). In these years he wrote his 'Oriental Symphony,' a youthful attempt, built up on Jewish melodies his father had sung to him, and consisting of four movements: 'Prayer,' 'The Caravan in the Wilderness,' 'Oasis,' and 'Funeral Ceremony.' In 1896 the violinist Marsick came to Geneva, and Bloch went to hear him play. Afterwards he sought him out in his hotel, played to him, and showed him works he had written, including a string quartet. Marsick was so struck by the lad's unusual musical gifts that he went to his father and drew his attention to them. Soon after, Bloch went to Brussels, where he studied the violin under Ysaye and Schörg and composition under F. Rasse (1897-1899). From 1899 to 1900 he continued his study of composition at Frankfurt-on-Main in the Hoch's Conservatoire, under Ivan Knorr, and from 1901 to 1903 he studied alone at Munich. Here he wrote the C sharp minor symphony (1901-1903). He then lived for a short period in Paris, without making any livelihood as a composer, and in 1904 he returned to Geneva and took up bookselling in his mother's shop. But he continued with composition in his spare time. At this period he wrote an opera, 'Macbeth,' to a text by Edmond Fleg, based on Shakespeare. It was given its first performance at the Opéra Comique in Paris on November 30, 1910, but it was not successful, partly because of its bold representational resources and modernistic music, partly owing to various influences to which Bloch succumbed. None the less he gained the sympathy of many who were struck by this new, strong personality in music. (It had its first performance in Italian forty years later, at Rome in 1953.) He had already composed 'Vivre-Aimer' in 1900; his symphony in C sharp minor (1901-1903); 'Hiver-Printemps,' two symphonic poems (1904-1905); and 'Poèmes d'Automne' for solo voice and orchestra or piano (1905-1906), all of these testifying to his marked gift for composition. In 1909 he conducted orchestral concerts at Neuchâtel and Lausanne, and from 1911 to 1915 he was teacher for composition and æsthetics at the Geneva Conservatoire. It was during this period that he wrote his first important compositions with Jewish subjects: the three 'Psalms' for voice and orchestra (1913-1914); the 'Three Jewish Poems' for large orchestra (1913); the 'Israel' Symphony for large orchestra, with soprano, alto, and bass soli and women's choir (1912-1916); and finally, *Shelomo*, a Hebrew rhapsody for violoncello and orchestra (1915-1916).

As early as the three 'Psalms' the original quality of Bloch's Jewish compositions was manifest, for he scored the psalm texts quite differently from the manner of other composers. He achieved a musical expression which is determined not so much directly by the words of the psalms as by the outburst of feeling and spirit which the psalms contain. This manner of handling the psalm texts is the result of a dramatic interpretation, as distinct from the lyrical or even epic interpretation of other composers. In their compositional technique the 'Psalms' exploit many elements that we recognise as drawn from dramatic music, and so their effect is rather 'secular,' 'profane.' None the less they are filled with religious emotion, expressive of passionate resignation and of belief in the righteousness of God. So these three 'Psalms' are also an expression of Bloch's religious attitude, since he seeks to comprehend everything positively. The psalm compositions were not directly and literally inspired by the Hebrew texts, nevertheless, the musical motifs correspond to the peculiarities of the Hebrew language, as is clearly shown in their tonal intervals and rhythms. Of the three psalms, two, Nos. 114 and 137, are for soprano or tenor, and one, No. 22, for baritone or contralto, all with orchestra. The 'Trois Poèmes Juifs' and the 'Israel' Symphony bring motifs created out of Jewish experience into small and large forms of orchestral music. 'Trois Poèmes Juifs' was completed in August-September, 1913, at Satigny, near Geneva. It is in three movements (1, Danse; 2, Rite; 3, Cortège Funèbre) and has a definite programme. It was the first work in which Bloch began to realise his expressive resources. But the orchestral sound is already characteristic of his writing. The 'Israel' Symphony, which Bloch began in 1912, then laid aside in favour of the *Shelomo* Rhapsody, and completed in 1916, was originally intended to be titled: 'The Jewish Festivals.' During the actual composition Bloch gave up this idea; later he employed some of its material in his *Avodath Hakodesh*, or 'Sacred Service.' However, the first movement of the symphony was inspired by the holy-day of *Yom Kippur*, the Day of Atonement, the second by *Succoth*, the Feast of Tabernacles.

The story of how *Shelomo* came to be written as a work for violoncello is interesting. Bloch originally planned to set passages from Ecclesiastes to music, and had already written sketches for this purpose. But the only language he considered suitable for such treatment in this particular case was Hebrew, and he did not know it well enough. Yet neither French, nor English, nor German met with his musical requirements. So the sketches were left undeveloped. At the end of 1915 Bloch went to a concert given by the violoncellist, Alexander Bariansky, and was struck by the idea of giving the solo voice of the Ecclesiastes texts to the violoncello. Thus he would avoid using any verbal text, and could interpret the Ecclesiastes thoughts which were gripping him in terms of pure music, expressing them in typical upsurges of feeling, and in a musically thematic manner rather than in terms of recitative or declamation. He quickly became a close friend of Bariansky and his wife Catherine, and in a few weeks he wrote a glowing rhapsody for violoncello and orchestra. (Meanwhile, Catherine Bariansky, who was a sculptor, modelled a small statue of king Solomon and dedicated it to Bloch.) Thus the *Shelomo* rhapsody is not a setting of texts; none the less in thought and mood it is in harmony with the spirit of the work which is said to have been written by king Solomon.

Bloch's first visit to America was made as orchestral conductor to the dancer, Maud Allan, in 1916. On March 23, 1917, at the invitation of Karl Muck he conducted his 'Three Jewish Poems' in Boston; in May of the same year Artur Bodanzky conducted the first performances of the three 'Psalms' and the 'Israel' symphony in New York. The 'Three Poems' were also performed at this concert. Bloch met with so much appreciation and interest in America that in the same year he decided to settle there. He became a teacher, first at the David Mannes Music School in New York, then privately, and in 1920 he went to Cleveland, where he founded and directed the Institute of Music. From 1925 to 1930 he was director of the Conservatoire in San Francisco.

In this period most of the compositions he wrote had a

non-Jewish content, though this is a term that is rarely completely applicable to Bloch. They include the suite for viola and piano, which he later arranged for viola and orchestra (1919) and which won the Coolidge Prize ; a sonata for violin and piano (1920) ; several pieces for piano ; the piano quintet (1923-1924) ; three Nocturnes for piano trio (1925) ; the ' Poème Mystique,' his second sonata for violin and piano (1924) ; a Concerto Grosso for string orchestra with piano obbligato, which he wrote in 1924-1925 for the students' orchestra at Cleveland ; the ' Four Episodes' for chamber orchestra, which first saw the light in 1926, and so on. Two other symphonies, besides the ' Israel' symphony, followed: the epic rhapsody for orchestra, ' America,' in 1926, and the ' Helvetia' symphony in 1928-1929. The three symphonies differ fundamentally from one another, in conformity with their pro-grammatic subjects. But, whether the starting point of his musical conception was his Jewish spiritual world with all its emotional feeling and mood, or his loyal and admiring attitude to America, or his attachment to his native Switzerland, always there is a central personality binding them together and welding them into an affinity of ideas: the distinctive personality of Ernest Bloch. His own philosophical outlook shapes all his work, and his own spiritual attitude is reflected in them. Thus we can always recog-nise the ' typical' Bloch.

His first String Quartet in B minor, begun in Geneva and completed in New York in 1916, is a majestic achievement. Bloch, a true master of modern chamber music style, combines its various archetypal motifs in typical manner. As one listens to this work one is frequently struck by its affinity to folk-lore music.

A number of Jewish compositions also came into being between 1923 and 1930: the ' Three Pictures of Chasidic Life' for violin and orchestra (pianoforte) (1923) called *Baal Shem* (after the founder of Chasidism in the eighteenth century) ; they consisted of *Vidui* (Confession), *Nigun* (Improvisation), and *Simchas Torah* (Rejoicing) ; the deeply expressive prelude, ' Recueillement,' for string quartet (1925). Then there was the too rarely heard *Abodah* (God's worship), a *Yom Kippur* melody for violin and piano (1929) ; and the ' Méditation Hébraïque' and three sketches ' From Jewish Life,' consisting of a ' Prayer,' ' Supplication,' and ' Jewish Song' ; both these works were for 'cello and piano, and were composed in 1924. They all combine East European Jewish religious and other melodic elements found in folk-song.

The events of the First World War and the absence of mutual understanding in the ensuing peace were so contrary to all Bloch's world of ideas that he felt spiritually at loggerheads with it. So in 1930 he left America and returned to Switzerland, where he took a small house in Roveredo Capriasca, a little village in the Ticino, and sought physical and spiritual recovery from the oppression of the world's disharmony. Here, close to Lake Lugano, in 1930-1933, he composed his *Avodath Hakodesh,* the Sabbath morning sacred service, scored for baritone (cantor), mixed choir, and large orchestra. It consists of five parts and is written to a Hebrew text based on the Sabbath liturgy according to the American Union prayer book. Since its composition it has had concert performances in many countries. From 1934 to 1938 he lived in the small village of Châtel, Haute Savoie, on the Swiss border. Here he wrote the pianoforte sonata (1935) ; also 'Voice in the Wilderness,' which was finished on January 26, 1936. Its expressive resources are akin to those of the 'Psalms' and *Shelomo,* but the orchestration is much more pellucid, without any loss of splendour in its tonal colour. It is a symphonic poem consisting of six meditations, which are built up as a manifold dramatic psalm. Originally it was intended for violoncello and piano ; later he orchestrated it and gave it the title 'Visions and Splendours.' There followed 'Evocations,' a symphonic suite for orchestra (1937) ; and his violin concerto (1937-1938).

In December, 1938, Bloch returned to America and resumed his active work in San Francisco. He settled in 1941 at Agate Beach, Oregon. Here he wrote the 'Suite Symphonique' (1944) for violin and orchestra ; the second string quartet (1945) ; and the pianoforte concerto 'Scherzo Fantasque' (1948). His most recent compositions include the magnificently written, noble sounding, 'Six Preludes' for organ (1949), which are particularly welcome for synagogal use. Also 'Four Wedding Marches' (1950) ; 'Meditation-Processional' for viola and piano or orchestra ; and the 'Suite Hébraïque' (Rhapsody, Two Processionals) for viola and piano ; both the latter in 1951. His most recent works are Concerto Grosso, No. 2, and 'Sinfonia Brève,' composed in 1952.

▼ Please detach and keep ▼

Christ Church
NASHVILLE

We are delighted to have you worship with us today! We are honored by your presence and pray that this service will be a blessing to you.

If you need to make a decision today, such as publicly confessing your faith in Christ or becoming a member of this church, we invite you to do so by responding to the invitation at the close of the service or by going to the Care Station (located at the main floor entry foyer of the church) where our Pastoral Ministers will be available to talk with you.

We are glad you visited Christ Church. Please come back soon. If we may be of service to you, please do not hesitate to call on us.

L.H. Hardwick

L.H. Hardwick, Jr, Pastor

Visitor Card

Christ Church
NASHVILLE

15354 Old Hickory Blvd. • Nashville, TN 37211
615-834-6171 • Fax 615-834-4463

We have listed only the most outstanding of Ernest Bloch's works, and we must add that his creative powers are by no means exhausted. We are too close to him in time to be able to form an historical estimate of his work; but already there can be no doubt of the great significance of this powerful composer in the sphere of Jewish music. Truly, like many another, in his youth he came under alien influences; his youthful imagination was fired and impressed chiefly by Debussy, Mussorgsky, Wagner, and Richard Strauss. But, like all composers of genius, he developed his own style, his own manner of expression. He is a man of wide culture and great spiritual and intellectual power, and this is reflected in his music. His orchestration is colourful, vivid, overflowing and intensive; his composition is frequently majestic and sublime; in lyrical passages his musical thought is intimate and warm, and it is always plastic in expression. Precisely because he has not made use of melodies and motifs from Jewish folk-song but has created Jewish musical motifs in his own imagination, his compositions are of all the more significance for the new Jewish music. He fixes his Jewish musical thought for us, and creates new, truly Jewish compositional elements which are part of our musical heritage.

We come now to a composer who, like Engel, may truly be said to represent, indeed to personify, the transition from the East European to the Palestinian branch of Jewish music. JOACHIM STUTSCHEVSKY, too, is a passionate pioneer and an ardent propagandist of the new Jewish music. But whereas Engel in his early years of advocacy had little or nothing on which to base his propaganda, Stutschevsky was able to profit by the published results of the earlier pioneering days, and was able to penetrate to the essence of the new national Jewish music, even though there was still comparatively little published at that time. He also occupied an outstanding position as a violoncellist and teacher in Central Europe.

He was born at Romny, in the Ukraine, on February 7, 1891, and studied music at Leipzig Conservatoire, where he graduated as Laureate of Professor Julius Klengel's class in 1912. From 1914 to 1924 he lived in Zürich, and it was there that he began his propaganda activity on behalf of Jewish music. He was responsible for the first concerts of Jewish music to be given in Switzerland.

At that time there was very little published music available, so he himself wrote arrangements and compositions for violoncello and piano, and for piano solo. In 1924 he went to Vienna, where he continued his activities, founding the 'Verein für Förderung jüdischer Musik,' which regularly arranged for the performance of such music. He also edited the publication of a 'Jüdisches Jugendalbum,' which contained twelve original compositions for pianoforte, and included works by Achron, Dessau, Rothmüller, Stutschevsky, and Thaler. In 1938 he went to Palestine, where he has been active ever since. Here he has composed many songs, which for him is a new genre. He was particularly drawn to song-writing through the influence of his wife, who is a singer. In his songs he has developed many new expressive resources. We must mention 'The Jolly Zoo' (to lyrics by Lea Goldberg), four colourful and vividly felt songs, composed in 1949 ; Shomer mah mi-leyl (to lyrics by Matityahu Shelem), rather freer and more boldly written ; and those of 'The Promise' (to lyrics by Natan Alterman), composed in June, 1951. So far he has written some twenty-five songs for voice and piano. In addition he has collected and published a hundred and twenty Chasidic melodies (1950) and has published a collection of East European Jewish folk-songs with words in the Hebrew translations of Shimshon Lezer, and Dov Shtok. There are also many children's songs among his compositions. The following works are regularly played with great success: 'Vier jüdische Tanzstücke,' 'Palästinensische Skizzen,' Riqqud (Dance Piece), and 'Bagatelles,' for pianoforte; Kinah (Elegy); 'Méditation Chassidique'; 'Freilachs' (dance paraphrase and improvisation); Dvejkut (Méditation Hébraïque); Eli, Eli (based on a folk-melody); Mechol Qedem (Oriental Dance); Shir Yehudi ('Jewish Song'); all for violoncello and pianoforte.

Although three distinct periods can be noted in his life—his residence in Switzerland, Vienna, and Israel—they do not find clear expression in his work, as there was not much change in his compositional technique. However, it is possible to observe an increasing degree of clarification in the invention and formulation of his Jewish musical thought.

His compositions since he went to live in Palestine include a Suite for violin and piano (1940) ; a Duo for violin and violoncello

(1940), dedicated to Joseph Achron ; 'Four Dances' for orchestra (1940) ; 'Israelian Suite' (1942) for violoncello and piano ; 'Improvisation' for flute and piano (1943) ; a Duo for violoncelli ; a piano suite ; an 'Old Chasidic Melody' written for violin and piano (1944) ; piano miniatures for children (1946) ; 'Chasidic Suite' (1946) for violoncello and piano ; songs for children (1949) ; 'Two Sefardic Prayers,' for voice and piano (1950). Taken as a whole the works he has composed in Israel are harmonically even bolder than those of his earlier periods. He has always built up his harmonies and dissonances unencumbered by the customary rules, and in this respect his latest works seem to have gone even farther. In these compositions the motif material is frequently no longer drawn from folk music, and this applies especially to the Duo for violin and violoncello. But in most of his works he has utilised charming Palestinian or Yemenite motifs, giving them a rich oriental ornamentation. His music is always expressive, colourful, and harmonised freely, with vivid rhythms, and conveying profound East European moods.

Apart from composition, out of his wide teaching experience he has published 'Studien zu einer neuen Spieltechnik' and a four-volume 'Violoncell-Spiel,' both of which works are officially used for instruction in the conservatoires of a number of countries. His concert arrangements of master-composers are well known. He has written many articles in support of modern Jewish music and has brought clarification to the subject in many respects. Before the foundation of the State of Israel he was the Inspector for Music of the Machleqet Ha-tarbut of the Vaad Leumi (Culture and Education Department of the Jewish National Council) and arranged the first concerts of Jewish music to be held in the Brenner House in Tel Aviv. His collected essays, published under the title of 'Mein Weg zur jüdischen Musik' by the Jibneh Editions, Vienna, in 1935, are valuable ; besides monographs on Engel, Achron, etc., the book contains polemical and discussional articles, and an appeal to Jewish composers. Stutschevsky has rendered valuable service in promoting the works of young Jewish composers and stimulating them to write.

France and Italy also have contributed to the main stream of modern Jewish music, both in the sphere of collection of traditional works and in that of original composition. As early as 1885 a volume of liturgical songs sung by the Jews of Comtat-Venaissin, in Provence, was published by Jules Salomon Crémieux and Hananel (Mardochée) Crémieux at Aix; this work has been continued by LEON ALGAZI, who, though known chiefly as a synagogue choirmaster in Paris, also conducts works in his own arrangements for sound-recording and is active as an editor and arranger of Jewish, mainly religious, songs. But the most distinguished of the French Jewish composers, one who has gained world recognition, is DARIUS MILHAUD, who was born on September 4, 1892, in Aix-en-Provence. He was a student at the Paris Conservatoire, under Gédalge, Widor, and D'Indy, from 1910 to 1919. Among his works containing Jewish themes are his Psalm 136 for baritone solo, male voice choir, and small orchestra; 'Poèmes Juifs'; 'Chants Populaires Hébraïques'; 'Liturgie Comtadine'; 'Chant de *Rosh Hashanah*' for voice and piano; and the Purim opera 'Esther de Carpentras.' In 1940 he went to America and worked as a teacher of composition, and he now, after a period at Oakland, California, lives in Paris. His compositions are marked with the characteristics of the contemporary French school, and this applies equally to those of his works with Jewish titles. In these he uses folk music only rarely, though he is a professing Jew and is wholly favourable to the idea of Jewish music. The same can be said of his recent liturgical work for the Sabbath morning synagogue service, 'Service sacré pour le Samedi matin avec prières additionelles pour le Vendredi soir,' written for baritone solo, reader, mixed choir and orchestra, or organ (Edition Salabert, Paris-New York, 1950), though it is closer to the traditional and customary liturgical melos than his earlier compositions of a Jewish nature. It is a highly interesting work, and is easier to perform and to apprehend than many of his other works. He has also published a few single compositions for synagogal use.

The composer MARIO CASTELNUOVO-TEDESCO was born in Florence on April 3, 1895, of an old Italian Jewish family. He received his first tuition in the pianoforte at the age of nine, and began to interest himself in Jewish musical material when he was thirteen, after discovering a notebook belonging to his grandfather, which contained religious songs. His first 'Jewish' work was 'Le Danze del Ré David,' for piano (1925), which he dedicated to his grandfather's memory. He describes it as a Hebrew rhapsody; it consists of seven episodes based on seven different themes. In 1926 he wrote 'Tre Corali su Melodie Ebraiche,' for piano, dedicating it to his mother; in this work he attempted to treat chorales in modern style yet in the manner of the Bach chorale; it is interesting in regard both to its compositional technique and its content. In 1931 Jascha Heifetz commissioned him to compose his second violin concerto, 'The Prophets,' in which he made some use of themes from the collection of Frederico Consolo, which we have mentioned in an earlier chapter. The concerto had its first performance in April, 1933, Heifetz playing the solo violin and Toscanini conducting the New York Philharmonic Orchestra. For many years past Castelnuovo-Tedesco has lived in the United States. He has written various works for synagogue use, and a complete 'Sacred Service.'

So far we have been dealing with the older, roughly the first generation of European Jewish composers. Now we come to a younger generation. In the search for new means of expression many of these have already given interesting and valuable demonstrations of their talent. But, just because they are younger, the composers of this later period are still in the first phase of their development, still struggling with the problem of expression, rather than already creating mature artistic works. None the less they represent a definite addition to the spiritual and intellectual values of the Jewish renaissance, and of modern Zionism.

ISRAEL BRANDMANN was born on December 1, 1901, at Kamenetz-Podolsk, in Podolia. His father was the conductor at the municipal theatre. He began to study the violin at the age of seven, and later continued his studies under Malkin. From 1913 to 1917 he was a student at the Petersburg Conservatoire, where he repeatedly performed in public. From 1917 to 1921 he was active in his home town as violinist and conductor. He started a Jewish musical organisation which gave chamber music concerts and performances with a large choir and orchestra. After a successful tour through Roumania, with a small choir, in 1921 he went to Palestine, where he expanded the group into a large choir, giving concerts with an orchestra all over the country. He resided in Palestine until 1924, working as a violinist, conductor, and music teacher. In 1924 he went to Vienna and devoted himself to the study of composition under Franz Schmidt at the Hochschule für Musik, and later worked with Alban Berg. He now proceeded to write the first of his works to attract attention, the most important being his Variations: the 'Variationen über einen Palästinensischen Volkstanz,' for string quartet (also arranged for orchestra); the 'Variationen über ein Volksthema,' for clarinet and piano (also for violin and piano); and 'Variationen über ein Thema von Engel,' for violin and string orchestra. His symphonic poem *Hechalutz* (The Pioneer) for large orchestra is also mostly written in variation form. He wrote two songs for high voice and piano, to words by Bialik; 'Palästinensische Hirtenweisen,' for mixed chorus and piano; 'Palästinensisches Tanzlied,' for mixed choir a *capella* (without words, for vocalising); 'Three Passover Melodies,' for clarinet and string quartet; 'Kinderstücke,' for piano; 'Palästinensische Melodie,' for violoncello and piano; an arrangement of the Jewish National anthem, *Hatikvah,* for solo, chorus, and piano; and some works with non-Jewish themes, which are to be regarded more as composition studies.

In his creative work Brandmann has fused his Russian musical education with that which he obtained in Vienna. His preference for the variation form may perhaps be most easily explained as a need to present the same musical thoughts in various forms and characters. He often uses an ostinato figure in his variations, and takes compositional ideas as a basic structure or theme-pattern to be worked up. In his melodic writing one comes upon an augmented second comparatively often, though both melodically and rhythmically he blends elements recognisable in Russian music with those of Palestinian songs, and other elements from Central Europe. His music is powerful in its effect, and his Jewish themes originate from a genuine folk melos. Occasionally there is some acerbity in his music, but in his later works this has tended to disappear. He has lived in Palestine since 1935, working as a teacher, violinist, and composer. For some years he did no composing, but has recently written choral works, songs, etc.

SHULA DONIACH can be regarded as entirely a product of British Jewry, for, although she was born in 1905 at Samara (now Kuibishev), on the Volga, in Russia, her parents brought

186

her to England when she was only a few months old. Her first language was Hebrew. She wrote her first composition at the age of ten, when she set a chapter of the Book of Isaiah to music. She studied at the Royal Academy of Music, where she made her debut as a pianist. She continued her studies at Berlin, Vienna, Budapest, and in Switzerland, and returned to England in 1934. Just before the second world war she spent two years in Palestine, and this was a most fruitful experience in her creative life as a composer. It was directly out of this experience that she wrote 'Voices of Jerusalem,' for soprano, baritone, oboe, string quartet and piano ; the texts were Hebrew poems by the Israeli poetess Sara Levi, by Ibn Ezra, A. L. Yaron, and S. S. Shalom, and two by herself (with versions in Hebrew and English throughout). Other works of hers include 'Rhymes from Carmel,' twelve songs for two or three voices with or without piano accompaniment, the texts by A. L. Yaron ; a rhapsody for violin and piano, several songs to English poems, etc. Her music is fresh, clear, rich in invention, and inspired by the true Jewish melos.

ARON MARKO ROTHMÜLLER,[1] who has used the pseudonym of Jehuda Kinor for some of his compositions, was born on December 31, 1908, in the small town of Trnjani, in Slavonia (Yugoslavia). In 1912 his family went to live at Zagreb. By the age of fifteen he was already collecting and publishing Jewish folk songs. At the High School of the Academy of Music, he studied composition and conducting under Dugan, Bersa, and Lhotka, and singing under Jan Ourednik. From 1928 to 1932 he continued his studies in Vienna, his teachers including Alban Berg and Franz Steiner. In 1932 he founded 'Omanut,' a society for the advancement of Jewish music (later the Society for the Advancement of Jewish Art), in Zagreb. From 1935 to 1948 he lived in Switzerland, as an opera singer. During this period he fostered Jewish music with all his powers, as singer, conductor, and composer. In 1941, together with a group of Jewish artists in Zürich, he founded the Zürich 'Omanut.'

Rothmüller's earlier compositions are marked chiefly by the free exploitation of folk music themes (Jewish or Yugoslavian), as in 'Sha, still!' (an East European folk-song), and Three

---

[1] As the following remarks relate to the author of this book, they are restricted to objective fact.

Palestinian Folk-songs; 'Aphorismen,' for harp; 'In Memory of Bialik,' for violin, viola, and violoncello; 'Rhapsodic string quartet' in D minor (on Yugoslavian themes); and a symphony for large string orchestra. The 'Praeludium and Fughetta' for organ, and 'Psalm 13' for baritone (or contralto, or mezzo-soprano), organ, harp, and string orchestra lead to his next phase, which was concerned with the compositional problems of a Jewish musical language. 'Kol Nidre' for solo voice and mixed choir; 'Four Sefardic religious folk-songs' for mixed choir *a capella*; 'Psalm 15' for voice and piano; and the Suite for two violoncelli complete this group.

Later his compositional technique became more complex and he began frequently to treat folk-songs in the style of art song. Here must be mentioned his 'Three Palestinian Love-songs' for voice and piano, his Trio for violin, violoncello, and piano; 'Phantasy' for piano; and, as transitional to the next group, the 'Psalm,' music for viola or violoncello and chamber orchestra. There followed a second string quartet and a pianoforte sonata; 'Three Scherzi' for violoncello and piano; the 'Elegiac Suite' for tenor, or soprano, oboe, two violins, two violas, violoncello, and piano; and the two ballet suites: 'Jewish Dance Suite' and 'From War to Peace.' Finally should be mentioned: Three Songs by Vladimir Nazor' (Yugoslavian); 'Pogledaj me!' ('Look at Me'), a Yugoslav folk-song from Slavonia, for voice and piano (also arranged for orchestra); songs to texts by Else Lasker-Schüler; two songs in twelve-tone technique, to texts by Karl Kraus; and various harmonisations of folk-songs.

One other name must be mentioned: Isco (Yitzchak) Thaler, whom we know through his piano works, published by Joachim Stutschewsky. Thaler was born at Bogorodczany, in Poland, on January 17, 1902, and studied music at the Staatsakademie für Musik in Vienna from 1917 to 1920. From 1920 to 1923 he attended the Staatliche Hochschule für Musik in Berlin, under Franz Schrecker. He is now living in Rome, and does a good deal of work for the radio.

*   *   *   *

The United States has seen the rise of two, and even three generations of Jewish composers, beginning with those who emigrated to that country in the early years of the century. As before, in discussing the works of individual composers we shall begin with the older generation.

LEO LOW was born in 1878 at Wolkowisk, which was then in Russia, and he is wholly rooted in the Eastern European Jewish world which he knew as a child; this East European spiritual element in his personality is always apparent in his work. As a boy of eight he helped his father in leading the prayers in the synagogue on *Yom Kippur,* the Day of Atonement. When he was twelve he himself led the prayers for the first time; three years later he was acting as choirmaster. After occupying various posts as choirmaster, e.g., from 1902 to 1920 at a Warsaw synagogue, he emigrated to the United States. His most important contribution to Jewish music has been in arranging folk-songs, and the composition of religious music based on folk-song. As a composer his merits are chiefly sincerity and clarity; his works are not overloaded, they are easily absorbed, and are written with warm feeling. Over the years his manner of writing, his style and technique have developed greatly.

JACOB BEIMEL, born in Russia in 1880, died in New York in 1944. He was a graduate of the ' Meisterschule für musikalische Komposition' of the Königliche Akademie der Kunst in Berlin. For synagogue use he wrote very expressive compositions, with fine, sometimes traditional, themes. Irreproachable in regard to harmony and counterpoint, they can be introduced into the synagogue service very effectively. His ' Organ Music for Jewish Worship: Five Preludes or Meditations,' published posthumously, fall within the same category. He wrote other works for voice, violin, chorus, and orchestra, and had articles on Jewish music published in English, German, Hebrew, and Yiddish.

ZAVEL ZILBERTS was born on November 7, 1881, at Karlin, near Pinsk, at that time in Russia, and in his youth worked as a cantor. He developed early as a composer of works for the Jewish sacred service. He studied singing at the Warsaw Conservatoire; from 1903 to 1907 he was musical director and conductor of the Hazomir Music Society at Lodz, in Poland; and from 1907 he was at the Central Synagogue in Moscow. He went to the United States in June 1920, and afterwards wrote many synagogal compositions, drawing on traditional motifs, and made exhaustive studies of Jewish folk music. He died in New York on April 26, 1949.

HEINRICH SCHALIT was born on January 2, 1886, in Vienna, the son of a Jewish writer. He began his musical studies at the age of eleven, under Josef Labor. Later, in 1903, he entered the Staatliche Musikakademie in Vienna, taking composition under Robert Fuchs. Meanwhile, he was studying the piano under Leschetitzky. In 1907 he went to Munich, where a number of his compositions of a non-Jewish character were performed, and where he continued his training as organist, begun in Vienna. The first world war caused a break in his career. As a musician he grew more and more conscious of his Jewish origin and character. This brought him to the writing of his ' Seelenlieder,' op. 16, for baritone and piano, to texts by Jehuda Halevy in German translation. There followed further settings of Halevy texts. From 1926 to 1933 he was organist at the Munich synagogue. The interest which he had already developed in Jewish liturgical music was now further intensified. He came to the view that the synagogal music of the Reformers, Sulzer and Lewandowski, customary in Germany, was spurious, and he devoted himself to study of the cantillation of the Torah and the chazzanut of the oriental Jews. These were more in tune with his own feeling, especially because of their psalmodic quality in the ancient modes. In 1930 and 1931 he visited the United States. On his return to Munich he occupied himself with study of Idelsohn's writings. In 1932 he produced his ' Freitagabend Liturgie,' for solo, choir, and organ (op. 29). At the end of 1933 he went to live in Rome, where he became a synagogue choir-master. He found the city stimulating, wrote several ' Psalms,' and finished the ' Chassidische Tänze,' which he had begun in Munich (a suite for string orchestra, or violin and piano). Later he spent two years in London, and in 1940 he went to America. There he lived first in Rochester, New York, then in Providence, Rhode Island, and Hollywood. Since 1948 he has resided at Denver, Colorado, as a composer and teacher. His ' Hymnische Gesänge' and ' In Ewigkeit' immediately revealed his distinctly religious manner of expression. The ' Sabbath Eve Liturgy,' for cantor, mixed chorus, and organ, published in America, is partly a revised version of his ' Freitagabend Liturgie' already mentioned. In it he employed a number of traditional tunes, some of them taken from the Idelsohn collection, and took care either to retain or—in his own, original work—to imitate the archaic character of the religious melodies. The work as a whole is an excellent, valuable contribution to this branch of Jewish music.

GERSHON EPHROS, Cantor of the Beth Mordecai Congregation in Perth Amboy, New Jersey, was born in Poland in 1890. He studied music and chazzanut under Idelsohn, Hermann Spielter, and Joseph Achron. He has rendered distinctive service to the cantor repertoire in the United States, enriching it partly with his own, partly with new editions of standard synagogue compositions. In his ' Cantorial Anthology ' he includes items by Sulzer, Lewandowski, and others, besides his own works. The fourth volume, which appeared in 1953, includes works by modern American and Israeli composers, which are most interesting and characteristic. Every cantor in the United States regards this anthology as his basic material. In his own music Ephros has sincere and beautiful melodic fancy, with very neat harmonisation, and clean, strict counterpoint. He has also written non-liturgical works, including a ' Children's Suite,' to words by the poet Chaim Nachman Bialik, for voice and piano (1936) ; these are excellent, attractive songs, worthy of being included in adult repertoires. His ' Three Jewish Folk-Songs ' are excellent arrangements for voice and piano ; the ' Biblical Suite ' for solo, chorus, and piano is very effective and technically well written ; other works include a piano sonata and, recently, ' Four Episodes ' for piano. But his main activity has been in the composition of works for the synagogue service.

FREDERICK JACOBI was born on May 4, 1891, at San Francisco, California. He studied music under Reuben Goldmark, Rafael Joseffy, Paul Juon, and Ernest Bloch. From 1913 to 1917 he was assistant conductor of the Metropolitan Opera, New York. He first attracted attention as a composer in 1923, with his quartet based on American-Indian themes. He has written a large number of works which are often performed, including many that he considered as Jewish, or as Jewish in inspiration. Among these are the ' Sabbath Evening Service ' (1930-31) ; ' Six Pieces for the organ for use in the Synagogue ' (1933) ; ' Three Biblical Narratives for string quartet and piano ' (1938) ; arrangements of Palestinian folk-songs (1939, 1940); 'Hymn' (to words by Saadiah Gaon), for male voice choir; 'Two Pieces in Sabbath Mood,' for orchestra (1946); 'Ode to Zion,' for mixed chorus and two harps (1946); 'Ashrey Haish' (arrangements of songs by Zeira), for mixed chorus and string orchestra (1949); and 'Three Preludes,' for organ. His composition is clear in texture, sometimes modernistic, sometimes conservative (especially in the case of synagogal works), and in almost strict counterpoint. He died on October 24, 1952.

PAUL DESSAU's early activities were in Germany, but he is now living in Hollywood, and his later work brings him into the American category. He was born on December 19, 1894, in Hamburg, and was the son of the celebrated cantor Moses Dessau. He studied the violin and composition, was conductor at a number of theatres in Germany, and wrote settings for several psalms, as well as a great deal of chamber music. His first symphony drew some of its themes from the traditional *Kol Nidre*. His later works include a 'Friday Evening Liturgy,' arrangements of Jewish folk-songs, and a full-length composition in oratorio-style, *Hagadah*, to a text by Max Brod.

ABRAHAM WOLF BINDER was born in New York on January 13, 1895, and in due course went to Columbia University (1917-20). Now he is teacher of liturgical music at the 'Jewish Institute of Religion,' and musical director at the Free Synagogue in New York (since 1923). He has written works of various kinds, especially hymns and orchestral pieces, which have been performed in America and by the Israel (Palestine) Philharmonic Orchestra. His orchestral work, 'Lament,' in memory of the defenders of the Warsaw Ghetto, was first performed in March, 1945. He has since written a 'Requiem,' *Yizkor*, for baritone (cantor), alto solo, mixed choir, and organ (1949). Other compositions include three suites for orchestra; an overture *He-Chalutzim* (The Pioneers); many compositions for the religious service, and many arrangements of folk-songs for choir or solo, etc. He is at his best in arranging folk-songs or other melodies. We may mention his 'The Jewish Year in Song,' a collection of songs, hymns, prayers, and folk melodies for voice and piano; and *Shire Chalutzim* (Pioneer songs of Palestine), for voice and piano. Of recent years he has written several works for the synagogue service. Harmonically these are simpler and clearer than his folk-song arrangements.

LAZAR WEINER comes from Russia. He was born in Kiev in 1897, studied at the State Conservatoire, and at the age of seventeen went to the United States, where he continued his musical education under Jacoby, Bennet, and Schillinger. His compositional technique always achieves the clear exposition of his thought. He sometimes employs more or less mathematical combinations. Simple, diatonic motifs are to be found in his music, but also complicated, chromatically rich motifs, often running in bold, yet well-proportioned passages. Similar motion with parallel fourths or fifths is frequent. Most of the texts he sets are Yiddish originals, or translations into Yiddish. They include 'To Thee, America' (Poem by A. Leyeless), for solo, mixed chorus, and piano (1942); 'Legend of Toil' (Poem by I. Goichberg), a cantata for soli, mixed chorus, and piano (1934); various compositions for piano; songs; a string quartet (1937); 'The Golem' (Prologue), by Leivick, for tenor, bass, chorus and orchestra (1950); many songs for the synagogal service; a three-movement 'Biblical Suite' for solo, choir, and piano; and the ballet: *Lag Baomer*.

REUVEN KOSAKOFF was born at New Haven, Connecticut, on January 8, 1898. After graduating from the Yale Music School he won a four-year scholarship to the Institute of Music Art of the Juilliard School of Music, where he continued his musical studies. Then he went to Germany, where he completed his pianoforte studies under Arthur Schnabel. He lives in New York as a concert pianist, composer, and teacher. He has arranged Jewish folk-songs ('Six Select Songs from Jewish Folklore,' 'Six Select Songs of Israel,' 'Two Ladino Songs') and 'Songs from the Bible.' These arrangements strike us as the most interesting of his works, since they present excellent treatment of distinctive musical motifs. He has also written a 'Concerto Palestina' for piano and orchestra; a number of compositions for the piano, including a 'Rhapsody,' a 'Caravan,' a *Hora*, and 'Yemenite Dance'; also works for voice and piano.

JACOB SCHÖENBERG comes of an Orthodox cantor family and was born on September 8, 1900, at Fürth, in Bavaria. He began to work at the piano very early in life, and also passed through a Jewish theological seminary. His Jewish compositions include a ' Chasidic Suite' for pianoforte (1937); several *Hora* dances for various instruments; a volume of arrangements of Palestinian songs, etc. He came to London to live in 1939, and in 1948 he went to New York.

ARKADIE KOUGUELL was born on December 25, 1900, in the Crimea. After a musical education at the St. Petersburg Conservatory and at the Vienna Academy of Music, he became, in 1920, Director of the School of the State of Crimea. Later he travelled as concert pianist and teacher in Europe and especially in the Middle East. He came to New York in 1951 and now divides his activities between the United States and Europe (Paris and Geneva). Only latterly has he begun to write music with Jewish subjects. He either uses musical motifs known to him since his childhood in Russia or from the cantoral chant, or he tries to create them. His compositions include chamber music, compositions for orchestra and several ballets. We mention here two rhapsodies (he is working on a third) for piano; Poeme, Lullaby, Oriental Dance for violin and piano; the ballet ' Jacob and Rachel'; the Hora Rhapsody for orchestra. His music is clear, melodic, and colourful. His style varies and reveals mainly Russian, Viennese, and French musical education.

AARON COPLAND, born on November 14, 1900, in Brooklyn, New York, studied composition with Reuben Goldmark, and later with Nadia Boulanger. He is regarded as one of the most significant of America's composers, and has written music for the films, radio, schools, and theatre, as well as for concert performance. Of late years he has begun to take interest in the Jewish element in music, especially since his recent visit to Israel, where he conducted the Philharmonic Orchestra.

ISADORE FREED, born in 1900, is another composer who can be considered as fully rooted in America. Having won a music scholarship at the age of eight, he graduated ten years later at the University of Pennsylvania. He continued his music studies under Ernest Bloch for composition, George Boyle and Josef Hofmann for piano, and Rollo Maitland for organ. Later he was at the Schola Cantorum under Vincent d'Indy. For fourteen years he was organist and director of music at Temple Keneseth, Philadelphia, and for the past six years has held a similar post at

Temple Israel in Lawrence, Long Island. Freed is a leader of the current musical renaissance in the United States. Besides his symphonies, two operas, chamber music, and other works, he has composed the ' Sacred Service for Sabbath Morning,' in which fine melodic motifs are excellently treated. Recently he has produced his ' Sacred Service for Sabbath Eve,' many parts of which are based on biblical cantillation or traditional prayer modes. In the same field are his ' Three Psalms ' for mixed voices with or without accompaniment, and his ' In Distress I called upon the Lord ' (from Psalm 118), for voice and chorus. Mention should also be made of his piano pieces: ' Prelude,' ' Canzonet,' and ' Caprice.'

HERBERT FROMM, who is now director of music at the Temple Israel in Boston, was born at Kitzingen-am-Main, in Bavaria, in 1905. He studied the piano, organ, and conducting at the Academy of Music in Munich. His teachers were August Reuss, Walter Courvoisier, Armin Knab, and Paul Hindemith. On concluding his studies he became a theatre conductor. In 1937 he went to the United States. Most of his works are for voice ; they include songs, choral works, and many compositions for the synagogal liturgy. His work is distinguished by a solid, progressive technique, not excessively modernistic or exploiting dissonance, yet of our time and colourful. His melodic invention often has affinities with the pentatonic scale of the *Neginot*. and this gives his compositions an attractive Jewish colouring. Mention must be made of his *Adath Israel*, for the Friday evening service ; the 23rd Psalm, for three-part women's choir and organ or piano ; the ' Song of Miriam,' for women's choir, baritone or contralto solo, and piano. This last work won him the Ernest Bloch prize for the best composition on a Biblical theme, in 1945. His ' Six Madrigals ' for choir are very interesting, forming a welcome contribution to the concert repertoire in this genre. Among his most recent works are a sonata for violin and piano (1949), and a concerto for flute and string orchestra.

An interesting young composer is JULIUS CHAJES, born in 1910, at Lwow (then Lemberg, in Austrian Galicia). Now he is a teacher of composition and an executant pianist, living at Detroit, Michigan. He gave public performances as a pianist at the age of nine, and composed a string quartet when he was eleven. In

1933 he won the prize for pianoforte in the International Music Competition held at Vienna. In 1934 he was conducting the pianoforte class at the School of Music in Tel Aviv. He went to the United States in December, 1937. He has written a large number of compositions, including chamber music, pianoforte works, many songs, choral works, pieces for violin or violoncello and piano, and orchestral works. In 1952 he published his 'Shabbat Shalom,' a Sabbath evening service, for cantor, mixed voices, and organ. 1952 also brought the first performance of his piano concerto, which was broadcast on the Vienna Radio on November 27, of that year. Generally speaking his compositional technique is distinctive and he has a pronounced feeling for the Jewish melos. His formal construction reveals his good, solid training.

He is particularly successful in employing or arranging Palestinian folk-songs or religious melodies. In this connection we must mention his 'Palestinian Dance' and 'Palestinian Melodies' for piano, and several psalms for soli and chorus. He has written a good deal of liturgical music. In 1951 he published a cantata, 'The Promised Land,' in English, for narrator, soli, chorus, and piano.

HERMAN BERLINSKI was born at Leipzig in 1910, his parents being of Polish-Jewish origin. He entered the Leipzig Conservatoire in 1927, studying pianoforte with Professor Otto Weinreich, harmony with Siegfried Karg-Elert, and counterpoint with Guenther Raphael. Graduating in 1932, he left Leipzig in 1933, and, after a concert tour, went to Paris, studying counterpoint with Nadia Boulanger at the Ecole Normale, and composition with Jules le Febre of the Schola Cantorum. In 1941 he went to the United States, and now lives in New York. Of his works we may mention 'The Golden Chain,' to a poem by J. L. Peretz, for 'Sprechstimme' and piano; 'David and his Friends,' suite for piano; and 'Serenade for the Peace of Mind,' for string quartet, piano, and *Ondes Martenot*, which he composed in 1951. In his work his Parisian training is clearly recognisable.

ARTHUR COHN, born in 1910, has written music for the bassoon ('Declamation and Toccata' and 'Hebraic Study'). The second movement of his 'Suite for Orchestra' has the superscription 'Hebrew Ritual.'

DAVID LEO DIAMOND was born on July 9, 1915, in Rochester, New York. Among his works are 'Mah Tovu' for cantor, mixed chorus, and organ; and a full Friday evening service; and 'Longing for Jerusalem,' to words by J. Halevy. He has written symphonies, concertos, etc. He writes very lucidly, diatonically, very rarely deserting the main key.

Three other Jewish composers in early middle age must receive brief mention. STEFAN WOLPE was born in Berlin in 1902. He began to study music at the age of fourteen, and later attended the Berlin Academy of Music and studied composition under Paul Juon. In 1934 he emigrated to Palestine, and this gave his creative work a new direction. There he wrote 'Twelve Palestinian Songs to biblical texts, and a sonata for oboe and piano. In 1939 he went to the United States and remained there. In his work he has been influenced by the twelve-tone technique, but he has developed his own style. HENRY BRANT was born in Montreal in 1913; MAX HELFMAN was born in Poland on May 25, 1901, and has lived in New York since 1909, acting as choirmaster as well as composer. His synagogal work 'The Holy Ark' (*Aron Ha-qodesh*) is rather daringly written music for the sacred service, and it makes considerable demands on performers and audience.

Among the youngest generation of American Jewish composers LEONARD BERNSTEIN has already achieved sensational success. He was born at Lawrence, in Massachusetts, on August 25, 1918. He studied composition under Walter Piston and Edward Burlinghame Hill at Harvard University, and graduated there in 1939. His pianoforte teachers were Helen Coates and Heinrich Gebhard. He studied for two years at the Curtis Institute of Music in Philadelphia, taking conducting under Fritz Reiner, and orchestration under Randall Thompson, while continuing with the piano under Isabella Vengerova; later he worked with Koussevitzky. He was quickly recognised both as an outstanding conductor and as pianist, and he had great success with his own compositions. The symphony 'Jeremiah,' in three movements (Prophecy, Profanation, Lamentation), which he completed at the end of 1942, witnesses to his powerful talent and solid musical training; in the third movement a passage given to a mezzo-soprano solo is taken from the Lamentations of Jeremiah. Only rarely in his works has he employed traditional Jewish motifs, and he follows Bloch's example in striving to achieve a true Jewish mood by the invention of his own musical themes. In his manner of treatment of the musical material, and especially his harmonisation and orchestration, he has written this symphony in the spirit of the modern age. Though he was only twenty-four when he wrote it, it must be considered a genuine achievement of the new Jewish symphonic music. He has written two ballets on non-Jewish subjects, both of which were performed in New York in 1944, and works for the synagogue service. In the spring of 1947 Bernstein visited the Near East to conduct the Palestine Philharmonic Orchestra. During the 1948-49 season he was artistic director of the Israel Philharmonic Orchestra and he acted as conductor to the orchestra in October and November, 1948. In the spring and in December of 1950 he again conducted the orchestra in Israel, and from January to March, 1951, during its tour in the U.S.A., he was joint conductor with Koussevitzky. In 1945 he wrote *Hashkivenu*, to a text from the Friday evening service, for tenor and mixed choir, with organ accompaniment.

JOSEF FREUDENTHAL, born March 1, 1903, has composed a number of works, chiefly on religious texts, but he is especially well known as a publisher (the Transcontinental Music Corporation of New York); also as an organiser of performances of Jewish music, and for his activities in the New York ' Jewish Music Forum.'

         ❖   ❖   ❖   ❖

In the course of this survey of individual Jewish composers, we have already mentioned more than one ·who emigrated to Palestine, either residing there for a time and then going on to America or elsewhere, or settling in that country, and who contributed to its musical life during their shorter or longer stay. Now we must complete the story of Palestinian-Israeli music by giving details of a number who have achieved distinction specifically as Palestinian-Israeli composers.

BARUCH KOBIAS was born in Krumau (Krumlow), Bohemia, on February 8, 1895. He studied the violin under Franz Drdla in Vienna, and under Suchy and Willy Szwejda in Prague, also composition under F. F. Finke at the Academy in Prague, and the history of music under Guido Adler, at the Vienna University.

He has lived in Palestine since 1941, and has written many works since, including a 'Divertimento,' for two violins and viola (1942); a Trio for flute, violin, and viola (1942); six string quartets, and orchestral works.

SHALOM AHARONI was born in December, 1895, in Belo-Tserkov, Ukraine, and is the son of David Shalom Mendels, a *Chazzan* and composer of religious music. He studied the violin in Chicago and later at the Institute of Musical Arts in New York. He has written chamber music, a concerto for violin and orchestra.

YITZCHAK EDEL was born at Warsaw on January 1, 1896, and was brought up in an Orthodox Chasidic atmosphere. His first encouragement to take up a musical career came from the well-known Jewish writer, Peretz. At the beginning of the First World War he went to Russia, and studied at the Conservatoire in Kiev, and later in Moscow. Then he returned to Warsaw, where he passed through the State High School for Music, under the direction of Karol Szymanowski. In 1929 he emigrated to Palestine, where he works mainly as a teacher. His Chasidic upbringing has found expression in his compositions, which include a 'Capriccio' for orchestra, an 'Elegiac Cantata' for baritone and orchestra, a 'Palestinian Dance' for orchestra (arranged for piano solo by E. Rudiakov), two string quartets, a wind and piano quintet, a wind quintet, songs, and other works.

Before emigrating to Palestine in 1933 PAUL BEN-HAIM (or Ben-Chayim) was Paul Frankenburger; he is one of the most prominent and characteristic composers in Israel to-day. He was born on July 5, 1897, the son of a Munich lawyer. At Munich he attended the high school and then the Akademie der Tonkunst, and the University. His teachers for composition were Friedrich Klose and Walter Courvoisier, and he was taught the piano by Berthold Kellermann, who had been a pupil of Liszt. Later he took up the career of an opera and concert conductor, but from 1931 onward he devoted himself chiefly to composition, though he also worked as a teacher. He went to Palestine at the beginning of 1933, and is teacher of composition and pianoforte at the 'Shulamit' Conservatoire in Tel Aviv. He occasionally acts as guest conductor of the Israel Philharmonic Orchestra and is engaged in organising activity in the Musicians' Union. All his works reveal a high standard of technical accomplishment, whether in the larger or the smaller forms of composition. The most outstanding of the works he has written in Israel are two symphonies, the first in 1939-40, the second in 1943-45; both of them are frequently performed and well received, because of their interesting, yet seemingly simple, themes, and especially because of the unusual orchestral combinations and brilliant orchestration. Other orchestral works include *Yizkor* (In Memoriam), a Poem for violin and orchestra; 'Pastorale Variée' for clarinet, harp, and string orchestra (1946); a 'Concerto for Strings' (1947); and a piano concerto (1949). His chamber music is frequently performed; it includes a string quartet (1938); 'Variations on a Palestinian Folk-Song' for violin, violoncello, and piano (1939); a clarinet quintet (1941); various works for violin and piano, and violoncello and piano; numerous songs, piano pieces, choral works, etc. His compositions for voice and piano, *Yerushalayim* (words by Jehuda Halevi), op. 24, No. 3; *Shim'u iyim elai* (' Listen, O Isles, unto me,' from Isaiah 49), op. 37; and his 'Twenty-third Psalm,' for contralto or baritone and string orchestra (op. 24, No. 1), make a vivid impression; and the music has some of the quality of the Sefardic songs originating from Spain. The 'Lullaby for Miriam,' to a text by Richard Beer-Hoffmann, translated into Hebrew by Ginsburg, also has some melodic phrases of a folk-song character. In 1950 he wrote a 'Liturgical Cantata' to the text of the liturgy; this is a very expressive work in five movements, for baritone solo, mixed chorus, and orchestra. His later instrumental compositions include a ' Nocturne' from op. 20 B; a 'Sonatina' (1946); 'Melody and Variations' (1950); and 'Five Pieces,' op. 34, all for piano. His '1949 Concerto' for pianoforte and orchestra, in three movements, is a strong and very interesting work which makes great demands on the orchestra and even more on the solo pianist.

He has also devoted much attention to the arranging of oriental Jewish folk-melodies, from the Yemen, Bokhara, Persia, etc., and his collaboration with the well-known and popular Yemenite Jewish folk-song singer, the Israeli-born Bracha Zefira, has been productive of much good music. Ben-Haim's significance for the new Jewish music is already indubitable; it remains for the future to appraise it exactly. Meanwhile, every new work from his pen is an enrichment of the treasury of Jewish music.

KARL SALOMON was born at Heidelberg in 1897, and has lived in Palestine since 1937, working as director and conductor of the Jewish radio-programme. His works include an opera, 'David and Goliath'; a set of variations on Palestinian folk-melodies, for orchestra (1937); a symphony, 'Nights of Canaan'; 'Partita' for strings (1948); 'Aria' (Nigun) for violin and orchestra; songs, etc. His compositions are frequently marked by their interesting and original colour.

The son of a doctor, ERICH WALTER STERNBERG was born at Berlin in 1898; he attended high school there and studied law. But he also took up music, and had Hugo Leichtentritt as his teacher in theory and composition. He visited Palestine in 1924 and finally settled in the country in 1932. His chief works are 'The Twelve Tribes of Israel,' a theme with variations, for full orchestra; 'Joseph and his Brethren,' for string orchestra; two works for chamber orchestra: the 'Dr. Doolittle Suite' and the *Amcha* Suite; the 'Story of David and Goliath' for baritone and chamber orchestra; the choral work *Yishtabach* (Vowed); a Jehuda Halévi cycle for six-part choir *a capella*; a *Hora*; also two string quartets, a piano trio, a wind quintet, a large number of pieces for piano, and songs with piano accompaniment. Some of these works have been performed abroad.

NAHUM NARDI (originally Narudetzky) was born at Kiev in 1901 and went to Palestine in 1923. He has arranged many Palestinian songs and has written music for the Habima Theatre.

ABRAHAM DAUS comes of an old Berlin family, and was born there in 1902. He attended high school, and began his musical education under one of Brahms' pupils, Edward Behm, then continued at the Munich High School for Music, studying composition under Walter Courvoisier. After some years as a theatre repetiteur and conductor he went to Palestine in 1936, and is there chiefly engaged as an accompanist, and as an orchestra and choir conductor. He has written a song-cycle to poems by Rachel, for mezzo-soprano, flute, and viola; 'Variations on an old Yemenite Theme' (Rondo and Passacaglia), for flute and piano; 'Overture to a Cantata' (The Sea Gate), for large orchestra, as well as chamber music, etc.

MOSHE RAPAPORT was born in 1903 in Chestohov, Poland.

Since the age of thirty he has lived in Israel as 'cellist in the Symphony Orchestra, and teacher of the 'cello. Among other compositions he has written a 'cello concerto in A minor. His home is in Tel Aviv.

MARC LAVRY, an Israeli conductor who is well known as a composer, was born in Riga on December 22, 1903, and studied first at the Riga and later at the Leipzig Conservatoire. His teachers included Glazunov for composition, and Hermann Scherchen for conducting. He became conductor at the municipal theatre of Saarbrucken in 1927, then conductor of the Berlin Symphony Orchestra and the Rudolf Laban Ballet, 1928-32, of the opera and symphony orchestras at Riga, 1932-35, then went to Palestine. Among the works he has composed there are the symphonic poem *Emek*; a violin concerto ; a *Hora* for orchestra ; *Shir Hashirim* (The Song of Songs), an oratorio to text by Max Brod ; an opera, ' Dan the Guard ' ; a piano concerto ; and music to various plays. We must also mention his ' Four Pieces ' for violin and piano ; and ' *Kukiah*, Variations sur un thème populaire Palestinien,' for chamber orchestra. He is a very productive and skilful composer. His work reveals the sound, practical, and well-trained musician. His opera, which has been frequently performed in Israel, and has had great success, is not actually based on Jewish folk-lore. It has a romantic flavour and is constructed very much in the style of Italian and Russian opera, with distinct arias, etc. Even so, it can be definitely regarded as a folk-opera.

Born on November 17, 1903, in Odessa, JOSEF KAMINSKY comes of an artistic family. His father Abram was an actor and theatrical manager in Warsaw ; his mother, Esther Rachel, was a well-known Jewish actress ; and his sister Ida also became a brilliant actress. Josef Kaminsky began to study music at the age of six, and developed his skill with the violin until he was ready to go on concert tours. His teachers were H. Heler, at Warsaw, Issay Barmas at Berlin, and Arnold Rosé in Vienna. He studied composition under Koch at Berlin, in 1922, and Hans Gàl in Vienna, in 1923-24. Then he returned to Berlin, for the years 1924-26. After giving recitals, etc., as a violinist in various cities he took a post as orchestral leader in Warsaw, and became leader of the Palestine Philharmonic Orchestra in 1937. While living in Europe he had composed a great deal, including incidental music for the famous Vilna Jewish Theatrical Troupe, songs with orchestra, etc. Among the works he has composed in Palestine and Israel are *Aggadah ve-Riqqud* for strings (1939) ; a 'Concertino' for trumpet and orchestra (1941) ; *Ha-aliyah*, variations for baritone solo and large orchestra (1943) ; a suite for violin, violoncello, and piano (1944) ; a 'Ballade' for harp and small orchestra (1945) ; a string quartet (1945) ; and the 'Comedy Overture' for large orchestra (1947). One of his latest works is a violin concerto in three movements.

AVIASAF BERNSTEIN, born at Vilna in 1903, studied the piano and from 1922 to 1927 was at the Staatliche Hochschule für Musik in Berlin, where he won the Mendelssohn Prize. He has lived in Palestine since 1935, and has written orchestral works for the Palestine Philharmonic Orchestra, etc. His works include the *Kinneret* Suite for orchestra ; 'Seven Preludes in memory of the fallen of Warsaw Ghetto' ; a violin concerto ; a piano concerto ; preludes for violin and for violoncello ; over eighty songs, etc.

VERDINA (Rachel) SHLONSKY (also spelt Vardina Chlionsky), born on January 22, 1905, at Kremenchug, in the Ukraine, is a highly gifted composer. She studied pianoforte under Petri and Schnabel in Berlin, and composition under Darius Milhaud. She has written many songs, orchestral works, and chamber music pieces, the cantata *Shirei Lechem va-Mayim*—Songs of Bread and Water (text by Abraham Shlonsky), for solo, chorus, and orchestra ; a three-movement symphonic poem, 'Jeremiah-David-Heroic March' ; and incidental music for the Habima and Ohel Theatres.

ALEXANDER URIA BOSCOVICH, born at Clausenburg (Cluj), in Transylvania, in 1907, studied in Vienna and Paris. In Palestine since 1937, he is seeking to create a new musical language—as indeed are most of his fellow-composers in that country. His orchestration is modern and he exploits the orchestral possibilities of instrumentation to the full. Among his works are 'Chansons Populaires Juives' for orchestra ; an oboe concerto ; a violin concerto ; and the 'Semitic Suite' for orchestra (also arranged for piano). He has written incidental music for the Habima Theatre, a number of piano pieces, and songs, including a setting of the Twenty-third Psalm for the popular Israeli singer Bracha

Zefira. He teaches harmony and counterpoint at the Israel Conservatoire.

OEDÖN PARTOS was trained as a violinist and composer. He was born at Budapest in 1907 and studied at the Academy of Music until 1924, the violin under Jenö Hubay and composition under Kodály. After several years as orchestral leader and solo violinist in Lucerne, Berlin, Budapest, etc., he settled in Palestine in 1938, taking the post of first viola of the Palestine Philharmonic Orchestra. He is now director of the Israeli Academy of Music. He has written chamber music, and *Yizkor* (In Memoriam) for viola and string orchestra (1946); 'Song of Praise,' a viola concerto (1948); and vocal works.

MENACHEM AVIDOM (Mahler-Kalkstein) is greatly esteemed in Israel. He was born in 1908 at Stanislawow, Eastern Galicia (then in the Austrian Empire, and later Polish). Since 1925 he has lived in Palestine, teaching composition and theoretical subjects at the Conservatoire in Tel Aviv since 1935. His works include 'Entretien Phantastique,' a concerto for flute and strings; the folk-symphony *Symphonia Amamit*; a string trio; a wind quintet; two piano sonatas; and vocal pieces. His compositional technique is thorough and his style progressive. Both his piano sonatas contain passages with themes based partly on folk-lore, treated polytonally throughout.[1] His 'Mediterranean Sinfonietta' won the Israel Philharmony prize in 1951.

YEDIDYA ADMON-GOROCHOV is one of the creators of the new kind of Israeli folk-song, alluded to above. His melodies are both rooted in traditional Jewish tunes and linked with the oriental motifs of the Bedouin and fellahin, as well as of the Yemenite and Persian Jews. He was born at Ekaterinoslav, in the Ukraine, on December 5, 1894, emigrating to Palestine in 1906. He became a pupil of A. Z. Idelsohn at the Teachers' Seminary, Jerusalem, continuing his studies in America from 1923 to 1927. Returning to Palestine he published his first songs, among them 'Gamal, Gamali,' which is still very popular. In 1930 he went to Paris to work with Nadia Boulanger. Among his works are many songs; a Cantata for soli, chorus, and orchestra; incidental music for

---

[1] Here 'polytonal' refers to passages in which the several voices are so laid out that they are simultaneously governed by different keys. The result is a brittle, dissonant-sounding music, with numerous false relations.

plays such as 'Jeremiah,' by Stephan Zweig, 'Bar Kochba' for Ohel Theatre; and for 'Mikhal, Daughter of Saul,' and 'Jephthah's Daughter' (Habimah Theatre). He has also written music for films.

One of the best-known writers of popular songs, many of which have become genuine folk-songs, is MORDECHAI ZEIRA. Born in Kiev in 1905, he went to Palestine in 1924. Until 1933 he lived in various *kibbutzim* (agricultural colonies). Since then he has lived in Tel Aviv. He studied musical theory with Salomo Rosowsky. Zeira has composed over two hundred songs, most of which have become part of the popular life in Israel. They are sung as folk-songs, and a number of them have been arranged and adapted by Jewish composers both in and outside the country. The songs *Kacha-kacha* (So-so), *Kinneret* (Gennesareth), *Layla-layla* (Night, night), the typically Palestinian *Hora* songs *Ad Or Haboqer* (Till the Morning Light), *Havu Levenim,* and others have achieved tremendous popularity. He has written children's songs, building-songs, Haganah songs (military marching songs), etc. The year 1951 saw the twenty-fifth anniversary of the appearance of his first song, *Paqad Adonay*. His melodies are a happy blend of East European Jewish and Palestinian-Bedouin musical elements, achieving a distinctive colour which imparts an original quality and makes them highly attractive to the Israeli Jews. If his songs had not found publication, but had been passed from mouth to mouth, they would by now have come to be regarded as anonymous folk-songs. In fact this has already happened to a number of them.[1]

Another well-known composer of popular songs, some of which have become genuine folk-songs, is DANIEL SAMBURSKY. Born in 1909 at Königsberg, East Prussia, he studied at the Danzig Conservatory and has lived since 1932 in Palestine. He has composed incidental music for the Matate Theatre, and for films. His song *Shir ha-Emek* (1934) for the film 'Land of Promise,' achieved great popularity. It is found below as Example 10 on page 234.

HANOCH (HEINRICH) JACOBY, born at Königsberg in 1909,

---

[1] In the case of *Paqad Adonay*, the present writer himself arranged the song, producing a somewhat modified version, thinking and stating it to be an anonymous folk-song.

studied under Hindemith and Wolfsthal at the Berlin Hochschule
für Musik. He went to Palestine in 1934, and works as violinist,
conductor, and composer. His works include two string quartets,
a concertino for viola and orchestra ; 'King David's Lyre' ;
variations for small orchestra ; 'Judean Hill Dance, Hora
Variations' for piano, etc.

Born at Warsaw in 1909, EMANUEL AMIRAN (Pugachov) soon
afterwards was taken to Russia by his parents, and the whole
family emigrated to Palestine from there in 1924. He studied
music in Palestine and London. At present he is with professor
Kestenberg as a teacher at the Music-Teachers' Training College
in Tel Aviv. He has written incidental music to several plays
for the Habima and Ohel Theatres, for films, etc.

JOSEPH TAL (Gruenthal) was born at Pinne, near Poznan, in
1910, and received his musical training at the Akademie für Musik
in Berlin. He went to Palestine in 1935, and is teacher for composition and pianoforte at the Jerusalem Conservatoire. His works
include a piano concerto ; a choreographic poem, 'Exodus,' for
baritone solo and large orchestra ; chamber music, piano works,
songs, etc.

HAIM (HEINZ) ALEXANDER was born in 1915 in Berlin, settled
in Jerusalem in 1936, and is a graduate of the Israel Conservatoire
of Music. He teaches piano and composition. His Passover
Cantata won the Robison prize in the Ein Gev Festival competition of 1951. The Six Israeli Dances (revised 1951) for piano
are character pieces written partly in the spirit of Israeli folk-
dances but without use of folk-lore material. It is a fine work and,
in spite of the modern style and some dissonant passages, the
rather transparent music makes a pleasant and interesting effect.

MORDECHAI SETER (Starominsky) was born in Russia in 1916 and
went to Palestine at the age of ten. Later he went to Paris to
study composition under Nadia Boulanger and Stravinsky, and
pianoforte under Lazar Levy. He returned to Palestine in 1937,
and settled there to work as composer and teacher. He has
written 'Children's Songs' for women's choir and orchestra, to
texts by Bialik and Pinkerfeld ; a 'Sabbath Cantata' for soli,
mixed choir, and string orchestra, to traditional texts ; an
'Improvisation' for violin, etc.

MAX BROD is internationally known as a literary figure, but

he has also composed various works. Born in Prague on May 27, 1884, he was a pupil of Adolf Schreiber. He has lived in Tel Aviv since 1939, and is drama adviser to the Hebrew Habima Theatre. His compositions include a 'Yemenite Song' and a 'Requiem Hebraicus' for baritone and small orchestra. He also wrote the libretti for Marc Lavry's opera 'Dan the Guard,' and for the same composer's oratorio *Shir Hashirim* (Song of Songs), etc.

This survey of some sixty Jewish composers of the past half-century does not pretend to be exhaustive ; there are others who may be regarded as on the borderline, and, too, the ranks are continually being increased. Nor do we claim any special merit in mere numbers. None the less, the list is impressive, not simply because it disposes of the deep-rooted prejudice that the Jew is 'only an executant,' but far more because it demonstrates the great and continually swelling stream of Jewish music being written to-day by Jewish composers.

CHAPTER XVI

RESEARCH INTO JEWISH MUSIC

THERE has been no lack of theoretical and analytical studies of the music of the Jews ever since biblical times. Strangely enough, the more advanced the age, the more absurd appear to have been the conjectures concerning the nature and kind of music produced in the ancient times; and it must be added that until recently the writers' aim always seemed to be to reconstruct or even revive that music purely for religious purposes.

The first steps towards sound scientific research into the music of biblical times were taken by Christian savants. However, from the historical aspect they could not but start from completely false premises, for only recently has critical biblical research made an agreed and credible chronological survey possible. And too often they attempted to reconstruct the type of instrument and even the music itself on the basis of the quite inadequate descriptions or even the bare mention in the Scriptures. For instance, in the eighteenth century Pastor Johann Christoph Speidel, of Waiblingen, in Swabia, wrote a work entitled ' Indubitable Traces of the Old Singing Art of David, according to their clearly differentiated voices, tones, tempi, notes, and repetitions, with an example for test; together with an investigation of the *dialogorum musicorum*, and fundamental indication of an accurate classification of the Psalms.'[1] In this work he speaks of a Hebrew Pentachord, i.e., a five-note scale; and he even composed a psalm in four-part arrangement in the ' ancient Hebrew' manner, although his only bases for all this elaborate structure were the Scriptures and contemporary synagogal music. By no means helpful, too, was the fact that until recent times Christian scholars often made use of translations of the Scriptures which, so far as the musical references were concerned, were even more unreliable than the Hebrew originals. A large number of

---

[1] Unverwerfliche Spuren der alten Davidschen Singkunst. Stuttgart, 1740.

writings on the music of the Old Testament exists in various languages, especially dating from the seventeenth and eighteenth centuries.[1] One of the richest collections of such writings is found in the thirty-four volumes of dissertations by various authors which was edited by Blasius Ugolino in Venice in 1744-1769: ' Thesaurus antiquitatum sacrarum. . . .' The 32nd volume contains ten chapters on Hebrew music. There are historical surveys of the subject in Johann Nicolaus Forkel's ' Allgemeine Geschichte der Musik' (Leipzig, 1788) and in August Wilhelm Ambros's ' Geschichte der Musik' (Breslau, 1862). Both these works deal thoroughly and fundamentally with the music of Biblical times, but later historical studies have rendered them out of date in many respects.

Towards the end of the nineteenth century, with the revival of national cultural life in Jewry and the awakened interest in a national Jewish music, Jews began to occupy themselves with the theoretical and analytical problems of their music, though at first rather unsystematically. In passing one must remark that if it is not pursued systematically at a Jewish scientific institution, a Jewish university or high school for music, such work must always remain restricted in its essence and scope. There have been large numbers of such unsystematic studies, and most of them have only restricted value.

By contrast, the importance and value of such a scientific work as that of Abraham Zvi Idelsohn can never be sufficiently appreciated. His serious and thorough musical research had results that on the one hand have served as a starting point for further research, and on the other have already been of extraordinary service to Jewish musicians. He devoted all his life to Jewish musical studies. He was born at Filzburg near Libau on July 14, 1882 ; in 1899 he became a student at the Königsberg Conservatoire, and, after a brief residence in London, in 1901 he went to study at the Stern Conservatoire, Berlin. He completed his studies as a pupil of Jadassohn, Krehl, Kretzschmar, and Zöllner, at the Leipzig Conservatoire. In 1903 he was cantor at Regensburg ; in 1904 he emigrated to Johannesburg in South Africa ; and in 1906 he went to Jerusalem, where he worked as music teacher and

---

[1] See ' Allgemeine Litteratur für Musik,' J. N. Forkel ; Leipzig, 1792, pp. 173-184.

cantor at the Teachers' Training College and the Jewish People's School, and began to study oriental music. In 1910 he founded the 'Institute for Jewish Music' in Jerusalem, and in 1919 a Jewish music school. In August, 1921, he travelled to Berlin and Leipzig, and in 1922 to America, where he began to make generally known the knowledge he had gained and the results of his gigantic work of collecting Jewish folk-music, giving lectures all over the country. In 1924 he became a professor at the Hebrew Union College in Cincinnati, Ohio. He died in Johannesburg on August 14, 1938.

Idelsohn's most important work is his 'Thesaurus of Hebrew-Oriental Melodies' ('Hebräisch-orientalischer Melodienschatz') in ten volumes. In it he published the Jewish vocal music which he had spent many years in collecting, noting down, and analysing, and even recording on gramophone records. In the foreword to the first volume he wrote: 'A systematic collection of the traditional songs of the oriental Jews is of great importance for the elucidation above all of synagogue singing, and not less for research into the original source of the Roman Catholic church vocal music. For both are rooted in the religious song of the oriental Jews, which has faithfully preserved its antique character, thanks to the strict conservatism of the Orient. The Jewish communities in the various lands and areas of the Orient live separated from one another, perhaps to a greater extent than one customarily realises. . . . These communities in turn have been separated from the Jews of Germany and Poland since the fifteenth to sixteenth centuries, and yet in their liturgical singing we find melodies and even whole types of song to be found also in the synagogal singing of the European Jews we have mentioned. This fact confirms our view as to the antique character of the oriental synagogal song. Further comparative research into Roman Catholic ecclesiastical singing provides striking analogies.' These deductions from and results of his research work determined all his later thought and activities. He also brought to light many facts of cultural history, and above all made a permanent record of an enormous number of Jewish songs, fixing their musical notation. Further, he investigated the varying styles and types of synagogal chants in different countries.

As we have said, Idelsohn's 'Thesaurus of Hebrew-Oriental

Melodies' is in ten volumes. A summary of their contents will reveal the vast range of their achievement. Volume one gives the songs of the Yemenite Jews, both synagogal and non-synagogal, and has an introduction, indications of Yemenite pronunciation of Hebrew, and notes on the poetry and song of the Yemenite Jews. The second volume was originally intended to cover the songs of the Persian, and the third volume the songs of the Baby-lonian Jews, but finally Idelsohn reversed this order. So volume two is devoted to the Babylonian Jews, and, besides notation of the songs, it contains an introduction, discussion of the names and the pronunciation of the Hebrew, discussion of the synagogal and non-synagogal song, and a thorough-going study of the motifs and the songs. Volume three contains songs of the Persian, Bokharan, and Daghestan Jews, with details of the history, the pronunciation, and of the songs themselves. The fourth volume brings together songs of the oriental Sefardim, and includes a survey of Arab music, and a treatise on 'Parallels between the Spanish and Slavonic folk-song.' The songs are classified into prayers, religious songs, and Spanish songs. The volume also contains historical details, notes on pronunciation of the Hebrew, and notes on the songs. The fifth volume covers the songs of the Moroccan Jews. He devoted his sixth volume to the synagogal singing of the German Jews ('Songs of the Ashkenazim') in the eighteenth century, based on manu-scripts: (section 1, the manuscript of Ahron Beer, Cantor in Berlin, written *circa* 1791; and section 2, manuscripts dating from 1765 to 1814, with an appendix devoted to Benedetto Marcello and others). Volume seven contains the traditional songs of the South German Jews, as they were customary in the eighteenth and nineteenth centuries in the communities of south and south-west Germany. In addition to historical material and details concerning the pronunciation of the Hebrew, it includes 'Comparative Investigations into Italian Synagogal Singing' and 'Research into the Steiger.'[1] A thorough survey of 'chazzanic'

---

[1] To-day no one really knows when the expression 'Steiger' came into use and what it means in musical respects. The Ashkenazi *chazzanim* used the word to indicate an established, traditional manner of singing (e.g., the *Adonoy-Moloch-Steiger*, the *Mogen-Ovos-Steiger*, etc.). Here 'Steiger' indicates not so much a mode, as a kind of motif or melody.

compositions together with biographical details is given in volume eight, which deals with the synagogal singing of East European Jews, drawn from various sources. The ninth volume brings together the folk-song of the East European Jews, the tenth the songs of the Chasidim; they both contain historical and analytical introductions, etc.

The 'Thesaurus of Hebrew-Oriental Melodies' was published in Hebrew, German, and English. Throughout the work Idelsohn kept his own personality in the background, and handled the material and investigated it as a research worker and scientist. From the musician's standpoint his analytical introductions especially are frequently too theoretical; and often the motif material is too dismembered. The work thoroughly deserves its title of 'Thesaurus' but in some instances the key-definition (the signature, for instance) is not fully elucidated for the musician. But the work has made a great wealth of vocal music available for scientific study as well as for utilisation by Jewish musicians and composers.

Idelsohn published other theoretical, analytical, scientific, and historical studies of Jewish music in addition to the 'Thesaurus.' They include 'Reste althebräischer Musik,' in 'Ost und West,' Berlin (June, September, November, and December, 1912, and March, 1913); 'Parallelen zwischen gregorianischen und hebräisch-orientalischen Gesangsweisen,' in 'Zeitschrift für Musikwissenschaft' (Leipzig, June-July, 1922); *Kele Ha-zemer Ba-tanach* (Biblical musical instruments) in 'Jahrbuch XIII,' Jerusalem; *Israel Nagara* (about Israel's Poetry and Song) in the monthly, 'Hashiloach,' Vol. 37, Jerusalem; '*Ha-chazzan be-Yisrael*' (History of synagogal precentors from the earliest times till the present), in the volume 'Ha-Toren,' New York (June, 1923); 'Synagogue Song in the United States,' in 'The Jewish Tribune,' New York, June 14, 1929; and articles in English and American journals, as well as in Yiddish and Hebrew. Another work of his was the publication, in English, of 'Jewish Music in Its Historical Development,' New York, 1929. This work summarises the results of his research while compiling the 'Thesaurus.' But in it, as elsewhere, he commits two errors: on the one hand he underestimates the extent to which Jewish music has been affected by time and the changes that have led to the present-day styles, and on the other he overestimates the possibility of recognising and isolating and classifying these modifications. He also believed it to be possible to establish the relative authenticity of the melodies, and at least in part to reconstruct them in their original form and style. He published some collections of Jewish folk-song, e.g., the *Shire Tefila* (Synagogal songs) for cantor and choir.[1] *Yiftach* (Jephthah) was a Biblical musical play with a Hebrew text, composed, written, and published by himself in Berlin, 1924. His other original compositions included two string quartets.

In the field of Jewish musicology the United States has become an important centre. Idelsohn was the first to popularise this branch of knowledge, but the Jewish immigrants of later days brought many eminent Jewish scientists to America, and in addition the American institutes and colleges are encouraging its development. In the sphere of Jewish musicology Eric Werner, who went to the U.S.A. in 1938, must be regarded as one of the greatest authorities of our time on this subject. He was born on August 1, 1901, in Vienna, but went to Saarbrücken to study music, taking composition under Franz Schreker. (His works include a string quartet, 'Psalms,' and songs.) He began research while still living in Germany, and has since covered many aspects of Jewish music. He has made a special study of Jewish music of the early Christian period, and its influence on Christian music. He is now Professor of Jewish Music at the Hebrew Union College Jewish Institute of Religion, and is also Chairman of the School of Sacred Music, both of which are housed in New York. He has been active as a composer, having written liturgical songs, etc., for the Friday evening service and for Jewish festivals, arrangements of folk-songs, the 'Symphony Requiem Hazkarah' (1943), and chamber music, most of which incorporates traditional liturgical tunes. Of his writings in the field of musicology we must mention his essay: 'The Music of Post-Biblical Judaism,' also 'Preliminary Notes for a Comparative Study of Catholic and Jewish Musical Punctuation,' and 'The Conflict between Hellenism and Judaism in the Music of the Early Christian Church.' Both the last two items were published by the Hebrew Union College, one in 1940 and the other in 1947.

---

[1] Jalkut Verlag, Berlin, 2nd ed., 1923.

Paul Nettl (born 1889), whom we have already mentioned in connection with his activities in Europe, is another prominent worker in Jewish musical research. He is now professor at the Indiana University, Boomington, Indiana. He has devoted himself particularly to the music of the Jewish secular musicians (minstrels) of the Middle Ages, and the music of the Jews in Bohemia. His writings include the work we have already quoted more than once: 'Alte jüdische Spielleute und Musiker' (Old Jewish Minstrels and Musicians), published by Dr. Josef Flesch, Prague, 1923, and 'Die Prager Judenspielleutezunft' (The Prague Jewish Minstrels' Guild) in 'Musik Barock in Böhmen und Mähren' (Baroque Music in Bohemia and Moravia), Brno, 1927. Also 'The Unknown Jewish Minstrel,' a chapter of his book 'Forgotten Musicians,' published in the Philosophical Library, 1951.

Joseph Yasser, who was born in Russia in 1893, possesses extensive knowledge of Jewish music. He has devoted himself chiefly to study of the music of the Russian Jews, has written a great deal on this subject, and has given many lectures, e.g., 'Hebrew Musical References in Russian Mediæval Ballads,' 'The Missing Chapter from the Jewish Music History in Russia, 1898-1918,' 'The Ancient Hebrew Melos and its Harmony Implications,' 'The Biblical Chant as Basic Material for Jewish Music,' etc.

The well-known musicologist, Curt Sachs, who was born in Berlin on June 29, 1881, and settled in New York in 1939, has also written much on the subject of Jewish music. His treatises on the musical instruments of biblical times especially have very valuable material relating to Israelite music; we may mention his 'History of Musical Instruments' and 'The Rise of Music in the Ancient World East and West,' published by Norton's, of New York, in 1940 and 1943 respectively. Other Jewish musicologists in the United States have written much on Jewish music and related subjects, and several research works are on the point of being published.

In Israel musical research appears to be largely confined to the transcription, recording, and study of songs, chiefly the songs of the Oriental Jews. In this connection Esther (Edith) Gerson-Kiwi must be mentioned. In addition, a number of musicians and musical theorists are writing on various aspects of Jewish music in periodicals, etc. Among these are Alice Jacob-Löwensohn (formerly of Berlin) and Menashe Ravina (Rabinovicz), both of whom have also done some composing. But the most outstanding of the writers on music is Peter Gradenwitz. He was born in Berlin in 1910, and settled in Palestine in 1936, to work there as a teacher, music critic, musicologist, and composer. In 1945 he published *Ha-muzikah Be-Yisra'el*[1] (Music in Israel, from its beginnings down to the present day). This volume of a hundred and ninety-eight pages and forty illustrations, includes an appendix containing a biographical index of five hundred names, a chronological table, a bibliography, a catalogue of Biblical sources, and the history of the Jewish anthem, *Hatikvah*. It has appeared in an English version, somewhat revised and enlarged, as ' The Music of Israel, its rise and growth through 5,000 years.'[2] It contains a great deal of material and its illustrations are valuable. The chapters on ancient and mediæval Hebrew music were written in collaboration with Ephraim Troche. In the section dealing with modern Jewish music Gradenwitz adopts the attitude that all composers of Jewish origin are covered by the concept ' the music of Israel,' even when they belong to non-Jewish cultural groups, e.g., Mendelssohn, Mahler, Korngold, and Schönberg. The book also makes mention of many executant artists of Jewish origin: conductors, instrumentalists, vocalists, etc. Gradenwitz's work as a composer includes ' Four Palestinian Landscapes ' for oboe and piano, in four movements (1946), also songs and chamber music.

Two further books should be mentioned. The first is ' Musikinstrumente und ihre Verwendung in Alten Testament ' (' Musical Instruments and their Use in the Old Testament '), by Eino Kolari, published in Helsinki, Finland, in 1947. This valuable study throws a great deal of light on this difficult problem, the author having collated and analysed all the available data on the subject. He has made great use of the etymologies of Oriental languages, no less than of researches into the general cultural history of this period.

---

1 Rubin Mass, Jerusalem, 1945.
2 W. W. Norton & Co., inc. N.Y., 1949.

The second book is ' Of Jewish Music, Ancient and Modern,'[1] by Israel Rabinovitch, expanded from his ' Musik bei Yidden,' published in 1940 in Yiddish. He was born on September 15, 1894, in Byten, Province of Grodno, Poland, his father being a *klezmer*, i.e., a player in a Jewish music band in Eastern Europe. He joined such a band at the age of eleven, but six years later went to Montreal, began his serious music studies, and eventually became editor of ' The Canadian Jewish Eagle.' Between 1931 and 1934 he was in fruitful contact with Idelsohn. His book is a collection of essays, part of it tracing the development of modern Jewish music from the days of the Russian ' Society for Jewish Folk Music ' down to the work of Ernest Bloch. There is also a valuable section on Jewish music in America. Rabinovitch's views are rooted in Yiddish culture, and this is apparent throughout his writing and strongly influences his views as to what can be considered as Jewish in music.

Our record of the history of the music of the Jews fittingly ends with mention of a work which is itself a considerable contribution to the study of that history. Dr. Alfred Sendrey's ' Bibliography of Jewish Music ' was published in 1951 by the Columbia and Oxford University Presses. Dr. Sendrey (also Aladar Alfred Szendrei) was born at Budapest on February 29, 1884, and studied music at the Royal Academy. He made a special study of musicology at Leipzig University, and took his Ph.D. there. He later conducted opera in various European and American cities. After the First World War he directed the Leipzig Symphony Orchestra. He left Germany in 1933 and lived in France until 1940, when he went to America. He is now teaching harmony, counterpoint, composition, and the history of music at the Westlake College of Music, Los Angeles.

His ' Bibliography,' which has involved immense labour and scientific devotion over many years, contains over ten thousand entries, including items of music, books, manuscripts, articles, notes, etc., wholly or in part devoted to Jewish music and music by Jews in all its possible aspects. It is classified in two main divisions of music and writings, which in turn are sub-divided into periods from the earlist times up to the present day, and

---

[1] Book Center, Montreal, 1952.

into the various categories of religious and secular music, etc. The book marks a new stage in Jewish musicology, and will enormously facilitate all further work in every section of this richly productive field.

Research into Jewish music is now, broadly speaking, concentrated in two countries, the United States and Israel. In America there is naturally more specialisation in religious music, ancient and modern. The Israeli musicologists, on the other hand, enjoy wider fields of investigation. For instance, they are also in a position to trace Oriental-Jewish melodies, their probable modification through the ages, and their influence on the modern music, as well as many other similar aspects of Jewish music.

CHAPTER XVII

ON 'JEWISH MUSIC'

EXCEPT when dealing with the modern composers of the national school, who tend to use the term 'Jewish music' in application to their work, this historical survey of the music made by the Jews has avoided reference to a specifically 'Jewish music,' even though, judged historically, all Jewish composers have consciously or unconsciously given their creations a bias in that direction.

It is obvious that, by the very nature of the thing, the author's personal attitude must play a greater part in the following discussion than it has in preceding chapters, even though the object of the discussion is to throw more light on the whole problem. At the same time, before proceeding to consider this very complex question, it must again be pointed out that the observations in this chapter must not be considered in isolation, but in association with all that has gone before; and they have validity only in such association.

Music has not been developed among the Jews, even those of Europe, as a branch of culture, as it has among other European cultural groups. In the story of European music, conveniently called Western music, a number of functions and forms can be distinguished during the centuries of its development. From its primitive function as part of the religious cult it was developed into a form of general artistic expression, in other words, into a form of art in the sense of Greek classic art. Then, from being a form of purely æsthetic expression, it later acquired the additional quality of being able to express and convey all human feelings and experiences, perceptions and sensations, even perceptions of a pictorial kind. The music which arose out of the Jews' cultural life did not pass through all these phases of development, nor did it possess all these qualities; or, at least, they were not so distinct as in the case of the Western peoples. The chief reason for this restricted development in Jewish music is to be found in the fact that generally speaking Jewish communal life was lived in unhealthy and unnatural conditions.

The fact of this restriction complicates the problem ; but with the very posing of the question, is there such a thing as "Jewish music"? the inevitable corollary arises: Is national music generally possible at all, since music can be regarded as supra- or ultra-national in its essence ? In the political sphere the term 'national' has had a very different meaning from that in the artistic sphere. For in politics 'national' necessities signify above all else political, territorial, economic, and cultural requirements ; but in national music, on the contrary, it is the popular, the folk-lore characteristics that come to the forefront, and such music is the bearer of the cultural perceptions of a people. Taking the largest possible cultural group, we recognise the folk-group (in the ethnical sense) as being the shaper of a particular culture, as the unit that constitutes the cultural group. So when using the word 'national' in this connection we are designating the distinctive, the typical folk-group. Then, when referring to French, German, Russian, Italian, Jewish, or other national music we mean the music that has emerged from these various cultural groups, and we simultaneously recognise that this music exhibits and reflects certain specific qualities of the people in question. Thus the concept, 'Jewish music,' on the one hand indicates the music of the Jews, music in which their folk characteristics and features are revealed ; and, on the other, the music of those Jews who belong to the Jewish cultural group. Furthermore, it can be taken to mean music through which a conscious and deliberate attempt is made to give expression to the folk, or the national qualities ; in this case, of course, the resulting product to be considered is more art-music than folk or 'folkish' music.

If a creative artist produces something which in kind, in content, and in form corresponds to his cultural community, so that through that product he can be accepted as belonging to, or in affinity with, that community, then the product can be regarded as belonging to that particular cultural group. The specific features of a nationally characteristic music must be judged not solely on the basis of the traditional and folk-music. The creative artist will discover or invent new expressive elements corresponding with his national cultural perceptions, and afterwards they will be recognised as specific to his people's type of perception, and will be accepted as such. This is evident, for instance, in the case of Debussy, Verdi, Wagner, Mussorgsky, Stravinsky, Smetana, Bartók, to mention only a few of the composers who have drawn on their creative faculties and their own perceptions to create music which is now generally recognised as typical of their national art, of their cultural group, and characteristic of their respective nations. It is unnecessary to seek the influence or the traces of folk-song in the works of Wagner, Verdi, or Debussy. They may be found or they may not ; in any case these creative musicians unquestionably belong primarily to their people's cultural group and only secondarily to humanity, since their works have specific peculiarities and characteristics which are rooted in the cultural perceptions of their peoples. But usually the relationship is formulated in the converse manner, namely: a creative artist is to be regarded as national (not always in the folk-lore, yet in the cultural group sense) if he draws his creations out of the cultural heritage and the cultural perceptions of his people, his group, working up the ideas he receives from the group and giving them artistic shape. But this second formulation is frequently inexact and unreliable. To begin with, a folk motif can be treated and worked up unorganically, artificially, without observance of the specific folk features, as innumerable arrangements and treatments of folk-songs have demonstrated. And in that case the result will be alien to the perceptions of the folk or the cultural group.

Moreover, this centrifugal formulation, so to speak, of the relationship between the artist and his folk community would, perhaps, exclude the possibility that works can be created which do not utilise folk-music elements, yet correspond to the perceptions of the cultural group. And that would be contrary to the previous argument. So we should accept both formulations in those cases where the artist can organically and integrally shape and invent his creations out of his own national or folk perceptions. By accepting both formulas we can comprehend the whole problem. Furthermore, we do not confine our classification into composers of any nationally homogeneous group solely to those who belong to a 'national school' based on folk-music ; we can discover the characteristics and peculiarities of a specific cultural

group even in composers who have not deliberately set themselves the object of expressing a folk, a national trend, provided
they are in spiritual affinity with their group.

In classifying and allocating a musical work according to its
national characteristics we usually apply two kinds of tests: the
test of our perceptions, in other words, classification by sensations; and the comparative test based on musical analysis. In
classifying music according to its national stamp of expression
our perceptions rely chiefly on psychic association. Consequently,
a highly important factor is the nature of the music which we
have first known and recognised as an example, as typical of a
particular national music. For through our perceptions we refer
to this early association, consciously or unconsciously, as a
criterion for all later reactions. Obviously, this perceptive,
associative method of classification cannot be objectively reliable,
though when applied alone it often seems subjectively adequate
to the person applying it.

The comparative method, based on musical analysis, consists
of investigating the characteristic music of any people in order
to determine and fix its specific features. The melodic principles,
the rhythm, the harmony are studied. The melody with its characteristic intervals, corresponding to the keys and modes customary
at any given period, but which can also be built up on the melodic
line of the language, often (like the language melodic line itself)
has its source in geographical conditions. A desert people, or a
people living in a low country, will use different intervals from
those used by a people living in a land of bold contours. The
rhythm and the metre also are usually influenced by geographical
peculiarities, as well as by the people's temperament. In a certain
sense this might also be true of the third main characteristic of
music, the harmony. Even if we were unable to conclude that
these objective influences play a decisive part in the formation
of the national music, the content and significance of national
life would themselves make it clear that homeland and speech
are objective, and folk elements with their own history and culture
are subjective, formative factors.

This approach must also be applied to the music of the Jews.
Granted that it is an open question whether these formative
factors were present in their case, and if so, how they operated,

Jewish musical expression was in any event shaped in conformity with geographical and social conditions. At any given moment of their history, the Jews achieved the musical expression that their circumstances evoked ; their musical characteristics were always moulded and formed by those circumstances, whether they were living in their own country or among strangers in the Diaspora.

In chapters one to sixteen we have dealt with these influences. But towards the close of the nineteenth century a new and extra-ordinary factor at last came into operation. A large number of Jews dedicated themselves to the Zionist idea ; they desired and desire to achieve the complete renaissance of the Jewish people and the Jewish nation. This began to influence the form of their musical expression, above all in art-music, since they deliberately sought to discover specific musical characteristics and to embody them in music corresponding with their musical perceptions.

These trends are to be found to-day in practically all cultural groups, and the fact that they have resulted in positive and mature achievement among the Jews is a proof of the existence of the criteria we have already mentioned, and which, indeed, are prerequisites to the creation of a national culture. Obviously, while the Jewish people were living in dispersal their environment and the above-mentioned physical factors could not have any similar healthy influence on the Jewish musical form of expression, since, so far as the Jews' own perceptions were concerned, they were among aliens. And, as they lived in varying environments, the effect on their cultural character was also varied in kind, and this explains the differences that existed among their own various cultural groups. The linguistic influences derived mainly from the peculiarities of Hebrew, but later also and especially from those of Yiddish. Jewish folk life developed out of the common cares and common interests of existence, religion, and culture which the Jews developed in their communities, many of which covered a considerable area and comprised whole urban settlements. To-day, owing to the resurgence of Jewish life in Israel, these factors have passed into a new phase ; for the new State centre of ' Jewish music ' presents far greater possibilities of development.

The idea of a ' new Jewish music ' thus grew at first very slowly, but gradually a Jewish music came into being which was characteristic of the people both racially and temporally. When the Jewish composers took over and applied to Jewish music the idea of national music as it had been evolved by the folk-music movement that followed the national movement, they found themselves at the dawn of a new musical epoch. And, as the history of music shows by innumerable examples, at such moments we often find a kind of childishness, irresolution, and a casting about in search of the ideal. This childishness finds outward expression in imitation, and in the desire to achieve a general independence with their own forces. The development of a national art is identical with the development of the national artists themselves. Where we find creative production, there we find an accretion to the folk group's cultural values ; where art was practised, art was developed and extended.

*　　*　　*　　*

In chapter thirteen, when discussing Jewish folk-song we mentioned certain of its characteristics. These are also largely characteristic of the art-music of the Jews. We need add only a little to what we have already said on the subject.

To attempt to define an individual mood, to analyse it on paper, is difficult enough ; to define a national or racial musical mood is, of course, practically impossible. And yet the music of certain Jewish folk-songs is so distinctive that no one, least of all a Jew, could mistake them for anything else ; they are Jewish if only in their specific manner of growing more and more rhapsodic, with the music rising to a more and more exalted intensity. Some Ashkenazi folk-tunes are songs of fervour, and their mood of rhapsodic fervour is specific to this Jewish music. And to a greater or lesser extent this same quality of rapture, often with pathos added, is present in most European Jewish folk music and, in a muted form, even in the lullabies. It is present, too, in much liturgical music, as well as in the concert performances of celebrated cantors. On the other hand, Israeli folk-tunes tend towards a gay and optimistic expression, which is mostly achieved by vivid rhythmic patterns.

When such a mood, whether derived from liturgical or from folk-music, is introduced and integrated into an original composition, then one can recognise that composition as specifically Jewish, even though one cannot analyse its Jewishness into its musical components. It is precisely this that Bloch achieves again and again in his music; although the tunes themselves are not traditional synagogal melodies in every case, those that are not are instantly recognisable as Jewish. One can hardly argue that Bloch is unoriginal in such melodies, just because their derivation, or rather inspiration, is so clear. Working strictly within the genre, each composer achieves a new, and individual contribution to the respective genre.

Some of the music being written in Israel to-day is not regarded by some people as Jewish in mood, even though the composer himself may think it is. Yet, here again, one must beware of hasty judgments. Music is organic, it grows or it dies; and its content varies according to time and place, age and clime. Israeli composers are trying to overcome the mood of mourning and brooding which derives from the Diaspora. They do not argue with their God for neglecting His Chosen People. Their tendency is to create a bright atmosphere corresponding to the clear air and sunshine of their country, and to express its high spirit and constructive purpose. Though their music may sometimes be a synthesis of the old mood of the Diaspora and of the new faith, the prevailing mood stems from the idea of a new way of life.

How have the composers of the 'national school' in Jewish music set to work to create 'Jewish' music? Do their works contain characteristics which express a specifically Jewish quality? There are a number of difficulties in the way of giving a clear answer to this question.

How would we answer such a question in relation to other music—Italian, French, German, or Russian, for instance, which possesses a recognisably national character? In addition to the specific qualities of the mood, we would also take into account the specific melodic, rhythmic, and possibly harmonic features. But it is well known that the recognised and naturalised specific features of any given music have mostly been introduced or developed by composers, and we know these features mainly from study of the works of those composers. Many of them correspond to distinctive features of the nation concerned, to its language, for instance, and often to its popular musical instruments, and so on. Yet these features change with time, and the present-day characteristics are not the same as those of the past. They, too, have been moulded by the spirit of the age and other factors making for development.

Idelsohn has said:

'. . . we see that the Jewish people has created a special type of music, an interpretation of the spiritual and social life, of its ideals and emotions. In this music we find the employment of particular scales, motifs, modes, rhythms, and forms, based on definite musical principles. These run through the music like a golden thread. Elements which do not conform to them have no hold on the music and consequently vanish from the body of that song.'[1]

Perhaps this is rather too definite a view. Both in Jewish folk and in Jewish art-music we see that these specific features are mingled with other, alien elements. It was the Jewish composers who tried to isolate these specific features, so as to allow them to appear in their original form and to develop them as an artistic expression.

Idelsohn had mainly the music of the Diaspora in mind, but Max Brod has made a special study of the music of Israeli composers. He has written in somewhat vague terms: 'The form Jewish music adopts is so manifold, so delicate in contour, that it is almost impossible to define it in words or even to describe it in abstract terms.'[2] But in speaking of the Israeli composers he goes on to ask:

'What have the works, written in this (Mediterranean) style, in common ? Their music is southern, infused with the bright light of the Mediterranean air, lucid, striving for clarity ; their rhythm is the harsh irregular beat, the obstinate repetition, but also the manifold, ceaseless variation which enchants by its apparent freedom from rule and its impulsive-

---

[1] 'Jewish Music in its Historical Development.' Henry Holt & Co., Inc. 1929. Tudor Publishing Co., N.Y., 1948, p. 488 conclusion.
[2] 'Israel's Music.' Wizo. Tel Aviv, 1951, p. 6.

ness. The structure of the movement is sometimes linear, unisonal, or at least not polyphonically overburdened. The influence exerted by the melodies of the Yemenite Jews, the neutralisation of the boundaries between major and minor keys, the return to ancient modes, the neglect of the augmented second so characteristic of the Diaspora—in all these respects lines of connection can be drawn with Arabic music and even with the particular consonantal structure of the Semitic languages. Climate and landscape, shepherd song, oboe, and clarinet, play their part.'[1]

This descriptive passage is interesting, because to some extent it reflects the general view in Israel itself. But as most of the present-day Israeli composers migrated to that country from elsewhere, all these influences can have only a restricted effect and enrich only the local musicians' means of expression.

Undoubtedly in the not distant future the music being composed in Israel will be written about more particularly than we propose to do in this book. It is undesirable that we should discuss the question to any large extent, since we cannot discover sufficient difference between this music and that of composers elsewhere to justify this treatment.

The problems of the means and the manner of creating Jewish national music were discussed when the first steps were taken in this direction at the beginning of the twentieth century. In those days there were three main opinions on the subject: first, that the Jewish folk-songs contained all the essentials of Jewish musical expression ; secondly, that the Neginot (tropes) provided the musical motifs, and that when utilised and interpreted these would lead to the end desired ; third, that by the employment of Bedouin-Arabic musical features (now to some extent replaced by the song of the Yemenite Jews), music in Israel has created motif-types which impart a Palestinian or Israeli colour.

Certain deductions and conclusions as to the specific features of Jewish music can be made.

(a) The minor mode predominates. There are various complicated modes with or without augmented seconds, and often with two augmented seconds.

---

[1] Op. cit., p. 57.

(b) Syncopation is the most striking feature of the rhythm. It takes different forms, which in general correspond to the structural peculiarities of the Hebrew language. These rhythms are also to be found in the music of other peoples, and as a rule, though not always, there too they can be related to the rhythm of the language. Here we have in mind primarily the peoples among whom Jews have lived and created their folk-song: for instance, all the Central and East European countries, Roumania, Poland, Russia, Hungary, etc.

(c) There are no specific features worth mention in respect of harmony. In general they derive from the minor and the ecclesiastical modes.

So far as the utilisation of folk-song is concerned we can point to the following facts. A number of folk-songs have been introduced into modern Jewish music in one form or another, either directly or in arrangement, or in conjunction with other, new themes; but in almost all cases they have been the folk-songs which the majority of the composers had known since childhood. However, during the pioneer period in Palestine under the Mandate, new Palestinian folk-songs were created, or certain alien songs were so completely naturalised that they can now be regarded as peculiar and specific to the country. Here by way of example we can again refer to the songs taken over from Palestinian Bedouins, or Arabs. More recently a new, popular song has developed, with new characteristics, out of all the elements we have mentioned.

All this has resulted in the creation of a Bedouin-Arab-Palestinian (Israeli) modern Jewish colour to which many composers are specially partial. In the works of Israeli composers, and of other composers spiritually associated with them, we can recognise a synthesis of all these elements, and that synthesis is historically justified. This relates above all to the musical, the compositional means, to the melody, the rhythm, and the harmony of their works.

Musical Examples

We are not in a position always to quote the most characteristic or most striking example. The reader must himself study the musical literature now available, if it is desired to go into the question more thoroughly. But we can adduce certain typical features. Our quotations are not taken from direct folk-song arrangements, rhapsodies, or paraphrases, as in such cases the characteristic feature is inherent in the folk-song itself, and can be studied therein, and then related to our examples, which form steps in the further development of Jewish art-music.

First we shall consider examples in which the main features of the folk-lore tinge are taken from East European Jewish folk-song and from the religious songs.

The following three examples illustrate various instances of the minor in melody, from simple to more complicated forms. We have here examples with two augmented seconds in the scale (marked ⌐ ⌐), e.g., in *Example 1* and *Example 2* (the E natural). *Example 3* is neither a pure B flat minor nor E flat minor. There are no special rhythmic features, except in *Example 2,* where the syncope at the beginning of the second bar, and in the voice part beginning of the fourth bar, is not the result of the rhythm of the words but simply a feature of Jewish tunes.

Ex. 1. From 'Romance,' by Jacob Weinberg.

Ex. 2. From 'Hakotel,' by Joel Engel.

Ex. 3. From 'Beker Teireni Dimati,' by Alexander Krein.

In the next two examples we note the influence of Jewish secular and the religious folk-song. Here the *Neginot* (Tropes) are clearly recognisable (compare musical examples in Chapter IX). The entire suite from which *Example 5* is taken is built up on *Neginot*, as we mentioned on pages 157 and 159.

Ex. 4. From 'The Vision of Ariel,' Op. 16, by Lazare Saminsky.

Ex. 5. From 'Children's Suite,' No. 18, by Joseph Achron (The Caravan).

Shepherds' songs in Israel revealed distinctive features quite early in the latest era of Jewish music. The songs of the Palestine Arabs were especially attractive and sensitively reflected the environment. The contact of modern Jewish composers with the music of the Bedouin shepherds has been a very fruitful one, as is shown in the next four examples. Further comment is added at the end of *Example 9*.

Ex. 6. From 'Shir Hagamal,' by Yedidya Admon-Gorochov.

Ex. 7.   *From 'Morning Song,' from 'Voices of Jerusalem,' by Shula Doniach.*

Ex. 8.   *From 'Shepherd's Dance,' from 'Piano Pieces for Youth,' by Alexander Uria Boscovich.*

Ex. 9. 'Tirza Yafa,' by Aron Marko Rothmüller.

Attention has to be drawn to the following points in the four preceding examples:

(a) *Melodic.* A minor mode corresponding to the Dorian or Hypodorian, and also the Myxolydian, is predominant. But various intervals are diminished or augmented by way of successive exchange. The result is an interchange of Dorian and Myxolydian modes. We note also the characteristic modal cadence, with a whole tone, instead of the semitone of modern major and minor modes, and often playing around the tonic, again with whole tone intervals.

(b) *Rhythmic.* There is much syncopation.

(c) *Harmonic.* It is striking that the harmonies are usually restricted to the bare essentials; there is a striving for simplicity in this respect, for a kind of primitiveness, in which much use is made of ostinato figures.

Example 10 represents another type of Israeli folk or popular song, and to some extent *Example 11* can be regarded as a modification of this or similar Israeli melody.

Ex. 10. ' *Shir ha-Emek,' by Daniel Sambursky (words by N. Altermann).*

Ex. 11. 'Preambulo' from 1st Sonatina for Piano, by Menachem Avidom.

As we have already said, the latest distinctive feature of Israeli music and of that of other Jewish composers, is the more frequent use of Oriental Jewish songs. *Examples 12* and *13* are instances of this.

In the last two examples we have a rhythmically free song very characteristic of the Orient. We find also various of the phenomena instanced in earlier examples. *Example 12* uses musical motifs of Yemenite songs, and *Example 13* is an old, traditional melody of Sefardic Jews from Adrianopolis (Bulgaria).

Ex. 12. From 'Israelian Suite,' by Joachim Stutschewsky.

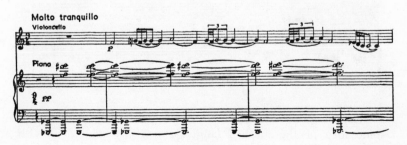

Ex. 13. 'Yerushalayim,' Op. 24/3, by Paul Ben-Haim.

The foregoing examples, though limited in number, will give some idea of the musical language used by modern Jewish composers, and indicate certain of their means of expression and the way in which their musical thinking has been shaped. Only rarely has a composer restricted himself to composing in one manner alone. All modern Jewish composers betray traces of most or all of these phenomena in their work, some taking up more advanced features, while others have restricted themselves to the more simple characteristics of this musical language.

It must be added that nowhere in this survey of Jewish music have we been tempted to reconstruct that music, in cases where it is unknown to us. Nor was there any object in our trying to awaken the music of Biblical times to new life, even if that were at all possible. Music, like any other art, is of value only if it is a living, artistic expression, the expression of a corresponding experience, an experience of the most varied trends, in the past, in the present, and surely in the future also; as well as an experience of the landscape and nature, of life, of culture. It is the spirit, the soul, the inner and outer expression of a musical thought that is indicative and decisive. In bringing this spirit, this soul, this expression under the comprehensive term 'music' we are indicating something akin to what, translated into literary terms, we call poetry; for we use the word 'poetry' not for the poem as a literary form but precisely and only for the poem's apprehensible mood and its purely emotional quality. Music binds together the notes of a composition just as poetry binds together the words and thoughts of a poem.

In brief, music is an expression of all that affects the human psyche and imagination. The means of expressing and shaping all this are of secondary significance, and whether those means are drawn from folk-music or are the result of a musical education, or are a formulation of a purely artistic musical language, seems to us a matter of indifference, to be left to the decision of each individual composer. No reconstruction of music that is past and gone can succeed. And yet, as we have always observed in the case of other peoples making similar attempts in this field, the Jews also, in their striving after a musical renaissance through which they would experience and recover what was past and over, have gained the stimulating power to create something new.

APPENDIX

Obscure Expressions used in the Psalms

The following expressions found in the Book of Psalms are generally considered to have some musical reference, but the meaning is lost, or is subject to various interpretations:

Hebrew	Transliteration	Meaning
למנצח	LA-MENATZTZEACH	Not known.
מנצח	MENATZTZEACH	T.: With the accompanist. B.: Of the choirmaster. L.: To lead the singing. W.G.: 1. To lead, direct; 2. In I Chron. 15, 21, it appears to mean: to play, to make music (in the liturgical sense); an abstract translation for the liturgical music performance.

Hebrew	Transliteration	Meaning
סלה	SELAH	W. G.: A music art-word customarily coming at the end of a homogeneous passage. C.: Probably a musical indication, perhaps a pause. B.: '. . . I have conveyed the unclarified "pause"-indication "selah" not by the customary but unintelligible "selah" (as in T. and L.) but by "on high" (empor); here the intention is rather to indicate an expressive "sursum," conveyed by the—somewhat swelling and protracted—tone of the instrumental accompaniment at the moment that the vocal part fades into silence.' K.: 1. Raising of voice, higher tone; 2. Pause, interlude; 3. Acrostic (a) סימן לשנוה הקול 'sign to change the voice.' (b) סב למעלה השׁה 'go back to the beginning, o singer' = da capo.
בנגינות על־השמינית	BI-NEGINOT AL HA-SHEMINIT	Perhaps (octave) lower neginot (=string playing, stringed instruments).
שגיון	SHIGGAYON	W. G.: Cannot be clearly indicated now. C.: A kind of song or tune. K.: 'dirge' (Assyr. shegû).

Hebrew	Transliteration	Meaning
נתית	GITTIT	C.: Musical instrument (apparently). W. G.: Statement of mode, or an instrument. In the Septuagint it is combined with a vat or winepress (Gat—נת = vat, or winepress). Also Gath—נת which was a town of the Philistines.
מכתם	MIKHTAM	W. G.: An obscure word. C.: According to some, a record or memorial. M.: 'Song of Expiation.'
משכיל	MASKIL	W. G.: The exact meaning is unknown. It is often translated: 'with art' (e.g., by B.). C.: Teaching song, participle of שכל = clever, prudent.
להזכי׳	LEHAZKIR	W. G.: Some explain it: to sing at the bringing of the Azkara (part of the sacrifice). T.: To the invocation. B.: To be borne in mind. L.: In memory (from Zachor—זכ־ = to bethink oneself, to remember).
על־שושנים or על־ששנים	AL SHOSHANNIM	W. G.: Cannot be explained to-day (shushan—שושן W. G.: Also means Susa, the Persian king's winter residence).

Hebrew	Transliteration	Meaning
עלמות	ALAMOT	W. G.: Plural of alma— עלמה (from 2nd part. עלם) a marriageable maiden. C.: It appears to be the name of a stringed instrument.
על־עלמות	AL ALAMOT	W. G.: Cannot be explained with certainty.
על־מחלת	AL MACHALAT	W. G.: A liturgical detail of unknown significance. Possibly connected with chalil—חליל = flute. Others: In a melancholy fashion (from חלה =to be sick), or: A melodic detail at the beginning of a song.
הגיון	HIGGAYON	W. G.: 1. Meditative, pensive ; 2. Perhaps the sound of the stringed instrument.
שיר המעלות	SHIR HA-MA'ALOT	W.G.: (from Maala— מע. ה [from עלה]=to rise, to exalt) a differentiating expression, in the psalms of the return from Babylon, or the Pilgrimage psalms ; *inter alia*, psalms with degrees of rhythmic stress, since a new passage repeats part of the preceding passage. B.: A rising song. Cp. II Chron. 20. 19 . . . B'kol gadol l'ma'ala בקול גדול למעלה . . .

Hebrew	Transliteration	Meaning
מני/מינים	MINNI, MINNIM	C.: Name of a musical instrument.

To the foregoing must be added the following expressions known to us from other writings ; of these the meaning is more or less clear:

מזמור	MIZMOR	W. G.: A song, when it is intended to have a musical accompaniment (hence, different from shir—(שיר). C.: A song; in the superscription of 57 psalms. T., B., and L.: Psalm. In the Apocrypha, it is used for ' Psalm.'
נגינה	NEGINAH	W. G.: 1. String playing ; 2. A stringed instrument ; 3. A mocking song. (Psalm 69, 13).
נחילה	NECHILAH	W. G.: To the flute, to flute-playing. C.: (Pl. n'chilot— נחילות) indication of an instrument or mode (*inter alia*, a band [musical]).
מחול	MACHOL	W. G.: (from chul— חול) to turn, twist, to move in a circle ; a dance, a round dance. C.: Round dance (cp. pp. 6, 10, 16, 57 f.n.).
ידידות	YEDIDOT	W. G.: (from ידד) Love.
שיר ידידת שיר ידידות	SHIR YEDIDOT	W. G.: Lovesong.

BIBLIOGRAPHY

The following list is not intended to serve as a complete bibliography. It simply indicates the main sources, chiefly German, on which the author drew when writing this book, together with a few additional works in English, for readers who wish to pursue the subject further:

CHAPTERS I TO VI

Ambros, August Wilhelm: *Geschichte der Musik*. F. E. C. Leuckart, Breslau, 1862. Vol. I.

Auerbach, Elias: *Wüste und gelobtes Land*. Berlin, 1932. Vols. 1 and 2.

Josephus, Flavius: *Jüdische Altertümer*, Trans. by Dr. Heinrich Clementz. Berlin-Vienna, 1923.

Dubnow, Simon: *Weltgeschichte des jüdischen Volkes*. Berlin, 1930. Vol. 1.

Gunkel, Hermann (—Joachim Begrich): *Einleitung in die Psalmen*. Göttingen, 1933.

Bible (in Hebrew). British and Foreign Bible Society, London, 1946.

Kautzsch, Prof. E.: *Einleitung zum Buch der Psalmen*. Halle a.d. Saale, 1910.

CHAPTER VII

Dubnow, Simon: Op. cit. Vol. 2.

Kautzsch, Prof. E.: *Die Apokryphen und Pseudoepigraphen des Alten Testaments*. Tübingen, 1900. Vol. 1.

CHAPTER VIII

Dubnow, Simon: Op. cit. Vol. 3.

Elbogen, Ismar: *Der jüdische Gottesdienst in seiner geschichtlichen Entwicklung*. J. Kauffmann Verlag, Frankfurt am Main, 1931.

CHAPTER IX

Encyclopædia Judaica. Verlag Eschkol, Berlin, 1928. Vol. 2.

Nettl, Paul: *Alte jüdische Spielleute und Musiker*. Vortrag gehalten in Prag, Juni 1923. Verlag Dr. Josef Flesch, Prague, 1923.

CHAPTER X

Elbogen, Ismar: Op. cit.

Zunz, Dr. Leopold: *Die gottesdienstlichen Vorträge der Juden, historisch entwickelt*. A. Ascher, Berlin, 1832.

Zunz, Dr. Leopold: *Der Ritus des synagogalen Gottesdienstes, geschichtlich entwickelt*. Julius Springer, Berlin, 1859.

Nettl, Paul: Op. cit.

Dubnow, Simon: Op. cit.

CHAPTER XI

Dubnow, Simon: Op. cit.

Friedmann. Aron: *Lebensbilder berühmter Kantoren.* Selbstverlag der Hilfkasse, Berlin, 1927. 3 vols.

Jüdisches Lexikon.

CHAPTER XII

Freigedank, Karl (i.e., Richard Wagner): *Das Judenthum in der Musik.* Neue Zeitschrift für Musik, vol. XXXIII, September 3 and 6, 1850. Also: Richard Wagner: *Gesammelte Schriften.* J. J. Weber, Leipzig, 1869. Vol. 5. Also: *Judaism in Music* (being the original essay together with the later supplement). Trans. from German by Edwin Evans, senior. C. Scribners Sons, New York; W. Reeves, London, 1910.

Von einem Unparteiischen: *Richard Wagner und das Judentum.* Sam. Lucas, Elberfeld, 1869.

Berl, Heinrich: *Das Judentum in der Musik.* Deutsche Verlagsanstalt, Stuttgart, 1926.

CHAPTER XIII

Kisselhof, Sussman: *Das jüdische Volkslied.* Jüdischer Verlag, Berlin, 1913.

Kaufmann, Fritz Mordechai: *Das jüdische Volkslied, Ein Merkblatt.* Jüdischer Verlag, Berlin, 1919.

Idelsohn, Abraham Zvi: *Hebräisch-orientalischer Melodienschatz.* Friedrich Hofmeister, Leipzig, 1932. Vols. 9 and 10.

CHAPTERS XIV AND XV

Sabaneyev, Leonid: *Die nationale jüdische Schule in der Musik.* Universal Edition A.G. Vienna-Leipzig, 1927.

Stutschewsky, Joachim: *Mein Weg zur jüdischen Musik, Gesammelte Aufsätze.* Jibneh-Musikverlag, Vienna, 1936.

Chiesa, Mary Tibaldi: *Ernest Bloch.* G. B. Paravia & C., Torino, 1933.

Paoli, Domenico D., and others (Henry Leigh, Leonid Sabaneyev, Josef Yasser, Leon Vallas): *Lazare Saminsky, Composer and Civic Worker.* Bloch Publishing Co., New York, 1930.

Neues Musiklexikon.

Jüdisches Lexikon.

CHAPTER XVI

Idelsohn, Abraham Zvi: *Thesaurus of Hebrew-Oriental Melodies.* Vols. I-X. Leipzig, 1914-32.

Other works detailed in this chapter.

GENERAL

Brod, Max: *Israel's Music.* Wizo, Zionist Education Department, Tel Aviv, 1951.

Gradenwitz, Peter: *The Music of Israel, Its Rise and Growth Through 5000 Years.* W. W. Norton & Co., Inc., New York, 1949.

Gradenwitz, Peter: *Music and Musicians in Israel.* Youth and Hechaluz Dept. of Zionist Organisation, Jerusalem, 1952.

Idelsohn, Abraham Zvi: *Jewish Music in its Historical Development.* Henry Holt & Co., New York, 2nd ed., 1929. Tudor Publishing Co., New York, 1948.

Rabinovitch, Israel: *Of Jewish Music Ancient and Modern.* The Book Center, Montreal, Canada, 1952.

Sachs, Curt: *The History of Musical Instruments.* W. W. Norton & Co., New York, 1940.

Sachs, Curt: *The Rise of Music in the Ancient World East and West.* W. W. Norton & Co., New York, 1943.

Saleski, Gdal: *Famous Musicians of Jewish Origin.* Bloch Publishing Co., New York, 1949.

Saminsky, Lazare: *Music of the Ghetto and the Bible.* Bloch Publishing Co., New York, 1934.

Sendrey, Dr. Alfred: *Bibliography of Jewish Music.* Columbia University Press, New York, 1951 ; and Geoffrey Cumberlege, London, 1951.

INDEX

247

4711 O